The Once& Future Faith

The Once & Future Faith

Karen Armstrong

Don Cupitt

Arthur J. Dewey

Robert W. Funk

Lloyd Geering

Roy Hoover

Robert J. Miller

Stephen J. Patterson

Bernard Brandon Scott

John Shelby Spong

Polebridge Press

The Once and Future Faith

Published in 2001 by Polebridge Press, P. O. Box 6144, Santa Rosa, California, 95406.

ISBN 0-944344-85-2

Contents

Contributors

Karen Armstrong teaches at Leo Baeck College for the Study of Judaism, London. She is the author of several books, including the bestsellers *The Battle for God* (2000) and *A History of God* (1993). A well-known commentator on religious affairs, she received the 1999 Muslim Public Affairs Council Media Award.

Don Cupitt is a Fellow and former Dean of Emmanuel College, Cambridge. He is the founder of the Sea of Faith network and the author of more than thirty books, including *Taking Leave of God* (1980), *Reforming Christianity* (2000), and *Emptiness and Brightness* forthcoming in Fall 2001.

Arthur J. Dewey is Professor of Theology at Xavier University in Cincinnati. He is the author of four books, including *Spirit and Letter in Paul* (1996) and *The Word in Time* (1990). His bi-weekly Friday morning commentaries are heard on NPR station WVXU.

Robert W. Funk is founder of the Jesus Seminar and Director of the Westar Institute. A Guggenheim Fellow and Fulbright Senior Scholar, he is the author of *Honest to Jesus* (1996) and co-author of *The Five Gospels* (1993) and *The Acts of Jesus* (1998). His new book *Jesus: Fragments of a Vision* is forthcoming.

Lloyd Geering is Emeritus Professor of Religious Studies at Victoria University of Wellington, New Zealand. Honored as Principal Companion of the New Zealand Order of Merit in 2001, he is a renowned and respected commentator on religion and the author of several books, including *The World to Come* (1999) and *Tomorrow's God* (reprinted in 2000).

Roy Hoover is Weyerhaeuser Professor of Biblical Literature and Professor of Religion Emeritus, Whitman College, and the recipient of the Whitman College Award for Faculty Achievement. He is co-author (with Robert W. Funk) of *The Five Gospels: The Search for the Authentic Words of Jesus,* 1993.

Robert J. Miller is Westar Institute's Scholar-in-Residence for the year 2001. A recipient of the Midway College Trustee Award for Faculty Excellence, he is the editor of *The Complete Gospels* (1992), author of *The Jesus Seminar and Its Critics* (1999), and editor of *The Apocalyptic Jesus: A Debate* forthcoming in Fall 2001.

Stephen J. Patterson is Professor of New Testament at Eden Theological Seminary, St Louis. His is author of *The God of Jesus: The Historical Jesus and the Quest for Meaning* (1998) and *The Gospel of Thomas and Jesus* (1993).

Bernard Brandon Scott is the Darbeth Distinguished Professor of New Testament at the Phillips Theological Seminary on the campus of the University of Tulsa. He is the author of several books, including *Hollywood Dreams and Biblical Stories* (1994) and *Hear Then the Parable* (1989). His new book *Re-imagine the World: An Introduction to the Parables of Jesus* is forthcoming in Fall 2001.

John Shelby Spong is the former Bishop of the Episcopal Diocese of Newark, New Jersey. An outspoken advocate for justice and human dignity, he is the best-selling author of many books, including *Here I Stand* (2000), *Why Christianity Must Change or Die* (1998), and *Rescuing the Bible from Fundamentalism* (1991).

A Faith for the Future

A New Phase of the Jesus Seminar

Robert W. Funk

We are about to embark on a new phase of the Jesus Seminar. We will be exploring the contours of a faith suitable for the third millennium and the global age we are now entering. Our immediate task is to form an agenda of topics and issues ingredient to that prospective faith.

Recall the initial commitment of the Seminar: We agreed to form an agenda of issues that mattered and then address those issues openly, honestly, and with the best scholarship we could enlist. We need now to repeat that foundational process.

A Cameo History of the Quest

As a way of peering into our collective future, I propose to retrace the steps we have come. The trajectory of our journey may afford us some clues about the issues before us in the next phase. It will also remind us of the stages through which we have passed and the critics we have produced. Opponents are helpful in pointing out our mistakes; but they are also useful in identifying the obstacles we have had to overcome.

The Aim of the Quest: To Free Jesus from Church Dogma

I want to begin with an outrageous claim: The Jesus Seminar has finally succeeded, after two hundred years of critical New Testament scholarship, in separating Jesus from the mythical matrix in which he was framed. Of course, I am aware we were not the first to do so. And I am aware that details of the divorce we have effected may need revision from time to time. But I know of no other group of scholars that has carried out the sorting process in such detail.

In an essay designed to launch the new quest of the historical Jesus in 1959, Ernst Käsemann wrote that for two hundred years "critical research has been trying to free the Jesus of history from the fetters of the Church's dogma." Amazingly, that statement is virtually axiomatic for all critical scholars of the gospels. It was and is undoubtedly the theoretical aim of most original questers. Yet the participants in the quest during the 19th century appear very reluctant, for the most part, to honor that goal. Most New Testament scholars beat a slow, reluctant retreat, giving up only such ground as they were forced to do so by each new stage in our understanding of the gospels. The devaluation of the Fourth Gospel, the priority of Mark, and the advent of the Q hypothesis mark such stages. Scholars tended to treat these hypotheses as obstacles to be overcome, rather than as incentives to carry through the separation of the historical Jesus from the mythical framework invented for him by the evangelists. Most scholars, who were still in the service of theology, were reluctant participants because they did not want to recognize the narrative framework of the New Testament gospels for the supernatural myth it was.

Only the rare visionary, like David Friedrich Strauss, was courageous enough to carry out a clean distinction between the Jesus of history and the Christ of the creed, between history and the supernatural. And we know Strauss paid dearly for his honesty. The original quest inched toward its goal with grave reservations on every hand.

The Arrest of the Original Quest

The slow progress of the original quest was arrested by Johannes Weiss and Albert Schweitzer at the end of the 19th century. Jesus was put down as an apocalyptic fanatic who thought the world was coming to an end in his own time. That made him useless for the liberal theology of Friedrich Schleiermacher and Adolf von Harnack then in fashion. The apocalyptic thesis was regarded as a triumph of historicism over theological accommodation. Scholars and theologians adopted the apocalyptic thesis and it became the dominant view in the 20th century. With an eschatological fanatic at the far end of the search, interest in the original quest began to wane.

Dialectical Theology and the Quest

As it became clear that the gospels are essentially declarations of faith in Jesus and not biographies, a radical skepticism about our ability to recover reliable data about the historical figure took hold. This skepticism was aided and abetted by the dialectical theology sponsored by Karl Barth. According to the dominant opinion, Jesus had been so completely filtered through the mythical matrix of the gospels that nothing could be known about him with certainty. The historical figure had been merged into the myth, or into the kerygma, as they preferred to term it. (Dialectical theologians piously renamed the supernatural framework of the gospels the kerygma, or proclamation.) The gospel of Jesus could not be distinguished from the gospel about Jesus. The original quest was dead.

Now Rudolf Bultmann was a dialectical theologian and a New Testament scholar of international stature. He also doubted that the New Testament gospels provide real access to the historical figure. In concert with Barth, he argued that we must not attempt to undergird faith in Jesus with historical knowledge. That would sully faith at its foundations. The quest was impossible for both historical and theological reasons.

Nevertheless, Bultmann himself appeared to know quite a bit about the historical Jesus. Yet for him Easter formed the ultimate barrier to significant knowledge, since Christian faith did not exist prior to Easter and the descent of the spirit at Pentecost. Jesus was the presupposition of faith, not its supposition. There was no such thing as Christianity on the far side of the resurrection. The resurrection was an 'eschatological' event, which meant that it occurred and occurs outside of history, beyond the space/time continuum. It is therefore in principle beyond the reach of historical analysis and evaluation. Since Jesus was the precursor of the faith, knowledge of his human history could function as no more than background to the emerging Christ cult.

The Quest in Reverse

At this point, two developments took place simultaneously. First, the skepticism of the German school precipitated a strong reaction on the part of an established body of scholars thoroughly critical in their approach to the gospels, but conservative theologically. In reaction, these scholars revived the quest as an apologetic or defensive tool. The prospect of the loss of the "historical reality of the revelation," as they thought of it, prompted them to renew the quest in order to maintain the connection between Jesus and the gospels. To put it simply, the original quest was first suspended (by Weiss and

Schweitzer) and then reversed. Its goal now was to join Jesus of Nazareth to the myth that had been created to cradle his story.

Rather than divorce Jesus from Christian dogma, the quest was intended to conflate Jesus with the mythical frame. Scholars like Joachim Jeremias, Oscar Cullmann, T. W. Manson, and C. H. Dodd became advocates of this version of the quest. The Bultmann school had produced its antithetical counterpart.

The Collapse of the Mythical Matrix

The second thing that transpired was Bultmann's remarkable declaration in 1941 that the mythical framework of the gospel was defunct. We can no longer believe in angels and demons, he wrote; the doctrine that sin is perpetuated through male sperm, that Jesus was born of a virgin, and that he rose from the dead on the third day and ascended into heaven are no longer credible. One of Bultmann's favorite sayings was that Jesus rose into the kerygma. By that he meant that Jesus' resurrection is expressed in the gospel, not in an empty tomb. The resurrection of Jesus takes place every Sunday morning between 10 and 11 a.m. In a nutshell, the myth is the message.

However, since the worldview undergirding the myth is no longer cogent, that myth has to be translated into modern terms. He called that process 'demythologizing.' In retrospect, we can see that Bultmann was about three decades ahead of his time in acknowledging the collapse of the mythical kerygma. He was also very orthodox in vesting the future of the faith in a translation of the myth.

The New Quest

The new quest was launched by students and friends of Bultmann in the 1950s. His followers decided that the message of Jesus had to sustain some vital link with the primitive Christian gospel, or the Christian faith could not be said to derive from Jesus of Nazareth. And they were convinced that the gospels did preserve some minimal historical data, in opposition to their teacher. So they inaugurated the new quest. That was the purpose of Käsemann's 1959 essay and a book by James M. Robinson. Günther Bornkamm, another student of Bultmann, had published his *Jesus of Nazareth* in 1956. The new quest was erected on two principles: the gospels contain some reliable data about Jesus, and a link between Jesus and the Christian gospel is theologically essential.

The new quest died aborning. It did so, in my judgment, because the comparison of the message of Jesus with the kerygma widened rather than closed the gap between the two. In addition, the new quest failed to develop adequate criteria for distinguishing the two. The new quest, like so many of its predecessors, failed in its attempt to reverse the aim of the original quest.

The Third Quest

The so-called third quest is an extension of the liberal/conservative quest of the pre-war days. The aim is to maintain the continuity of Jesus with John the Baptist, on the one hand, and with the orthodox evangelists, on the other. The third questers I have labeled THE APOSTOLIC PARTY because they hold the view that the message of Jesus is in essential continuity with that of the so-called apostles of the New Testament. They are also advocates of the view that the myth is the message. And they are staunch advocates of a reverse version of the goal of the original quest.

The Jesus Seminar

We come now to the Jesus Seminar.

The immediate context of the formation of the Jesus Seminar were the radical shifts in the paradigms that informed the scholarly disciplines ingredient or ancillary to NT scholarship. Those shifts prompted many of us to reconceive our approaches to the gospel tradition, or the Jesus tradition, as I prefer to call it. Amos N. Wilder was the precursor of these developments. As a consequence, we formed the parables movement and founded a new journal *Semeia* devoted to these new methods in 1972. A second parent of the Seminar was the work of C. H. Dodd and Joachim Jeremias on the parables of Jesus. But we reversed their apologetic attempt to reconcile Jesus with the gospel of the primitive church and resumed the original quest. We held the organizational meeting of the Seminar in 1979. My health and departure from the SBL/AAR caused us to delay further work until the spring of 1985.

Meanwhile, two scholars who were originally outsiders, Marcus Borg and Thomas Sheehan, anticipated much of the Seminar's agenda. Sheehan published his ground-breaking work, *The First Coming: How the Kingdom of God Became Christianity* in 1986, and Borg published his *Jesus a New Vision* in 1987.

The upshot of this story is that the Jesus Seminar finally succeeded in carrying through in elaborate detail the separation of the historical Jesus from the primitive Christian proclamation. We published our reports as *The Five Gospels* (1993) and *The Acts of Jesus (1998)*. And, so far as I know, the individual scholars who carried through the divorce are all associated with the Seminar. After two hundred years of backing and filling, we finally managed to carry the ball across the goal line.

Digression: A Brief Review of the Basis of Our Decision-Making

We began with the scholarly consensus that the narrative framework of the New Testament gospels was essentially fictive. Historical data, if any, were to be found in the individual pericopes — anecdotes or compendia of teachings — and not in the narrative connectives. It was also common scholarly conviction that a large number of the legendary stories were inventions suggested by the cultural milieu in which the gospel was being promulgated. It does not sound seemly to pious ears, but it is basically correct to describe the gospels as religious propaganda designed to persuade and convert. Miraculous birth, mountain top revelations, voices from the sky, martyr's death, and immortality were all themes alive and well in popular culture in the Roman first century.

Within individual stories and miniature collections of sayings, however, are pearls of wisdom that contrast starkly with the surrounding prosaic terrain. We discovered the parables originally with the help of the new criticism, which enabled us to recognize these short, short stories as works of literary art with their own integrity. As critics bent on escaping from the literalist/dogmatic reading of them, we learned to read them non-literally at more than one level. We took them to be astute observations on the ordinary and everyday. They were so constructed as to satirize the received world and contrast it with Jesus' vision of a counter-reality, as Brandon Scott terms it. Later we discovered the aphorism, the twin of the parable. The aphorism is subversive of conventional wisdom and thus of the proverb. It undermines the old traditions, religious, social, political. Familiarity has robbed us of the ability to see that "Love your enemies" is incomprehensible in a tribal society. We no longer appreciate the fact that "Congratulations, you poor! God's domain belongs to you" is a huge irony for those who sought the restoration of the

Davidic kingdom. Fragments like these provided us with the essential clues. We followed them up diligently, rigorously, item by item through more than 1500 versions. A glimpse of the historical figure began to emerge, and he was not at all what the orthodox tradition had taught us to expect or indeed what we had learned to expect from our mentors.

The Final Set of Barriers

With the historical Jesus liberated from the gospel frame, we were able to break through the Easter barrier. We rejected the notion foisted off on us by our neo-orthodoxy predecessors that there were events that historians dare not assess by historical standards. The empty tomb became one of the early fictions generated by an adoring movement sometime between the death of Jesus and the creation of Mark around 70 C.E. The Sayings Gospel Q and the Gospel of Thomas show no trace of that story.

To the consternation of many, we abandoned the thesis of Weiss and Schweitzer that Jesus was an apocalyptic fanatic. The parables and aphorisms simply do not support that thesis. As Sheehan wrote in 1986, "Strictly speaking, it appears that for Jesus the future did not lie up ahead. . . . The future kingdom had already dawned and the celebration could begin." We took the non-apocalyptic interpretation of Jesus to be "the more difficult reading," which guides decisions in textual criticism: It is easier to hypothesize that apocalyptic sayings were put on the lips of Jesus than to conclude that the non-apocalyptic parables and aphorisms were incorrectly ascribed to him.

We found very few examples of genuine parables in contemporary literature, and we observed that they are exceedingly difficult to imitate. That is not a residue of the Christian assertion that Jesus was a god/man; it is no more than the recognition of Jesus as a wisdom teacher of considerable rhetorical power. We think it only goes with other insights of Jesus that looked a long way into the future. He appears to have observed the fall of Satan and the end of the demonic powers. He seems to have looked beyond tribalism, ethnic privilege, and nationalism. His concern for the birds and flowers may even have foreseen that God's domain was transhuman. He certainly thought the kingdom was transreligious, as Paul Tillich liked to say. The importance of these discoveries can scarcely be exaggerated. It enabled us finally to divorce Jesus from his mentor, John the Baptist, and from the early Jesus movement fueled by former followers of John. Jesus was free at last.

The final barrier that had to come down was the canon. The authority of the New Testament gospels is the ultimate defensive line of orthodoxy. Once Q is admitted into the picture, and the Gospel of Thomas becomes an independent source, the mythical matrix created by the narrative gospels stands out in bold relief.

These then are the achievements of the Jesus Seminar in concert with our mentors and many friends. We should take them as the foundation of the quest for an authentic faith for the new age.

We must take care not to be distracted by the poison barbs of our critics. They have elected to retreat behind the canonical gospels, behind the physical resurrection, and behind the second coming. These are all elements of the supernatural framework, the mythical matrix of the gospels. They have speciously claimed that apocalypticism is what makes Jesus historical and Jewish. That claim, together with a mindless insistence that Jesus could speak only Aramaic, goes together with the politically correct flattening that is so characteristic of our time.

The Transition to a New Agenda

Divorcing Jesus from the mythical matrix by which he was framed is not the end of the story. Somewhere along our journeys — individual and collective — to that conclusion, it dawned on us that the mythical matrix of the gospels had lost its purchase on the modern mind. The confession of Bultmann in 1941 came home to roost.

It is quite possible, even likely, that the collapse of the credibility of the old myth is what opened our eyes to a Jesus emancipated from the mythical overlay. I see no reason to deny the convergence of the two epiphanies. In any case, recognition of the collapse of the myth is what distinguishes us from many of our critics, who seem to think the modern mind can still embrace elements of the old myth.

In spite of its collapse, some Fellows and Associates apparently think that the mythical matrix, when understood as a myth, continues to serve us well. Reduced to shorthand, the myth is still the message. All it wants is appropriate translation and it will provide the basis for the Christian faith into the next millennium. In the Christmas message from *The Center for Progressive Christianity*,

James R. Adams asks, "Cannot perhaps the supernaturalist scheme survive at least as part of the 'magic' of Christmas?" He has John A. T. Robinson answer for him: "Yes, indeed it can survive — as myth. For myth has its perfectly legitimate, and indeed profoundly important, place. The myth is there to indicate the significance of the events, the divine depth of history. And we shall be grievously impoverished if our ears cannot tune to the angels' song or if our eyes are blind to the wise men's star." All that is needed, it seems, is to understand the old myth precisely as myth and all will be well. That appears to be the view that Marc Borg represents. We will undoubtedly want to concede that myth in some form will always be with us. But will it be the same mythical elements — miraculous birth, sacrificial death, bodily resurrection — or will it be some new form of the story more compatible with modern sensibilities? That is the first issue we must clarify in this new phase of the Seminar.

There is a second, related issue. It concerns a rather more sweeping view of the origins of the myth. Can we agree that the Christian myth is a human creation? If it is a human creation, then it is not revealed truth as the church has claimed for all these centuries. It is no more than a mythic shelter devised to house ancient admiration for Jesus. With that change in status, we must adopt as a part of our new quest the search for adequate symbols and the stories in which to house them.

The third issue on our new agenda concerns the relation of Jesus to the mythical matrix. It follows actually from our success in divorcing Jesus from that matrix. If Jesus is contrasted with the mythical frame, can we also say that our profile of Jesus clashes or diverges in significant ways from that matrix? Without being too specific, I think we should test this statement. The outcome will impinge on the agenda we form for the future.

The Historical Agenda

The discovery that historical knowledge has its consequences was the avenue along which we began to recover our public. Scholars in the humanities, and in the theological disciplines in particular, had lost their public. The On-the-Road programs we developed inadvertently opened our eyes to the possibilities and to the need. We discovered that very few scholars in the humanities had bothered to convey the knowledge they possessed, or to interpret it in useful ways, to non-specialists. It was this discovery that prompted us to form this new phase of the Seminar, a quest for a faith for the future.

Meanwhile, we should not, we must not, lose sight of the historical agenda that has brought us this far. In this context I can do no more than list the projects we have yet to finish or which lie before us.

- We need to rewrite the history of the quest for the historical Jesus.
- We need to produce a new history of the gospel (better: Jesus) tradition.
- We need to issue a new New Testament in multiple versions.
  a. One version of a new New Testament should contain only the voices of the original strong poets, Jesus and Paul.
  b. A second version should contain the customary twenty-seven books, plus the Gospel of Thomas and a few others, arranged chronologically.
  c. A third version should contain all the extant documents of the early Christian movement.
- We should issue a new Bible in which an SV translation of the LXX replaces the Hebrew Bible, thus reinstating the original scriptural legacy of the early Christian community.
- We need to pursue the quest for Christian origins in the period 30 C.E. to 70 C.E.
  a. We need to finish work on the quest of the historical Paul.
  b. We need to finish work on a color-coded Acts.
  c. We need to launch a study of Q for the data it yields for Christian origins.
  d. We then need to produce a synthesis of the data we have collected.
- We need to produce a Scholars Version of *The Complete Letters*.
- We need to produce a Scholars Version of *The Complete Acts*.
- We need to launch a quest for the historical Israel. Our only goal would be to determine when the real history of Israel begins by color-coding the so-called historical books as we go.
- We need to contribute in basic ways to the revision of the infrastructure of the discipline.
  a. Daryl Schmidt and colleagues need to complete work on a new Blass-Debrunner-Funk.
  b. We need to finish work on reference tools, such as New

Gospel Parallels, Sayings Parallels, Acts Parallels, in both English and original language versions

c. We need to produce an original language version of *The Complete Gospels, The Complete Letters,* and *the Complete Acts.*

- We need to develop a curriculum series for the Westar Institute as the basis of our On-the-Road programs and for the Westar Academy.
- We need to produce a documentary film depicting the work of the Seminar.

The Future Agenda

The lectures and essays prepared for the March 2001 meeting of the Seminar and published in this volume have identified a number of basic themes and issues that will have to be on our agenda for further exploration.

Karen Armstrong suggests that we are even now in the midst of a second axial age. The first axial age witnessed the birth of numerous religious traditions in various parts of the world. After the great prophets of Israel, the Buddha, Lao Tze, Confucius, and others, nothing was ever the same. As we enter the global age, following the Enlightenment, those ancient traditions, as vigorous as they are, will undergo a radical transformation. The new axial age will constitute a new beginning.

Lloyd Geering proposes that we reconsider the doctrine of the trinity as a secular doctrine. The three members of the new trinity are the self-creating universe, the self-evolving human species, and the new global consciousness. Those three correspond to the Father, the Son, and the Holy Spirit. Rather than simply giving up the doctrine of trinity, Geering thinks we may salvage it by a bold reinterpretation to bring it in line with what we know of the physical universe.

Armstrong and Geering have challenged us to clear away the debris of the first axial age and be prepared to start over again.

Don Cupitt, Jack Spong, and Roy Hoover all call for a Reformation.

Don Cupitt also thinks we must clear away the debris from Christian orthodoxy. We should challenge orthodox Christianity on its own grounds and show the inner contradictions in its premises. In the process we will want to exchange church-religion for kingdom-religion, as he terms it. Kingdom religion is ethical and this-worldly. It is concerned to dedicate itself to life and to neighbor in the present, as Jesus taught. The church, on the other hand, substituted a mediated religion that was institutionalized as a salvation machine. We must now reverse that process.

Bishop Spong believes the church can be reformed if it recovers the original response to Jesus by his first followers. That response, as it turns out, presupposes a Jesus that is not greatly different from the Jesus uncovered by the Jesus Seminar in the course of its critical work. But the departure from orthodoxy that Spong proposes is no less radical than the program of Don Cupitt. Spong affirms the reality of God but believes all responses to God are human contrivances. Yet the God we meet in Jesus as the Christ calls all our preconceptions into question.

Roy Hoover joins this chorus of voices in calling for a recovery of the tradition in the light of the findings of historical-critical scholarship and the paradigm shift that has taken place. He believes we have inherited an incredible Christ; what we need now is a credible faith that will bear the weight of the future.

We have assumed that the genuine words and deeds of Jesus offer some promising clues for constructing a faith for the future. Ferreting out those clues is perhaps one of the first items on the agenda for gospel scholars. Robert J. Miller asks why critics of the Seminar have clung tenaciously to an apocalyptic Jesus — a Jesus who thought the world would come to a catastrophic end, followed by a new golden age. Miller exposes some of the investment our critics have in the old view. Among the most devastating is the proclivity to retain divine violence as a basic principle: a God who will wipe out evil by destroying evil persons.

Brandon Scott takes a bold step into our future agenda by asking whether we can derive an ethic from the parables of Jesus. Utilizing the parable of the leaven, he suggests that Jesus' God may be "unclean," which is the reason Jesus embraced the unclean in his society. Scott draws the conclusion that the phrase "kingdom of God" embodies a huge irony: God's domain is nothing like the Roman Empire or the Davidic kingdom it references.

Arthur Dewey and Stephen Patterson address one of the most difficult and pervasive issues in Christian theology: How are we to understand the death of Jesus? Dewey argues that we should read the passion narrative non-realistically. In this he is following the lead of Don Cupitt. The orthodox tradition understands the story of Jesus' death realistically: that tradition believes Jesus died at the behest of God for the sins of humankind. A non-nealistic reading reads Jesus' death in a variety of ways, depending on the community in which the story is being interpreted. That opens up the possibility that Jesus was a martyr in the tradition of the Maccabees and other Jewish heroes.

Stephen Patterson adopts this suggestion and provides it with the historical context of the understanding of the death of the hero in hellenistic times. Plato interprets Socrates' death as a noble death: he dies rather than compromise his position. Jesus, too, dies for a cause — the truth he has enunciated about the empire of God. Thus, in related ways Patterson and Dewey have opened up the delicate issue of why Jesus died. Both are attempts to move beyond accusations regarding who killed Jesus into new territory. The reformation of Christianity, if it is to succeed, must tackle this paramount problem.

My own modest proposal for our future agenda is this: We need to conceive a faith that reconciles our need to know historically and scientifically with our need to create symbols and form myths. That means we must explore the parameters of a faith inspired by Jesus on a much broader front, including the biological, environmental, psychological, and social sciences. And we must include architecture and the arts, visual and aural, as well as performing.

The initial problem we face is the extent to which what we know, or think we know, contravenes the myths we have inherited. As scholars of the Christian tradition, we are in a quandary. Many of the biblical myths we have inherited are at odds with aspects of our knowledge of the physical universe. We simply cannot ignore those discrepancies. My fear is that we will fudge the discrepancies, paste over them, and extend the proclivity to bask in the past.

Our first brush with these larger issues occurred more than a century ago in connection with the creation story in Genesis. Our record as interpreters of scripture has not been stellar; we have been content to let scientists fight the battles with the creationists, while we remained silent on the sidelines. Consider this recent statement by Stuart Kauffman, a biologist and MacArthur Fellow at the Santa Fe Institute:

Until Copernicus, we believed ourselves to be at the center of the universe. . . . To pre-Copernican Christian civilization, the geocentric view was no mere matter of science. Rather, it was the cornerstone evidence that the entire universe revolved around us. With God, angels, man, the beasts, and fertile plants made for our benefit, with the sun and stars wheeling overhead, we knew our place: at the center of God's creation. The church feared rightly that the Copernican views would ultimately dismantle the unity of a thousand-year old tradition of duty and rights, of obligations and roles, of moral fabric.[1]

Biblical scholars have long since acknowledged the mythic character of the Genesis account. We know that Adam and Eve do not represent individuals created at the beginning of time. But we have not been as clear that the myth itself is flawed. In addition to the fact that its cosmology is mistaken, it assigns a special place in creation to humankind, and thus assigns a lower status to all other living creatures. It endorses the subordination of women to their male partners. The myth reflects the kind of human hubris that now threatens the future of the planet.

The Genesis story needs to be replaced by one that sponsors evolutionary and ecological humility. Life existed on this planet aeons before humanoids appeared. We are no more than a late bubble on the evolutionary pond. This story, moreover, became the source of the "fall" and "sin" and "redemption" that helped give birth finally to the church as a bureaucratic salvation machine, to use Don Cupitt's phrase. At one point in its history, the "fall" became a fall into sexuality, the consequence of which, according to Augustine, was that Adam's sin was transmitted to all his progeny through male sperm. If we could perpetuate the human species without sexual intercourse, without the conjunction of female egg and male sperm, I suppose we could eradicate sin and restore the garden in a single generation. But of course we can't. And I imagine we don't really want to. Yet these strands of the Genesis myth have dire implications for how we understand ourselves and the world. There is thus a great deal that calls for correction beyond the recognition that the story is not history but myth.

As Anne Primavesi sums it up, "The 'beginning,' that putative moment indelibly inscribed on Christian consciousness, is no longer

---

1. Kauffman, *At Home in the Universe*, 5.

a sure source of knowledge about ourselves now, or about our present relationship with the world or with God."[2]

Traditional Christian theology has ignored the implications of evolutionary theory by reducing the story of human kind to one species, homo sapiens, and then further reduced the critical account to a particular people at a particular time and place in history. The story of the chosen people is all too often a picture of conquest, slaughter, pillage, and violence directed towards both the land and those conquered. All in the name of a God who has favorites. All three branches of the Abrahamic tradition are guilty of this narrowing. We can no longer accept this pre-Enlightenment view.

We have steadily refused to acknowledge the status of our species. We continue to insist that human beings are a special creation, with certain inalienable rights in relation to the rest of creation. And we have built the Christian myth on this premise by insisting that our messiah is a special creation of God via the virgin birth, without the benefit of normal sexual contact, and that he is unique among all God's creatures. God reveals the divine through a human vessel, which once again asserts that the human species is the only part of creation really akin to God. The doctrine of the incarnation is the siamese twin of the creation myth: they are joined at the heart.

Christian theologians have traditionally held that Jesus is God. If Jesus is not God, or at least the son of God, we will have to revise our notions of God. However, the old concept of God has suffered erosion in and of itself.

We can no longer understand God as the creator of the species. We can no longer understand God as an interventionist tyrant as he is depicted in the Old Testament. The creator God stands at the beginning of history, while the interventionist God meddles in history midstream. God as judge, God of the apocalypse, stands at the end of history. That God, like the Second Coming, no longer plays a role in our mythical heavens.

God has become mostly unemployed as the old doctrines have atrophied. At the same time, our notions of the physical universe have left God homeless. For a time we assigned God to the depths of the psyche. The depths gave way eventually to God as the equivalent

---

2. Primavesi, *Sacred Gaia*, 39. (Anne Primavesi has accepted our invitation to become a Fellow and will make a major presentation at our March 2002 conference.)

energy diffused throughout the universe. Panentheism became the in concept.

The problem we face is that God is not a primary datum. God is derivative of the human imagination. We do not know God directly; no one has seen God, or heard or smelled God. Those who claim to know God can only give us an account of their experiences. An experience of God, or a revelation from God, is an interpreted experience, since there is no such thing as an uninterpreted experience. It seems we have invented God in our own image.

Rebellion, Revolution, and Reform

We have a revolt underway, perhaps even a rebellion, against the elitist conspiracy of scholarly secrecy. But we should turn our rebellion into a revolution. To do that we will unfortunately require organization. We will have to modify the format of the Seminar in order to accommodate more Fellows representing a wider range of expertise. We will probably be forced to break up into smaller working seminars before reconvening as a committee of the whole. The sessions will require careful preparation and disciplined conversations.

In the next phase, we will want to enlarge our Associates base. At the same time, we will need to increase the interface with Associates, who will assume a much larger role in the direction of the Seminar. We may want to develop a special section for clergy, who have joined us in increasing numbers.

We will need to create a curriculum of short books and study guides to assist with the training of teachers. In that connection, many of us think we have a Westar Academy in our future — a center for our conferences and short courses.

We have talked of a conference of outrageously successful liberal churches. The purpose of such a conference would be to showcase models that have proved workable. We have imagined a conference of ecclesiastical leaders who are willing to break silence and speak out.

In all of this it is imperative that we retain the present core of the Seminar and maintain its integrity. The constant temptation will be to give in to soft judgments and easy accommodation. We must keep the gyroscope of Christian self-criticism spinning in order to sustain our course.

I can imagine that we will develop regional chapters of the friends of Westar, such as those forming in Arizona, Alabama, and Florida. These local groups will become the hubs of On-the-Road programs in those regions. With their aid, we will infiltrate and undermine the smugness of the mainline churches with knowledge of the past and prospects for the future. We will take no dissembling prisoners; we will create space for honesty and candor. The best thing we have going for us is our critical purchase on the past and our wide-angle perspective on the present and future.

The future of the Christian faith may turn out to be a minor aspect of the cultural shifts that are shaping our global future. The themes that have dominated the institutional churches may no longer be of central concern to us. But no matter. Yet at the heart of the old faith tradition there are topics and themes that are central to the human condition and the fate of the planet in the next millennium. Our task is to locate those themes and set them in a new and broader context.

Finally, it is well to remind ourselves that our task is not messianic. It may turn out not to be very important. Yet we must act on what we know, or think we know, at this moment in history. To do anything less would be to betray the faith we have.

Works Cited

Kauffman, Stuart A. *At Home in the Universe: The Search for Laws of Self-Organization and Complexity.* New York : Oxford University Press, 1995.
Primavesi, Anne. *Sacred Gaia: Holistic Theology and Earth System.* London-New York: Routledge, 2000.

Suggestions for a Second Axial Age

Karen Armstrong

We have been asked to propose an agenda for a radical reformation of Christianity. Any reform movement looks back to the origins of a tradition or to a Golden Age before the present troubles set in. We seek inspiration from the past, when the faith was strong and luminous, in order to correct the abuses of our own time and to find hope to pass on to the next generation. Religion and spirituality are difficult. There is no need for each of us to invent the wheel afresh each time we seek renewal. Some difficulties are perennial, some past solutions can be applied, with modification, to our own situation. In fact, this happens all the time. Any tradition represents a constant dialogue between the transcendent reality that is the goal of its quest and the constantly shifting conditions of this world. As we struggle to find meaning and value in an inescapably flawed existence, each generation has to examine the tradition it has inherited and make its scriptures speak to its unique circumstances. This is a constant task, not limited to our own day. So Christianity is indeed a "once and future faith." It is rooted in the past; we need the past to give light to the troubled present, but we cannot allow ourselves to be imprisoned by doctrines and concepts that were formed in a completely different world. If the faith is to have a future, we must be creative and selective with our scriptures and doctrines, as religious people have always been.

In the sixteenth century, the Protestant reformers looked back to primitive Christianity and to the Fathers of the Church. But I want to look back to a more distant period, to that era of history which the German philosopher Karl Jaspers called the Axial Age, because it proved to be pivotal to the spiritual development of humanity. The Axial Age began in about 800 B.C.E. and had come to an end by 200 B.C.E. In three core areas — China, India and the Eastern Mediterranean — religious geniuses shaped traditions which have continued to nourish human beings to the present day: Taoism and Confucianism in China; Jainism, Buddhism and Hinduism in the

19

Indian subcontinent; monotheism in Israel; and rationalism in Greece. Christianity — like Rabbinic Judaism and Islam — was a later powerful and eloquent latter-day expression of this Axial spirit Why am I going back so far in time? Because I believe that possibly the greatest religious gift of the 20th century was our new understanding of other faith traditions. For the first time in human history, we had the opportunity to recognize the profound unanimity of the religious quest in all cultures. This is not to say that all religions are the same. Each has its particular genius, each its peculiar failings, but beneath all the challenging differences, there are strong and arresting similarities.

Until the late nineteenth and early twentieth centuries, most people knew little about other religions. Travelers brought back exotic tales of bizarre religious practices, but now improved communication means that we can begin to understand the faith that lay behind them, a faith which bears close similarities to our own. We have not yet begun to appreciate the profound significance of this development. We shall never be able to think of our own or other people's faith in the same way again. It is becoming increasingly difficult — I would say, impossible — to believe that any one tradition has the monopoly of truth. Already, without abandoning the faith they were born to, people are seeking help from more than one religion. Christians read Martin Buber; Jews read Paul Tillich and Harvey Cox; Jesuits study meditation with Zen monks. To dismiss this as "pick and mix" religion its to trivialize an important and potentially enriching development, an inevitable consequence of living in a global society. To consider Christianity in isolation is to deny one of the major religious realities of our time. If Christianity is to survive in the twenty-first century and beyond, it must consider itself in relationship to the other great traditions. Indeed, Christians can learn a great deal from them which could be helpful in their present dilemma. So to look back on Christian origins alone during our proposed reformation would be parochial. Let us look back instead to the fathers of faith as we know it and consider the spirit and circumstances in which they reformed their old pagan traditions during the Axial Age and thus led their people into a transformed and enlightened future.

After the Axial Age, nothing was ever the same again. There have only been two other comparable periods of change. One is lost to us in the obscurity of prehistory. It has been called the Promethean Revolution, because it marked the "moment" when men and women discovered how to harness the element of fire to their needs and thus gained a measure of control over the physical world. It was the beginning of technology and a new era of material efficiency. The second period of major change is what is known as the Great Western Transformation, which began in Europe during the sixteenth century and is still in progress. It inaugurated a wholly new kind of civilization, one based on technology and capital investment instead of upon a surplus of agricultural produce like all the previous premodern cultures. Our modernity has shattered old sanctities and radically altered human life in ways that we are only just beginning to appreciate. It has seemed inimical to traditional faith and that is why we are holding this conference. As a result of the Great Western Transformation we cannot be religious in the same way as our ancestors. There was a similar crisis at the time of the Axial Transformation, and people needed new insights to help them to make sense of their radically altered circumstances. It has often been said, therefore, that today we are living through a Second Axial Age, when yet again the old religious ideas no longer make sense and new solutions are necessary. But I am beginning to conclude that what the West actually unleashed in the sixteenth century was a new Promethean Revolution, a new age of technology, and that we have not yet begun the hard creative work that is essential if we are to inaugurate a second spiritual revolution. We have had scientific and religious geniuses, but no religious leaders of the stature of the Buddha, Isaiah, Plato or Lao Tzu. But their example can at least help us to see what we are up against. We cannot copy them exactly, any more than the Protestant reformers could reproduce the Primitive Church in the early modern period. But we can see the spirit which enabled these men to break so completely with the past that they were able to bring a lasting new spiritual perception to the world.

Today we often feel that we are living on the brink of catastrophe, and fear the new world order that is coming into being. So too did the people of the Axial Age. It was a time of immense social, political and economic upheaval. China was caught up in centuries of internecine, warfare, anarchy and political strife. In the Ganges basin in North India there was a major economic and social revolution, accompanied by the emergence of powerful and aggressive monarchies that violently absorbed the older republics and kingdoms. Like all social change, this brought with it great fear and insecurity, not to mention untold suffering as people were caught up in the incessant warfare. In the Middle East, the rise of mighty empires led to the obliteration of smaller states and massive deportations during which whole peoples were forcibly resettled thousands of miles from their homelands. Greece had an initially more peaceful introduction to the new world order,, but then almost unwittingly began a political transformation which has left an indelible impression on the Western world. In the course of these change, old and precious ways of life were annihilated and the traditional religions could no longer provide adequate answers. Some scholars call the Axial Age the "Great Reversal" because the old mythologies seemed to have failed and the sense of holiness, which had once permeated the whole of life, had apparently departed from the world. There was alienation, terror and despair. In the three core Axial areas, life seemed drained of the meaning that human beings, who fall very easily into hopelessness, need if they are to survive. New solutions were essential.

The old gods began to lose their appeal during this crisis. These deities gradually receded from the consciousness of the more thoughtful people. In Israel, prophets and psalmists turned on the old gods in fury. The Bible makes it clear that for centuries the Israelites had worshipped other, so-called pagan gods alongside their own tribal god Yahweh. They worshipped the Canaanite gods Baal, Asherah, and Astarte; some were devotees of Mesopotamian astral cults, which had even penetrated the Temple in Jerusalem. But as the Axial movement developed in Israel, reformers such as King Josiah tore down the altars of these gods and murdered their priests. Others simply excoriated them: these gods, they claimed, were merely homemade deities, knocked together by a craftsman in a couple of hours. They consisted simply of gold and silver; they had eyes that did not see, ears that did not hear; they could not walk and had to be carted about by their worshippers. They were brutish and stupid subhuman beings that were no better than scarecrows in a melon patch. The pagans and Israelites who worshipped them were fools and Yahweh hated them. In other Axial countries, people did not turn against the old gods. In India and Greece, they either reinterpreted the old theology or turned the gods into symbols of an absolute transcendence or else saw them as projections of purely human states of mind.

There are clear similarities with our own dilemma. Today we have lost the ability to think mythologically, as people by and large did in the premodern world. In the eighteenth and nineteenth centuries, scientific rationalism made such huge strides and achieved such astonishing results in the West that reason and logic became the only valid means of arriving at truth. The more intuitive approach of myth was discredited.

As a result, in popular parlance, a "myth" simply means something that is not true. This means that we interpret our scriptures in a wholly literal way, instead of seeking the metaphysical and allegorical interpretations that mystics, kabbalists and theologians relished before the advent of modernity. Not surprisingly, the mythos of the Bible has become incredible to many people. So has God. In my country, in Britain, only about 8 percent of the population attends a religious service on a regular basis. Churches are being turned into warehouses, theatres and art-galleries. And people tend to inveigh against God and religion as vehemently as Hebrew prophets of the Axial Age lambasted the pagan deities. The chattering classes of London may be very liberal in some matters, but can be positively bigoted on the subject of faith. It is so discredited that people in general do not want to hear that there might be another way of looking at religion. To reject violently the symbols of a faith which has failed one is a common response in the history of religion. In much the same spirit, some of the radical Protestants of the early modern reformation in Europe smashed the statues of the saints and vandalized Catholic and Anglican churches. Here in America my impression is that people are not so given to this type of verbal iconoclasm, but are more prepared, like the Axial sages of India and Greece, to reinterpret the old theology and give it a new significance.

But there is no doubt that a void has been an inescapable part of the modern experience. The vehemence of fundamentalism often seems like a desperate attempt to prop up the old beliefs. Whether one calls it the death of God (as Nietzsche did) or speaks, like Sartre, of a God-shaped hole in our consciousness, we feel our loss in much the same way as, some 4000 years ago, during the Axial Age, people suffered their Great Reversal. But we have something more in common with this distant period, because the prevailing forms of Christianity (and perhaps other faiths) bear a very strong resemblance to some aspects of the old religion that the Axial sages were trying to reform. We lack the vibrant holism of the pagan vision, in which the divine was felt to be all-pervasive and in which no painful gulf yet yawned between the gods and the mundane world. But the churches, it seems to me, often go out of their way to reproduce some of the less positive characteristics of primordial religion.

In most cultures, pre-Axial faith gave sacred significance to the status quo. There was a divine order which all beings had to obey and which was beyond question. There was no need for a religious quest, because sacred knowledge was a given, received from outside, cast in stone and already in place. Religion often had a magical character: prayers and sacrifices, for example, could change the weather and were thought to keep the world in existence. Nearly all sacred lore was esoteric, the preserve of a priestly elite and kept from the masses, who were required simply to follow their leaders. Based as it was on a timeless order, there could be no alteration of the religious ethos and, indeed, for millennia, there seems to have been little spiritual change. This static type of faith gave people a sense of security in a world where progress was slow and imperceptible. Does this religious stasis sound at all familiar? Our priests do not perform animal sacrifice like the Indian Brahmins or the priests in Jerusalem. We may not even have a priesthood in our particular church. But most churches have an elite that believes itself to be the guardian of sacred, immutable truth. In the interests of preserving this truth, they are perfectly ready to conduct heresy trials, to excommunicate or expel those who challenge this holy order. The status quo still has sacred significance; it is still regarded by many as beyond question. The churches don't really like the idea of a quest because the faith has been revealed already, once and for all. If the people do not understand this sacred lore or complain that it seems incredible, they are told — often sharply — to "take it on faith." and accept the view that is called "orthodoxy." The churches often talk theology in such archaic and abstruse ways — using concepts and language so far removed from ordinary modern ways of thinking and speaking — that it might as well be esoteric. Isolated in this way, it is not surprising that a good deal of what passes for "faith" is really magical thinking: a prayer, it is thought, can cure cancer, or at least ensure good weather for the Sunday School picnic.

So what changed ? Was the Axial Age a failure? People still revere Confucius, Socrates and the Buddha, as Christians revere Jesus. They have even deified these men in ways that would have seemed shocking to their contemporaries in the Axial Age. Yet this exaltation of these reformers shows that we recognize their immense significance and the value of what they taught or achieved. These paradigmatic figures can still fill us with intense emotion; this, we feel, is how human beings are supposed to be. Even secularists tacitly acknowledge this, when they praise Jesus as a revolutionary thinker, or, so limited is their view of religion (thanks in no small part to the behavior of the religious) they deny that the Buddha or Confucius were religious men at all. They want to claim them for their secularist camp. But despite the esteem in which they are now held, very few of their contemporaries could really follow the Axial teachers. Their position was often too radical. There is always a temptation to scuttle back to the old static forms of faith and take refuge in a religion of immutable truth that absolves us from the painful duty of change. Many religious people who revere Isaiah, the Buddha or Lao Tzu would be shocked by some of their views, because they have little in common with the popular view of faith in the modern world. Very few of the Axial sages believed in the supernatural; none were much interested in an afterlife; they refused to provide the faithful with obligatory doctrines, and gave their disciples none of the certainties that people often expect of religion today.

The greatest of the Axial thinkers had no time for a timorous adherence to the status quo. They questioned everything; nothing was safe from their scrutiny. In their teaching, old values and doctrines, hitherto accepted without demur, were overturned. The Axial Sages smashed into the old orthodoxy. One need only think of Socrates, who was never content to accept traditional certainties as final, however august they might be. Instead of receiving knowledge passively from heaven and submitting to mysterious divine decrees, each individual must find the truth within his or her own being. Socrates called everything into question, infecting his interlocutors with his own perplexity, since confusion was not a sign of spiritual weakness but the beginning of the philosophical quest. Everybody, Confucius declared, must work things out for himself. Lao Tzu believed that all values, all morality, all truths were relative; all our human doctrines and rituals were provisional, imperfect reflections of the eternal Tao, which remains opaque to human understanding. The Buddha refused to accept any of the teachings of the past as final; he also rejected the doctrines of all the great spiritual leaders of his own day, when he found that they did not bring him to the enlightenment of Nirvana. He insisted that his disciples must have the same potentially rebellious attitude. They must test every aspect of his own teaching empirically, accepting nothing on hearsay or at second hand. He would have been horrified at the idea of "taking things on faith." If a teaching did not resonate with one's own experience and did not help the seeker to make progress, it must be rejected. No human doctrine could be final or permanent — not even his own. He liked to compare his teachings to a raft, telling the story of a traveler who had come to a great expanse of water and desperately needed to get across. There was no bridge, no ferry, so he built a raft and rowed himself across the river. But then, the Buddha would ask his audience, what should the traveler do with this raft? Should he decide that because it had been so helpful to him, he should load it onto his back and lug it around with him wherever he went? Or should he simply moor it and continue his journey? The answer was obvious. "In just the same way, monks, my teachings are like a raft, to be used to cross the river not for holding on to," the Buddha concluded. "Letting go" is one of the keynotes of the Buddha's teachings. A religious idea could all too easily become a mental idol. The enlightened person did not grab or hold on to even the most authoritative instructions. Everything was transient, and until his disciples recognized this in every fiber of their beings, they would never reach Nirvana.

Even though, in some respects, monotheism was initially less advanced than some of the other Axial ideologies (catching up later in Rabbinic Judaism, Christianity and Islam), the great prophets were just as iconoclastic as the Buddha, overturning many of the old mythical certainties of ancient Israel. God, they taught, was no longer automatically on the side of his people, as he had been at the time of the Exodus from Egypt. He would now use Gentile nations to punish the Israelites, each of whom had a personal responsibility to act with justice, equity and fidelity. Salvation no longer depended upon external rules; there would be a new law and a new covenant inscribed in the heart of each individual. The notion of personal responsibility was crucial to the Axial Age. Nobody should revere a religious authority but was responsible for his or her own salvation: this notion of liberty and independence was also vital in Greece, India, and China, as well as in Israel. Similarly, Jesus, as presented in the gospels, also shows scant respect for authority or tradition per se. He is constantly shown consorting with the wrong people, antagonizing the establishment, violating purity conventions, offending expectations, even — like some of the prophets — belittling the sacred institution of the Temple, without which the religious life of Israel was at this point unthinkable. Over and over again, the evangelists present him as an iconoclast, shocking his contemporaries and, finally, being convicted of blasphemy. In this, Jesus had fully imbibed the Axial spirit. To create a new religious vision, perhaps, we have to be ready to be as offensive as Jesus seems to have been, overturning old sanctities and reaching creatively for a new religious solution that is no longer enmeshed in the shibboleths of the past.

It is interesting that Christianity has been so particularly concerned about the doctrinal formulation of ineffable truth. It is very difficult to find a single doctrinal definition in the teaching of Jesus, who, like the prophets, Lao Tzu and the Buddha, seems remarkably insouciant about theology. We do not hear him pronouncing definitively on any of the dogmas that are now held to be essential to the faith: Original Sin, the Incarnation, the Trinity, the Atonement. One suspects that Jesus might have been rather surprised by some of these theological ideas, since most of them evolved centuries after his death. St. Augustine's doctrine of Original Sin, St. Athanasius's formulation of the Incarnation, the Cappadocian Fathers' Trinitarian dogma, or St. Anselm's theology of the Atonement all seemed a good idea at the time. All were highly inventive — and sometimes rather controversial ways of making the Christian tradition address the difficult circumstances of the theologians' own day. But if they do not speak to our own condition, perhaps we should treat them like the Buddha's raft, put them to one side, with gratitude, and continue on our way. Just because they have once been very helpful to Christians in the past does not mean that we need to lug them around with us forever. All too often such doctrines can become a mental fetter, impeding us from enlightenment. Like Augustine, Athanasius and Anselm, we should perhaps create our own ways of speaking about Christianity. We should also be creative and inventive with the tradition, as they were, but in the certain knowledge, that when they have served their term, these new "doctrines" of ours should also be let go.

To make sure that we do not throw out the baby with the bathwater, we could try to see what lies at the heart of each of these cherished doctrines and whether they contain some core insight that is worth preserving. Thus at the center of the Greek Fathers' doctrine of the Trinity was a salutary vision of the absolute mystery and ineffability of the reality that we call God, whose essence is always beyond our ken. The Trinity à la Grecque is a reminder to Christians that they cannot think about God as though "he" were a simple, single personality, that the mysterious and ineffable God could only reveal himself in a mysterious and incomprehensible manner. If the Trinity was irrational and contradictory, that, for the Greeks, was the whole point. The Greeks later developed a maxim: every theological statement should be paradoxical, to remind us that when we are speaking about God we are at the end of what thoughts and words can do and that the divine cannot easily be contained within a human system of thought. Further, Greek Trinitarianism is incomprehensible outside the context of liturgy and contemplation; it cannot be understood "cold", in the same rational way that we can follow a mathematical equation. We have to train ourselves to read it, as though it were poetry — which, indeed, it is. This was the useful insight that informed the Greek formulation of the

Trinity in the fourth century. It is clearly not conveyed in Western Trinitarianism, which often degenerates into an empty jingle: "Three in One and One in Three". which leaves us baffled and frustrated. Certainly, the ineffability of God is not much stressed in a good deal of conventional Western Christianity. Many church officials and preachers seem entirely confident about the nature of the divine, can second-guess God, explain his will, pronouncing definitively on his likes and dislikes, which often bear an uncanny resemblance to the preacher's own prejudices.

One attitude that we can certainly learn from the Axial sages is reticence when speaking of the Ultimate. "The Tao that can be spoken of is not the eternal Tao; the Name that can be named is not the eternal Name." This is the way Lao Tzu opens the *Tao Te Ching*. Confucius refused to speak about the Tao at all, preferring to maintain a reverent silence. When asked whether Nirvana existed, the Buddha replied that this was an inappropriate question, because normal words and concepts are inadequate to describe this final Reality. If no description can define the Tao, Nirvana or God, then no theology can be definitive, whatever the churches claim. Monotheists have conceived of God as personal, but not always, as we have seen, as a single personality like ourselves, writ large, with likes and dislikes similar to our own, which can simply become an idol, created in our own image and likeness. The personalized God is not the only way of speaking about the divine or the Sacred. The Axial thinkers described the Ultimate in many ways: as ineffable, impersonal (beyond personality as It is beyond all other human categories) as Mother rather than Father, as Emptiness, as the Void, as Nothing, because it bears no relation to any of the other "things" we know. It is not another Being. It is found in the depths of one's own self, as well as "out there." It is experienced as the immanent *atman*, the Self, as the peace of Nirvana which rises up from the roots of our own psyche at the moment of enlightenment. If Christians have problems — as many do with the notion of God as a personality — they are in tune with some of the greatest mystics of the Axial Age. Even the Hebrew prophets, who did see God as a thinking, speaking personality, experienced this holiness as a near lethal shock, beyond any other human experience. Second Isaiah, the first prophet to enunciate a clear and unequivocal monotheism in the mid-sixth century B.C.E. makes God say: "For my thoughts are not your thoughts, my ways are not your ways; As high as heaven is above the earth, so are my thoughts above your thoughts, my ways above your ways."

So how do we reach this Transcendence? The most insightful of the Axial thinkers insisted that people had to enter deeply into their own conscious and unconscious minds and grapple with the obscure roots of pain and desire. With varying degrees of intensity, they introduced their fellow men and women into their inner worlds. They were pioneers of the hitherto uncharted realm of the psyche. In India, especially, the yogis had discovered the unconscious millennia before Freud and Jung. In this sense, the Axial Age saw the initiation of humanity into its self. For the first time, human beings became acquainted with the deeper recesses and complexities of their condition. The sages all reinterpreted the old myths and cultic practices of their culture to give them a more interior, spiritual dimension, undeterred by the fact that that they were flying in the face of a more literalistic and externally-oriented tradition. They broke through to a new realm of interior experience and found that in the course of the meditative and liturgical practices they evolved, men and women were fundamentally changed. The aim was not to impart privileged information or obligatory doctrines, but to transform the way in which human beings thought and felt. In India, Buddhists and Hindus cultivated a sense of the Sacred by means of yoga. Plato insisted that the philosopher trained his mind by the disciplines of philosophy, especially mathematics, which would teach him to turn from the external world and concentrate on the inner abstract laws and forms of existence. He would then wake up to a more profound level of his own nature, to an ecstatic union with the divine. This was what the Buddha had called "direct' 'knowledge: not based on hearsay, on information received at second hand, but a knowledge in which nothing interposed between the sacred and the individual psyche and the truths of religion became a living reality. But all the sages were aware that this demanded hard work. The sense of sacredness had to be cultivated as assiduously as we cultivate a sense of art or music, or the ability to appreciate the beauty of mathematics. Without this special mental training, we cannot gain this direct apprehension of the divine, which requires a more intuitive and disciplined type of approach than truths which are immediately perceptible. The Axial transformation was, therefore, not a doctrinal but a spiritual reformation. Here too, it can help us in our present dilemma. Many are so weary of doctrines and orthodoxies that they feel alienated from faith itself. A spiritual renewal should be the hallmark of any new reformation today. We should follow the Axial sages in valuing spirituality more than theology. One of the chief aims of Axial contemplation was to restrain the egotism which, the reformers believed, holds us back from the Ultimate. The disciplines of Yoga were not designed to improve our posture, help us to lose weight, or make us feel more comfortable with ourselves, as Yoga is often understood in the West today. It was a devastating and systematic assault on the ego, which took the "P" out of the yogin's thinking. Confucius taught that by surrendering to the ancient Chinese rituals and liturgies, the individual would do violence to his natural inclinations, overcome pettiness and achieve a transcendence of self. By laying aside the demands of the clamorous greedy ego, the seeker would find a liberating peace which would bring him or her into what monotheists would call the Presence of God.

Much institutional religion, however, seems chiefly concerned to prop up the ego that we are supposed to transcend. Churches that are obsessed with their own survival have lost the plot. They might benefit from the Buddha's teaching of *anatta* (no-self) which suggested that living as though the self did not exist would bring a monk to Nirvana, and that we are most fully ourselves when we give ourselves away. Or they could remember Jesus' words: "Unless the grain of wheat die, it remains nothing more than a grain of wheat; but if it dies, it brings forth much fruit."

Yoga and ritual was an important way of mitigating egotism, but the chief means taught by all the Axial leaders was the disciplined practice of compassion, which demands that we dethrone the self from the center of our universe and place other beings there. The Axial philosophers lived in violent times. They recoiled in horror from the aggression of their society and evolved different ways of moderating the desire to injure other creatures in the struggle for personal survival. The Hebrew prophets insisted that religion was pointless unless the Israelites took care of the orphans, the widows and the oppressed. Centuries before Rabbi Hillel and Jesus enunciated the Golden Rule, Confucius had insisted: "Do not do unto others what you would not have done unto you." Buddha taught the same rule. He also taught monks and layfolk alike a meditation in which they directed thoughts and feelings of compassion and sympathetic love to all four corners of the earth, not omitting a single creature from this radius of benevolence. . . . By practicing compassion, Buddhists would reach *cetto-vimutti*, a "release of the mind," a phrase which in the Buddhist scriptures is a synonym for the supreme enlightenment

So for Christians who fear that science has discredited their traditions or who feel crippled by ancient doctrines that make no sense, the Axial thinkers offer a salutary alternative. Instead of obedience to authority, they preached independence and even rebellion against the constraints of the status quo. Instead of accepting abstruse dogma on faith, they advocated a "direct" knowledge, that was the result of spiritual disciplines. Their religion consisted not of theology and conformity but depended solely on a spirituality that taught disciples to explore the inner world and encounter a Sacred Peace or Presence there; if they laid aside selfishness and practiced the compassion that would teach them to value others as themselves, they experience a liberation and transcendence We cannot imitate the Axial Sages in toto. They were not perfect. One of the great flaws of the Axial Age was its denigration of women, who were reduced to second-class status in all these faiths. New forms of Christianity must rectify this imbalance between the sexes, which has been a blot on the history of all the churches. And perhaps women can draw on their experience of exclusion in the restoration of the true values of a Christian tradition which claims to have a special message for the marginalized, the poor and the downtrodden.

This brings me to my final point. The Axial Age brought the suffering of humanity to the top of the agenda, and, it seems, without an appreciation of this suffering, the Axial transformation was not possible. Scholars have long puzzled over the mysterious fact that Axial movements only occurred in the three core areas of China, India and the Eastern Mediterranean. Why did neither Egypt nor Mesopotamia, both of which had civilizations of great majesty and beauty, evolve an Axial ideology at this time? It seems that one of the threads that links all the Axial regions together was their experience of suffering. Indeed, without acknowledging the ubiquity of suffering in our own lives, we will find it impossible to recognize adequately the suffering of other people. This will make the essential virtue of compassion impossible and so bar us from the salvation and enlightenment we seek. Even the Greeks, who did not initially suffer as greatly as the other Axial cultures, had early developed an extraordinary sensitivity to the poignancy of human suffering, as we can see in the great Tragedies. Not only is compassion the keynote of the New Testament; not only is faith worthless without charity; but the central image of Western Christianity is the crucified Christ, a terrifying depiction of the difficulty and pain involved when we try to implement a divine imperative in the flawed and tragic conditions of human life.

In the modern world, we are confronted with suffering on an unprecedented scale. It pours into our living rooms night after night, through the medium of television news. We are deluged with global suffering, witnessing immediately the deprivations of the developing world and the hideous injustices within our own society. We often feel helpless. It sometimes seems to me that we Westerners are becoming Pollyannas, endlessly and feverishly looking for the bright, the positive side, panicking if we cannot find an instant solution to life's ills, or simply putting the suffering we cannot help out of our mind. But the Axial sages, like Jesus, taught us that a faith that excludes the suffering of the whole world is inauthentic. It is all too easy to immure ourselves in a safe heartlessness, denying the pain that surrounds us on all sides, but if we do this, we cannot even begin our spiritual quest. One of the legends that developed about the Buddha's decision to renounce the world shows this clearly. His father had carefully shielded him from all suffering; until he was 29 years old, he had lived in a carefully guarded palace, where all spectacles and images of suffering were excluded. Then the gods decided that he had lived in this fool's paradise long enough and sent three of their number into the pleasure park disguised as an old man, a sick man and a corpse. The Buddha was horrified and finally resolved to leave home, become a monk and devote his life to suffering humanity. His pleasure-palace is a striking image of the mind in denial. As long as we persist in closing our minds and hearts to the universal pain which surrounds even the most privileged of us on all sides, we remain locked in an undeveloped version of ourselves, incapable of growth and spiritual insight. The young Buddha was living in a delusion, because his vision of the world did not coincide with the way things really are. The first of the Four Noble Truths he enunciated when he attained Nirvana was "that all existence is suffering." This was the starting point of any spiritual quest. Once we have allowed the suffering that is an inescapable part of the human condition to break through the cautionary barricades that we have erected against it, we can never see the world in the same way again. The Buddha had allowed the spectacle of suffering to tear his world apart. He had smashed the hard carapace in which so many of us encase ourselves in order to keep sorrow and pain at a distance, but once he had let the suffering in, his quest could begin.

And in the same way, our own quest for a renewed Christianity can also begin. We should resolve to conduct a reformation which is not solely inward-looking, not simply examining our doctrines and finding clever ways of reconciling past teaching with postmodern conditions, but which also looks compassionately at the rest of the world, in the spirit of the greatest Axial thinkers, because it is by forgetting our own selves that we will recover our spiritual vision.

The Secular Trinity

Lloyd Geering

We are here to discuss the faith of the future and discern how it is linked with the faith of the past. We are rightly using the term 'faith' rather than 'religion' or even 'Christianity'. These latter terms have become too objectified. As Wilfred Cantwell Smith showed in 1962 in his seminal little book called *The Meaning and End of Religion*, it is a modern and quite misleading practice to think of religion in general, and Christianity in particular, as objective things. He urged us to turn back to the concept of faith. 'Faith' is a much more universal term. It refers to the personal attitude of trust and hope which we humans manifest as we interpret the world in which we live and respond to its demands.

Faith is an essential component of the human condition. We may have only a little faith or we may have great faith but without faith of some kind we do not live as humans. Each person and each community, during their respective lifetimes, may be said to walk a path of faith. Along each path the inner experience of faith comes to expression in all sorts of external forms and structures – such as myths, rituals, holy writings, theological systems, moral codes, social institutions and so on. These objective data reflect the social and cultural environment through which the path is moving, and consequently they are diverse and also subject to change. For all of these external objects which develop along a path of faith Smith coined the term the 'cumulative tradition'. He warned us against the danger of identifying faith with the cumulative tradition or any part of it. Doctrines, rituals and other religious institutions are not the content of faith; they are the products of faith and they serve as markers of the particular path which certain people of faith have trodden.[1] To

1. Smith's analysis of religion is reflected in the difference between two titles of textbooks widely used in the study of the religions of the world. Both books cover much the same ground. The first was written by J.B. Noss, appeared in 1949 and was called *Man's Religions*. The second was written by J.H. Hutchison, appeared in 1969, and showed the influence of Smith by being entitled *Paths of Faith*.

regard any of these markers as the object of faith is to fall into the error of idolatry.

Christianity is a general term referring to a particular path of faith. It is only one of several major paths which humans have trodden, though for a long time Christians regarded it as the only true path and referred to it simply as 'the faith'.[2] This path originated long before the man Jesus, whose title of 'Christ' it now bears. Jesus himself spoke of faith as that which makes us whole and healthy. From what we can gather, Jesus was very much aware that he was walking on a path of faith which stretched back not only to Abraham but even to Adam.

During the last four thousand years of what we may call the Judeo-Christian path of faith each new generation of people has learned from the generation before it how to live by faith. The particular beliefs and practices of the cumulative tradition, in which faith has been expressed, have changed greatly in the course of time. Abraham, Jeremiah, Jesus of Nazareth, Augustine, Aquinas and Luther were all people of faith, walking along that path, but the words and deeds in which they expressed their faith varied tremendously. So, as the cumulative tradition progressed, some elements dropped out of sight, new elements appeared and many things changed.

The ancient Israelite prophets gave the path its initial direction. Then it went through quite a shift of emphasis in the Babylonian Exile, partly because it came under the influence of the Zoroastrian path of faith emanating from Persia. That is when Judaism and the institution of the synagogue came to birth. Some centuries later a radical change of direction took place from within the Jewish path, as a result of the influence of Jesus of Nazareth. The path soon divided into two, and somewhat later into three — the Jewish, Christian and Islamic paths.

During the first five centuries of the Christian era Christian thinkers from Paul onwards set out to clarify the character of the new path of faith. Of necessity they were much influenced by the Graeco-Roman culture in which they lived but at the centre of their thinking was the continuing influence and memories of Jesus, now worshipped as the Christ. They constructed the framework of thought and practice which shaped the Christian path of faith for the

---

2. Note 'the faith which was once for all delivered to the saints', Jude 3.

next fifteen hundred years. For simplicity they expounded this in the great creeds; these received the stamp of authority from a succession of ecumenical councils, of which Nicaea was the first.

In some respects there are some very real parallels between this conference and the Council of ancient Nicaea. There are of course some very big differences also. We are not under the dominating chairmanship of the Emperor Constantine, bent on achieving a unified statement that can be used to uphold and promote imperial power. Nor are we the official representatives of the many church bodies into which the once great universal church has now become fragmented. If we represent anybody at all other than ourselves, it is an anonymous host of genuine enquirers who value the Christian spirituality of the past, but who wonder where the path of faith is now leading.

The chief parallel between Nicaea and this Conference is this. The Christian thinkers of the first centuries lived in the religiously fluid aftermath of the Axial Period. We live in the equally fluid and uncertain aftermath of a Second Axial Period.[3] Let me explain. The term 'Axial Period' is now widely used to refer to cultural and religious changes of a radical nature, which took place between about 800-200 BCE. That period gave rise, both directly and indirectly, to those paths of faith that are today known as the 'World Religions'.

These new paths were pioneered by prophets, philosophers and teachers who dared to hold up their cultural past to critical examination. Prior to the Axial Period, faith consisted of following meticulously in the footsteps of one's tribal ancestors. From the Axial Period onwards faith called for some self-critical reflection and personal commitment. Each of these new post-Axial paths transcended the exclusively ethnic limitations of the cultural traditions of the past. They did this by enunciating a set of principles or ideas which had the potential to unite all humankind in a common path of faith. In this respect the Buddhist, Christian and Islamic paths have been the most widely successful in crossing ethnic boundaries.

The second Axial Period occurred in the Christian West between 1400–1900, with the Enlightenment marking the irreversible threshold of no return. The Christian path of faith, after reaching an apex of flowering in the High Middle Ages, initiated a second period of

---

3. Fuller explanations of these two Axial Periods are to be found in the author's, *Christian Faith at the Crossroads* and *Tomorrow's God*.

radical questioning. This gave rise to the modern, global and secular world.

Both Axial Periods necessitated radical changes in the way faith has been experienced, understood and expressed in words. This may be illustrated by the changes which took place in understanding a basic religious concept — that of god. This concept originated in the pre-Axial Period where it was created to explain the mysterious forces of nature which were found to dominate human existence. The gods (and other spirits) came to be conceived as an unseen order of spiritual beings who operated behind and through all visible phenomena and who ultimately controlled human destiny.

During the Axial Period the reality of these gods was questioned. The Israelite prophets iconoclastically rejected them as having no substantial reality. Plato and the Hindu seers, in their respective ways, saw the gods as ephemeral reflections of a deeper and unfathomable reality. The Buddha simply ignored them as irrelevant to the path of faith. But, whereas the Buddhist path of faith thereafter abandoned the use of the god concept altogether, the Jewish, Christian and Islamic paths retained the term but began to use it in a radically new way. The Jews treated the plural word 'gods' (*elohim*) as a singular, the Holy One,[4] translated by Muhammad as *al-Wahid*. This god was quite different from the gods it replaced. As the ban on graven images makes clear, this god was beyond being visualised or objectified.

What has been too often overlooked is the fact that, whereas each of the former gods had a special name and function, the new use of the word god in the singular left it without any specific meaning or content. That is why, in Biblical usage, we find frequent reference to 'the god of . . .', as in 'the god of Abraham', 'the god of Israel', 'the god and father of Jesus Christ', 'my god' and 'your god' and so on. What this implied was that, if you want to know anything more about, say, 'the god of Abraham', then you must look at the path of faith which Abraham walked and see what were his values and goals. That is the only way to know the character of 'the God of Abraham'. In other words the God of Abraham consists of all which motivated Abraham along his path of faith.

This further explains why the word 'God' came to mean different things to different people. Jews, Christians and Muslims are all said to be monotheists. They each believe there is only one God; yet they

4. Note how the Shema (Deut. 6:4) affirms 'YHWH our god is one YHWH'.

do not worship the same God. To Jews, for example, God is the one who brought their forefathers out of Egypt, gave them the Torah and led them to the land of Promise. To Muslims, Allah is the one who revealed his Will to Muhammad in the Qur'an. To Christians God means the One who became incarnate in Jesus of Nazareth.

The difference between the Jewish God and the Christian God is made abundantly clear by the Creeds of the early Christian centuries. During this formative period the Christian path of faith abandoned the pure monotheism of Judaism (later to be revived by Islam) and replaced it, after much debate and no little dissension, with the twin doctrines of the Incarnation and the Holy Trinity.

Many influences entered into the turmoil, including even ideas from Zoroaster and Plato. But the chief ingredients of these twin doctrines were three areas of their experience they believed to be vital:

The inheritance from their Jewish origins of the oneness of God. This of course was pure monotheism and was expressed as: 'I believe in One God the Father Almighty, Maker of heaven and earth, and of all things visible and invisible'. But this is not where the Creed stopped.

The Creed proceeded to modify this form of theism quite radically in the light of what they had inherited from the apostles — namely, the influence of the man Jesus of Nazareth. His presence, his deeds and his teaching were believed to radiate the divine in such a way that this man had to be fitted into their understanding of God. The way they did this is called the doctrine of the Incarnation. It was expressed particularly in the words 'and was made man' and became by far the longest section of the Creed.

To this was added a third concern. They experienced an inner vitality at work within the fellowship of the church. This they called the Holy Spirit, or power of God within human minds.

The doctrine of the Holy Trinity attempted to preserve the unity of God, while doing justice to these three experiences. The doctrine of the Incarnation bridged the gulf between divinity and humanity, which existed in both polytheism and pure theism. By affirming both the divinity and the humanity of Jesus of Nazareth the ancient Christian thinkers, in this most daring fashion, found a way of building humanity itself into the content of the God symbol.

These twin doctrines, finalized by the fifth century, served the Christian path of faith very well for the next 1000 years. Although they were never anything more than humanly devised formulas, they came to be used as sacred mantras. This is well illustrated by the hymn known as St. Patrick's Breastplate – 'I bind unto myself today the strong name of the Trinity'. They were treated as divinely revealed truths and tended to be taken more and more literally. What started as the *personae* or masks of the invisible and non-objective deity came to be perceived as personalized and objectified. God the Father was even referred to as the Supreme Being – a personal being – for whom God was now the proper name. Then came the visual representations, starting with the icons and images of Jesus and the Virgin Mary. This process reached its climax when Michelangelo at last transgressed the ancient prohibition of the visualizing of God and painted a portrait of God the Father on the ceiling of the Sistine Chapel.

This was on the eve of the second Axial Period and may even be taken as symbolic of how, by the High Middle Ages, Christian orthodoxy had over-reached itself. The whole framework of Christian thought constructed in the first five centuries thereafter began to disintegrate. The Renaissance, the Protestant Reformation and the Enlightenment followed in quick succession. The doctrines of the Incarnation and Trinity, as traditionally understood, came under strong criticism. Diversity and confusion resulted and the unity they provided for the Christian path of faith was increasingly lost.

In place of the doctrine of the Holy Trinity a non-Trinitarian theism began to appear at one pole of thought and atheism at the other, with deism, pantheism and panentheism at various points in between. The most vigorous defenders of Christian orthodoxy today are theists rather than true trinitarians. The ancient Gnostic heresy of Docetism, which asserted that Jesus was a divine figure who only appeared in human form, finally prevailed in much popular Christian devotion. The humanity of Jesus was largely lost sight of. The short life of the human Jesus had been almost completely replaced by the figure of Christ as the glorified Son of God sitting at the right hand of God the Father. The daring and paradoxical character of the Incarnation and the Trinity has been largely lost in traditional Christianity.

It is tempting to conclude, as many do, that the doctrines of the Incarnation and the Trinity are now outmoded and are to be discarded. I wish to suggest rather that what is to be discarded is the way in which these doctrines had come to be understood by the eve of the second Axial Period which brought about their undoing.

Further I wish to suggest that, paradoxical though it may seem, it was the daring and innovative character of the doctrines of the Incarnation and of the Holy Trinity, which eventually led to the Second Axial Period. Further, they constitute the reason why the modern secular world emerged out of Christian Europe rather than elsewhere. So, far from judging these doctrines to be obsolete and meaningless, they may be seen as having an unexpected new relevance in the global, secular world to which they have led.

The full humanity of Jesus is once again being acknowledged, thanks to the work of biblical scholars from Strauss to the Jesus Seminar. The recovery of the footprints and voiceprints of the historical Jesus show he was truly human in every way, even to being a man of his own times. This makes it necessary to look at the doctrine of the Incarnation in quite a new light. It re-opens the question of why the pioneers of the Christian path of faith dared to incorporate humanity into the concept of God. To restrict the incarnation of the divine to one human person, namely the man Jesus of Nazareth, is to miss its full significance. The idea that God could become enfleshed even in one special person was more than most Jews could accept at the time, so much so that all pure monotheists, such as Jews and Muslims, continue to reject it to this day.

The idea that God could become enfleshed in humanity as a whole is more than even most Christians have been able to accept. Yet the seeds of this more extensive interpretation of incarnation were already present in the New Testament. Jesus was at first was not separated from his fellow-humans by a great gulf in the way the glorified Christ later became. Jesus was seen rather as the one who had brought God down to earth. His teaching and manner of life enabled people to sense the presence of the divine in the affairs of ordinary daily life.

Even Paul spoke of Jesus as the representation or embodiment of the whole human race. Just as the first Adam (meaning 'humankind') embodied the whole human race, so the Christ figure evolving out of Jesus was said to be the New Adam, (i.e. the embodiment of the new humankind). "For as in Adam all die, so also in Christ shall all be made alive'.[5] That is why Paul spoke of all Christians as being 'in Christ'. They were conceived as participating in the continuing incarnation.

5. 1 Cor 15:22.

Thus, from the beginning, and continuing in later hints, there has long been the seed-thought that humanity itself was to be the enfleshment or incarnation of the divine. This is why it later became common to speak of the Christian life as one of 'sanctification' and why the Eastern Orthodox Church speaks of the Christian life as the process of 'deification'. Even Aquinas said, 'The Incarnation is the exaltation of human nature and consummation of the Universe'.

The doctrine of the incarnation is therefore to be applied to the whole of humankind. David Strauss regarded the Incarnation of God in Jesus Christ, not as a unique historical event but as a symbolic portrayal of the spiritual process of the cosmos. This has been in operation from eternity and consists of the humanization of God and the divinization of humankind.[6]

The first modern theologian to expound at some length this way of understanding the Incarnation was Ludwig Feuerbach. This he did in his book, *The Essence of Christianity*, where he contrasted the False or Theological Meaning of the Incarnation with the True or Humanistic Meaning of the Incarnation. In Christian orthodoxy the humanity of Jesus had been taken up in to heaven and lost in the Holy Trinity. For Feuerbach the Incarnation meant that the divine had come down to earth to reside permanently within humanity. Following the example of the New Testament declaration that 'God is love', Feuerbach took the being of God to be nothing else but the moral values, such as love, justice and compassion, and these, henceforth, were to be manifested within the human race. The doctrine of the incarnation spelt the end of theism. The God who was mythically conceived by theists to be sitting upon a heavenly throne has come down to dwell in human flesh — in all human flesh.

This means, first, that we humans must live without the divine heavenly props thought to exist in the past. 'We must be mature as God is mature', to quote the words attributed to Jesus.[7] It means, secondly, that we now have to play on the earth the role which theism had assigned to an objective, supernatural god. Not only is the heavenly throne empty but heaven itself is an empty void. As Feuerbach saw it, the incarnation, properly understood, marked a turning point in human history; yet not until it had led to the Second Axial Period have we been able to realise it. The emergence of the modern secular

---

6. See my *Christian Faith at the Crossroads*, p. 80.
7. Matt 5:48.

world is thus to be seen as the logical consequence of the doctrine of the incarnation and the legitimate continuation of the Judeo-Christian path of faith.

Feuerbach was so far ahead of his time that he was completely rejected and his insights lost sight of for more than century. Yet he was not the only one to see a connection between the doctrine of the incarnation and the coming of the modern secular world. In 1889 Charles Gore edited a symposium of Essays on "The Religion of the Incarnation' called *Lux Mundi*. They were written, he said, out of the conviction that the epoch in which they lived was 'one of profound transformation, intellectual and social, abounding in new needs, new points of view, new questions', an epoch which meant that 'theology must take a new development'.[8]

One of the contributors, J. R. Illingworth, regarded secular thought, not as the enemy of Christianity, but as that which 'often corrected and counteracted the evil of a Christianity grown professional and false and foul'. 'Secular civilization has co-operated with Christianity to produce the modern world. *It is nothing less than the providential correlative and counterpart of the incarnation'.*[9]

In the secular world, on this side of the Second Axial Period, we are in a position to appreciate, as people after the First Axial Period were not, that the cumulative tradition of each path of faith is a human creation. All human languages, all philosophies and doctrines, and all religious concepts, such as the gods and God, are of human creation. The heavenly world was a creation of human imagination.

As we now walk by faith into the future we have to decide how much from the past path of faith we find useful and how much we must leave behind. For example, what are we to do with the concept of 'God'? The theistic use of the term has now become obsolete but this does not necessarily mean it has to be discarded any more than it had to be abandoned at the First Axial Period. To walk the path of faith we still need religious symbols with which to express our quest for spiritual fulfilment even though we must now acknowledge their symbolic character and their human origin.

But if we continue to speak of god then, as at the first Axial Period, we must again learn to use the term in a radically new way.[10]

---

8. *Lux Mundi*, ed. by Charles Gore, p. viii.
9. J. R. Illingworth, 'The Incarnation in Relation to Development' in *Lux Mundi*, p. 155 (italics added).
10. For a fuller discussion see *Tomorrow's God*, chapters 9–10.

God is a symbolic word which originated in ancient mythology. By this term we refer to whatever concerns us in an ultimate way, to use the well-known phrase of Paul Tillich. Even Martin Luther was aware of this, for he said, 'faith and God have inevitable connection. Whatever your heart clings to and confides in, that is really your God'[11]. Don Cupitt put it this way; 'God is the mythical embodiment of all that one is concerned with in the spiritual life'[12]. Similarly Gordon Kaufman says 'The symbol of God claims to represent to us a focus for orientation which will bring true fulfilment and meaning to human life. It sums up, unifies, and represents in a personification what are taken to be the highest and most indispensable human ideals and values'.[13] Thus, if we continue to speak of God, we are pointing to the values, goals and aspirations which motivate us on the path of faith.

The Christian thinkers of the first five centuries expressed their values and aspirations by speaking of their God as the Holy Trinity — Father, Son and Holy Spirit. What motivates us on our path of faith? What are the highest values and aspirations to which we respond in faith?

To answer these questions we must acknowledge that the world we live in looks very different from the way it looked to the ancient Christian thinkers. People both before and after the first Axial Period felt they were surrounded by, and often in close touch with, a world of spirit. Today we use the word 'spirit' metaphorically, if we use it at all. Where they talked about spirit as the substance of reality, we talk about physical energy. Where they explained natural phenomena in terms of gods and spirits, we do so in terms of electrons, quarks and nuclear forces. Where they explained living creatures as fleshly embodiments of spirit or of a life-principle, we talk of organisms, identifiable by DNA and chromosomes, immune systems and amino acids. We see ourselves as human organisms, who feel through our bodies and think through our brains and nervous systems.

So we are much more focused on the physical world than were the ancients. Reality for us is what we can confirm with our senses and what is open to public investigation. All the rest, including religion, philosophy and science, is human interpretation and this

---

11. *A Compend of Luther's Theology*, ed. by Hugh Thomson Kerr, p. 23.
12. *Taking Leave of God*, p. 166.
13. *The Theological Imagination*, p. 32.

remains open to continual review. Reality for us is the physical universe and, compared with how people perceived it even up until only 200 years ago, this has expanded in time and space beyond the ability of our minds to contain it.

The universe is one enormous bundle of energy. This is the basic stuff of reality. We do not quite know what energy is but we know a lot about how it works. The universe is awe-inspiring, not only in its dimensions but also in its capacity to create out of itself ever more complex and beautiful patterns of energy. First came the 'big bang', then the slow accumulation of gases into stars, then the explosion of supernovas into star dust, then the formation of planets out of star dust, and finally, to date, the evolution of life on at least one planet. The universe has been a continuing process of change, manifesting both growth and decay over some fifteen billion years. At any one moment the universe may appear to be a static changeless thing but, viewed by the dimension of cosmic time, it is dynamic and alive.

Although we speak of the universe as having had a beginning, there was never a time when it did not exist, for time and space themselves only came into existence with the universe itself. So the universe is all there is; there is nothing outside of it as there was nothing before it. It is now illogical to postulate the prior existence of a Creator. The universe has to be self-explanatory. It is from the universe itself we must learn what it can tell us about itself and how it works.

We are not only *in* this universe but we are an integral part of it. Our very existence and our continuing life are dependent upon it. That is why our pre-Axial ancestors believed their destiny to be in the lap of the gods, one of whom was Mother Earth. In modern times, in recognition of the fact that we are dependent on the processes of nature, we are still inclined to speak of Mother Nature, even though we are aware we are speaking metaphorically. Moreover within the Christian path of faith there has long been a thin line of mystical tradition, starting with the ancient Neo-Platonists and continuing through such people as Jakob Boehme, Bruno and Spinoza, who identified Nature with the divine. Schelling (1775-1854) saw Nature as an infinite, self-developing super-organism which is realizing itself in finite matter and coming to consciousness though human consciousness.[14]

14. See my *Christian Faith at the Crossroads*, p. 65.

Many of the processes of nature, which ancient humans found awesome, can be readily explained by us in quite mundane ways; yet they have been replaced in our new picture of the universe by other mysteries which are just as awe-inspiring. We know extremely little about what takes place in the rest of this universe. We have no idea, and we may never know, whether there is life anywhere else within it. Life on our planet has apparently been evolving over some three billion years. Our human species emerged out of a myriad of evolving living species. It did so only very recently, relative to the story of the Earth, and more by accident than by any apparent design. There is no obvious reason why we have evolved as we have, or even why there should be any life at all on this planet. The origin and purpose of human existence remain a mystery.

Because we are so dependent on the physical universe as a whole, and on this planet earth in particular, the natural world itself must be the first focus of our faith. In his later and lesser-known book, *The Essence of Religion* (1848), Feuerbach acknowledged this when he said: 'that upon which human beings are fully dependent is originally, nothing other than Nature. Nature is the first, original object of religion'.[15]

The most pressing concerns of our dependence upon nature are very basic. They are largely the same as those we share with the other animals — the need for air, drink, food, shelter, survival, and the regeneration of the species. Built into every species, including humanity, are the instincts to survive and to procreate. These basic needs and animal instincts were the starting-point from which our primitive human ancestors set out on their path of faith, slowly and unconsciously creating human culture. We too must go that far back. We are today relearning that the need for pure air, clean water, healthy food, adequate shelter, the regeneration of the species and the overcoming of all threats to human survival have once again become the ultimate or religious issues to which we must 'devote' ourselves.

It is not sufficient to acknowledge our dependence on the world. We have to learn to trust it — to put our faith in it — in much the same way as our Christian forbears put their faith in its supposed Creator. There is much about the world that fosters faith. It has an awe-inspiring capacity to produce order and design out of chaos, to create beauty, to bring forth life. It is true that there are earthquakes,

15. Quoted by Van A. Harvey, *Feuerbach and the Interpretation of Religion*, p. 166.

storms and disease — what we call natural disasters. Yet the changing seasons keep bringing renewal. The story of evolution itself is
spellbinding. The beauty we see through the microscope is breath
taking. There is so much about the world to inspire awe, to foster
faith and to renew hope.

No one has expressed this more dramatically than the devout
Jesuit priest and scientist, Teilhard de Chardin, when he wrote, 'If as
the result of some interior revolution, I were to lose in succession my
faith in Christ, my faith in a personal God, and my faith in spirit, I
feel that I should continue to believe invincibly in the world. The
world (its value, its infallibility and its goodness) — that, when all is
said and done, is the first, the last and the only thing in which I
believe. It is by this faith that I live. And it is to this faith, I feel, at
the moment of death, rising above all doubts, I shall surrender
myself'.[16]

When Teilhard spoke of his faith in the world he was not referring merely to rocks and rivers, nor even less to atoms and electrons.
To appreciate what he meant one needs to read his magnum opus
The Phenomenon of Man,[17] preferably at one sitting. This is one of
the great spiritual classics of modern times. Here is an unfolding
vision of the evolving universe in all of its breath-taking grandeur
and awe-inspiring mystery. It is a vision of cosmic creativity on the
grandest possible scale, surpassing any description of the glory of
God written during the ages of theism.

Most impressive of all is the way Teilhard builds into his vision of
the evolving universe two great thresholds of change. First came the
transition on this planet from non-life to life, resulting in the emergence of the biosphere, similar to but distinct from the lithosphere,
the atmosphere and the stratosphere. Within the biosphere, and only
in the species homo sapiens, came the transition from life to reflec-
tive thought, resulting in the emergence of the noosphere. Teilhard
coined this term in 1925 to refer to the layer of self-critical thought
covering the already existing layer of life, which in turn covered the
inorganic lithosphere.

Such is the creativity present in the self-evolving universe that it
has the potential not only to become alive but also to think. This

16. *Christianity and Evolution*, p. 99
17. Since this was published in English translation in 1959 it has been succeeded by
many similar books such as *The Universe Story* by Brian Swimme and Thomas Berry.

potential, Teilhard argued, must have been there from the beginning and present within the energy which constitutes the basic stuff of the universe. As energy organized itself into ever more complex patterns, so its potential for consciousness reached ever higher levels. In the growing self-consciousness of humankind the universe is becoming aware of itself. Our minds become the mirror through which the universe sees and understands itself.

This whole new way of understanding reality is today's equivalent of the traditional doctrine of the Incarnation. It used to be said that the divine Creator Father had become incarnate in human flesh. Now, and on a much grander scale, we may say that cosmic creativity has enfleshed itself in the earthly species we call humankind. What is more, whereas cosmic creativity seemed to be blundering along blindly for so long, lacking any clear purpose, it has now through the medium of human consciousness manifested itself in purposeful activity.

In the traditional doctrine of the Incarnation the man Jesus was seen as the prototype of the new humankind, or the expression of the 'new being', to use Paul Tillich's term. The subsequent elevation of the man Jesus to divine status, which took place in ancient Christian thought, may now be interpreted as a symbolic premonition of things to come. The verbal imagery of Jesus sitting on the right hand of God, wielding divine power and responsible for ultimate judgment, is a quite daunting parable of the grave responsibilities now coming to rest upon the shoulders of the human race after the Second Axial Period. As Jesus was once assumed to be able to think with the mind of God, so, on this particular planet, the collective human mind is the organ of thought through which the universe can now direct the process of future evolution on this planet. Now that the human race is being forced increasingly to play the role of God with regard to the sustaining of earthly life, the doctrine of the incarnation, interpreted in this way, has taken on a striking new relevance for this global, secular and ecological world.

The evolving process is far from having reached an end. Indeed, mankind, as Nietzsche suggested, is an unfinished animal. There are many signs that the evolving process is now accelerating. Yet there is no guarantee of ongoing progress.

From the 'big bang' right up until now, what came forth at each step was due to the potential possibilities already there. But that does not mean that everything was predetermined. There was no necessity for potential possibilities to be realised. The majority of possibilities have either not been realised or have ended in blind roads. But as the evolving process has proceeded there has been what Teilhard called a 'cosmic drift'. As the level of consciousness rose, chiefly in the human species, the evolutionary process came to depend more on personal choices. On the one hand this made the future less predictable, but on the other it made possible a more purposeful future.

As we humans evolved to reach our present state of self-consciousness we have found that that we are only a tiny part of a self-evolving universe in which we ourselves are a self-evolving species. From one point of view we are a self-made species. For what makes us human is not our DNA, the majority of which we share in common with the other higher animals. What makes us human is what we have collectively created, including language, ideas, culture, knowledge, religion and science. All this is so much a part of what we are and what we live in that we have no particular name for it. It not only shapes the way we see reality but it also largely becomes the world in which we live. The philosopher Karl Popper called it World 3, to distinguish it from World 1 (physical world) and World 2 (consciousness).[18] World 3 is a human product, resulting from human reflection and creativity, and mainly generated after the advent of the noosphere.

There are some further interesting parallels between the traditional doctrine of the Incarnation and what is here being described. When the traditional doctrine of the Incarnation began to evolve in the first century there was at first no clear distinction between the continuing influence of Jesus, the work of the Holy Spirit and the mind of the church.[19] Similarly we find it difficult to distinguish between the human species and what the human species has collectively created; yet without World 3 we could not be human. This leads to a further oddity; because the content of World 3 developed differently in a variety of geographical areas it means that there have been different ways of being human — e.g. a Maori way, a Chinese way, a Christian way, a Muslim way, etc.

As a result of the globalizing process which followed the Second Axial Period all these different ways of being human are losing their absolute distinctiveness and there is slowly emerging for the future a

18. For a fuller discussion see Chapter 4 of the author's *Tomorrow's God*.
19. E.g. 'It has seemed good to the Holy Spirit and to us...' (Acts 15:28)

common way of being human. This is coming about through the widening and maturing of human consciousness to what may be called global consciousness. This process is currently being fostered at an accelerating pace by the interchange of reliable knowledge, the mass media of communication and the Internet. Global consciousness is the modern equivalent of the Holy Spirit in the New Testament context. We could well be living on the eve of an awe-inspiring new leap — a mutation — in the process of cosmic evolution. Yet there is no guarantee of this at all. We could just as readily be living in the last days before the human species brings about its own destruction.

As the primitive Christians looked into the future with faith based on their current experience, they expressed the substance of their faith, in the form of the Holy Trinity of Father, Son and Holy Spirit, for the reasons described earlier. We in turn must draw on our basic experiences of reality to express our faith for the future.

Our experiences of reality are very different. Yet, strangely enough, they also lead to a trinity — what we may call a secular or this-worldly trinity.[20] First, there is this self-evolving physical universe, which as we understand it, encompasses the whole of reality. Secondly there is the human species that has evolved out of this creative universe and which has brought us into existence. Thirdly there is that which the collective consciousness of humankind has in turn brought forth — the body of cultural knowledge (earlier referred to as World 3), without which we could not be human. These three constitute the God in whom **we** 'live and move and have our being'.[21]

In the traditional doctrine of the Trinity the ancient thinkers went to great pains to keep the Father, the Son and the Holy Spirit clearly distinguished from one another and at the same time to affirm their essential unity. So it is with us. We distinguish clearly between the physical universe and the human species which lives within it, as its highest product known to us. We also distinguish clearly between ourselves and the body of cultural knowledge which we inherit from our species and to which we contribute. Yet these three are so essentially one reality that they cannot exist in separation from one another.

20. The secular trinity here described is similar to what Don Cupitt called 'Being, Man and Language' (*The Revelation of Being*, p. 11), and interestingly referred to as 'the secular trinity' by Nigel Leaves in an unpublished thesis, *A Prophet of this World, A Defence of Don Cupitt*, Murdoch University, Western Australia, 2001.
21. Acts 17:28

As Father, Son and Holy Spirit were conceived as 'three in one' because of the Incarnation, so the self-creating universe, the self-evolving human species and the emerging global consciousness are all one because of the cosmic creativity which manifests itself in all three. This understanding of the secular trinity owes not a little to the earlier affirmations of the Incarnation and of Holy Trinity. The more we humans become an harmonious global society, relating in a healthy way to one another and to the planet, the more confident we can be about the future. This hope rests upon putting our faith in the secular trinity of the world, humanity and global consciousness.

Works Consulted

Cupitt, Don. *The Revelation of Being*. London: SCM Press, 1998.

Cupitt, Don. *Taking Leave of God*. London: SCM Press, 1980.

Harvey, Van A. *Feuerbach and the Interpretation of Religion*. Cambridge-New York: Cambridge University Press, 1997.

Hutchison, John A. *Paths of Faith*. New York: McGraw-Hill, 1969.

Geering, Lloyd. *Christian Faith at the Crossroads*. Santa Rosa, CA: Polebridge Press, 2001. Originally published as *Faith's New Age* in 1980.

Geering, Lloyd. *Tomorrow's God*. Santa Rosa, CA: Polebridge Press, 2000. Originally published in 1994.

Gore, Charles, ed. *Lux mundi*. London: John Murray, 1891.

Kerr, Hugh Thomson, ed. *A Compend of Luther's Theology*. Philadelphia: Westminster Press, 1943.

Kaufman, Gordon D. *The Theological Imagination: Constructing the Concept of God*. Philadelphia: Westminster Press, 1981.

Noss, John B.. *Man's Religions*. New York: Macmillan, 1949.

Swimme, Brian and Thomas Berry. *The Universe Story: From the Primordial Flaring Forth to the Ecozoic Era—A Celebration of the Unfolding of the Cosmos*. 1st ed. San Francisco, CA: HarperSanFrancisco, 1992.

Teilhard de Chardin, Pierre. *Christianity and Evolution*. Trans. René Hague. London: Collins, 1971.

Teilhard de Chardin, Pierre. *The Phenomenon of Man*. Trans. Bernard Wall. New York: Harper, 1959.

Reforming Christianity

Don Cupitt

In March 1965 John A.T. Robinson, the author of *Honest to God*, published a small book called *The New Reformation?* based on lectures that he had given recently at various places mainly in the USA. That moment in the mid-1960s was the high-water mark of confidence that it might yet be possible to reform and renew Western Christianity, and Robinson was surely justified in seeing his own much-publicized work as being only part of a larger movement, not only in the Churches, but also in popular culture generally.

While it lasted the mood of utopian optimism was intoxicating, but it did not last long. In the Roman Catholic Church Pope John XXIII was already dead, and the Second Vatican Council was scarcely wound up before his successor Paul VI had begun to back-pedal. Today, under John-Paul II, it is as if the Council had never happened at all, and the Roman Catholic Church is dying of spiritual asphyxia. The other strands in Sixties culture have fared equally badly. Its popular youth culture — still new and fresh in those days — has now become cheapened and coarsened. Student political idealism is extinct. The liberal protestantism that powered the ecumenical movement and the World Council of Churches seems to be a spent force; and the particular form of religious humanism that inspired John Robinson's own thinking, and which he drew chiefly from Martin Buber,[1] has become a quaint period piece.

There are some respects in which John Robinson's concerns are still ours. He was right to point to the rapid secularization of culture, to demand a theology led by the concerns of lay people, and to insist that the old supernaturalism and the old clericalism must go. He was right to stick to the principle that Christians should be sexual liber-

---

1. See *Thou Who Art* (1945), Robinson's unpublished doctoral dissertation about Martin Buber, in the Cambridge University Library.

als. But in other respects the modern reader is surprised to see how much he leaves out. His many writings include almost nothing about feminism, nothing about the environment, and very little about multiculturalism and race relations. This liberal Christian moralist missed many of the most important moral changes that were taking place in his own time. And his case well illustrates what the conservatives love to tell us: people have been demanding the reform of the Church and the modernization of Christianity at least since the days of John Wycliffe in fourteenth century England, but like science-fiction novels such demands always reflect the values of the time when they are put forward, and very soon come to sound old-fashioned. Meanwhile, the old Church takes no notice but simply chugs on, *semper eadem*, always the same. In the end it tends to win, for 'the Church is an anvil that has worn out many hammers'.

True, there was once a *successful* reformation; but it too illustrates the justice of the conservative criticism. Luther and Calvin were surely right to see the importance of printing and the new possibility of putting a vernacular translation of the Bible into each layperson's hands. But their theology of personal faith, of God's Word written and of private judgment was formulated just before the rise of the modern historical consciousness and just before the take-off of modern science. They missed some of the most essential features of modernity, even though it was already beginning in their time. Their new Protestant confessions and church polities made no provision for the coming knowledge-explosion and the vast cultural changes that it would bring about. They saw themselves as restoring the faith of the early Church, and they saw no need to leave room for future doctrinal development. The result has been the steady decline of Protestantism into pietism, literalism and (eventually) fundamentalism. What began as the most progressive force in Western culture thus steadily declined until it became the most reactionary. Certain moral and political changes in society at large that were first heralded by Protestantism are of course still with us, and still precious: but *as religion* the Protestant reformation has sadly turned out to be a long-term failure. It has been brought down by the obsolescence of the very ideas from which it started — the ideas of justification by faith and of the Bible as the written Word of God whose message is transparent to the honest reader — and today no fairminded commentator would claim that the Protestant version of Christianity is intellectually in any better shape than the Catholic. In Catholicism the Papacy is an institution that makes it possible for the Church to evolve over time in response to historical change; whereas Protestantism is stuck. It has no theory of, and no built-in machinery for bringing about, its own doctrinal development.

What then of us? We live at a time when the intellectual and moral standing of mainline Western Christianity is weaker than it has ever been. In most Western countries the historic denominations are contracting at a rate of around 2% per annum. Good leadership seems quite unable to arrest the decline: thus in Britain the late Basil Hume was universally reckoned to have been a very sure-footed Roman Catholic leader, but during his twenty-year tenure as Cardinal Archbishop of Westminster, English Catholicism halved nonetheless. Amongst the very young, religious belief is disappearing almost entirely, and several denominations are threatened with near-extinction within one or two generations. In Europe, Christianity is already becoming a forgotten religion — as badly decayed as (for example) Buddhism is in Hong Kong, whose professedly 'Buddhist' temples turn out to be concerned only with fortune-telling. The United States remains the world's leading Christian country, but I don't need to tell an American audience that a good deal of popular religion in the USA is of very low quality, makes little serious difference to the culture, and could vanish without trace very quickly.

Yet in this dire situation the principal religious bodies are tending to become more conservative as they contract. There is almost no debate about reform, and the great majority of Christians, whether they are Oriental, or Orthodox, or Roman Catholic or Evangelical Protestant, continue to regard their own faith tradition as objective and immutable Truth. In their own way, most Christians are just as traditionalist as are Muslims and Orthodox Jews. Any reform proposals from us will be dismissed by them as trendy and ephemeral nonsense, and I have already admitted that the track record of past reformation-attempts is not encouraging.

Can we then learn from past mistakes, and do better this time? I suggest that if we are to make any impression upon the Churches we must not think it sufficient merely to upbraid them for being out of touch with modern reality, for they will reply that they are in touch with eternal reality, which they say is all that counts. We will only succeed in unsettling them if we can expose serious internal contradictions within *their own* position: and that is what I propose we should do. This will require us to start from premises they accept, and to use types of argument whose validity they themselves already acknowledge.

I shall argue, then, that modern Christianity is in dire trouble because it will not face up to something that theologians have been aware of for more than a century.[2] The received orthodox faith of the Church is in various ways now known to be badly wrong. The historical Jesus, the Jesus who actually lived, has been shown beyond doubt to have been a quite different figure from the Divine Saviour of the developed ecclesiastical faith; and the 'kingdom religion' proclaimed by the original Jesus was a different religion — and indeed, a quite different *kind* of religion — from the religion of eternal salvation in the heavenly world above that is still taught by the Church. The Church claims to be founded upon Jesus Christ, but when we look into the matter we discover that its connection with him is very tenuous.

There is an intellectual muddle and a disastrously-bad misreading of Jesus at the very centre of Christianity. We know this clearly now, but the Churches cannot admit it or do anything about it, and our theology departments mostly operate as conspiracies to fudge the issue. Nobody is allowed to say too clearly what everybody knows: and *that* is why Christians are demoralized. We are being brought down by intellectual muddle and dishonesty.

The Church's traditional image of Christ was formed at a time when the authority of all four Gospels, and their consistency, both with each other and with standard doctrine, was taken for granted. Traditional thinking worked in that way: it simply added the whole of received tradition together, harmonizing it and assembling it into a loose system.[3] But then in the nineteenth century scholars began to see the Gospels in their historical context, to look closely at how they differ from each other, and to develop theories about how the various traditions must have evolved historically. It soon became apparent that only in St John's Gospel is Jesus seen as the Word of God Incarnate who has come to earth to reveal his divine glory to us; and that St John's Jesus is a different figure who talks an entirely different

---

2. See especially Johannes Weiss, *Jesus' Proclamation of the Kingdom of God* and Albert Schweitzer, *The Mystery of the Kingdom of God*. The full text of the much-enlarged and revised Second Edition of Schweitzer's *The Quest of the Historical Jesus* is now at last available in a sound English translation.

3. All these points are very clearly made by Dennis Nineham in his Foreword to *The Quest of the Historical Jesus*, First Complete Edition, cited above.

language from the Jesus of the Synoptic Gospels of Matthew, Mark and Luke. For these latter gospel-writers Jesus is a human figure, an exorcist, a teacher and a prophet of the Kingdom of God, a new religious order which he believes is already beginning to phase itself in. Some of Jesus' contemporaries go further, and see him as the Messiah of the Jews. After his martyrdom they begin to think of him as having been raised to heaven and there declared by God to be the Messiah-designate who will soon return to Earth in glory.[4] He has come once with his Messiahship veiled: he will return with it manifest to all.

After D.F. Strauss in the 1830s scholars were becoming clear about the difference between the historical Jesus and the Son of God Incarnate who does the talking in St John's Gospel, and the way was open for them to construct a theory of the development of early Christian doctrine. As they worked it all out, the scholars could also explain an old puzzle well pointed out by the dissident Roman Catholic scholar Alfred Loisy. It is this: Jesus came preaching the Kingdom, but what we actually got was the Church. How did this happen? How is it that Christianity has arisen on the basis of a disappointment?

The answer soon suggests itself. After Jesus' death the full arrival of the Kingdom seemed to be delayed, and the return in glory of Jesus himself was also delayed. Meanwhile it seemed that his surviving disciples were in charge. Renamed Apostles, they organized Jesus' followers into a disciplined, vigilant society of people, looking up to the heavens for the Lord's return. They used the old baptism of John as an initiation-rite, and a fellowship meal in Jesus' own favoured style as a way of anticipating the feasting that was to come in the Kingdom world.

Thus the Church began to take shape. Jesus' Kingdom had been ethical and this-worldly. It was about committing oneself ethically to life and to one's neighbour here and now, in this world, and in the present. But the Church developed as being in many ways the opposite of the Kingdom. The longer Jesus' return was delayed, the more the Church became a disciplined army, 'the Church Militant', governed by a class of high priests and oriented towards long-term salvation in the heavenly world after death. Long after New Testament

4. Acts 2:36.

times, Jesus himself gradually became the coequally and coeternally divine Son of God.[5] It came to be claimed that he himself had commissioned the Apostles and their successors. The Church's rituals became 'sacraments', controlled by the clergy and guaranteed by Christ. These sacraments were means of grace, and the Eucharist in particular was 'the medicine of immortality'. The Church thus gradually evolved into a huge salvation-machine, which claimed to have been founded by Jesus himself. It guided human beings *en masse* through the various changes and chances of this life, purifying their souls from sin and preparing them for eternal blessedness after death.

The Church thus became a great system of long-termist, institutional, mediated religion. Salvation was mediated to the believer by the whole disciplinary apparatus of the Church, the clergy, the sacraments, doctrine, scriptures, moral training, canon law and so on. It is true that the Church continued to pray 'Thy kingdom come on earth . . .', but in practice the Kingdom-religion of the original human Jesus was quite forgotten. His teaching is unmentioned in the Creeds, and his own categories of thought were almost wholly lost. The divine Saviour of St John's Gospel had in effect blotted out the original Jewish teacher. The Church had by this stage not merely forgotten the kingdom: it had also forgotten the original Jesus.

I need to emphasize the extent to which the religion of the fully-developed Church became the exact opposite of the religion of Jesus.

First, as the Church became established, its religion became more and more cosmology-based. The Church's teaching took the form of a Grand Narrative of cosmic creation, Fall and Redemption, a narrative that also provided ideological underpinning for the moral order, for the State and for the Church. Jesus' religion was the exact opposite. He wanted us to live *without* a cosmology, and as if we stood at the very end of the world. For him, everything is radically contingent and transient. His outlook is a strange mixture of nihilism and radical humanism. We must be intensely and urgently focussed upon the Now and upon ethical commitment to the neighbour in the Now, as if nothing but the Now exists. That is the way we should live.

So the Church wants us to live on the basis of a sacred cosmology, whereas Jesus wants us to live without a cosmology. The Church became a great system of mediation, founded upon the divine Christ

---

5. In John, the Son is represented as being co-eternal with the Father (e.g., 17:5), but he is not co-equal (e.g., 14:28). Not even John teaches the orthodox Christian doctrine.

who is its guarantor, whereas Jesus himself was a fierce critic of all the apparatus of religious mediation and died opposing it. In short, Church religion is mediated, long-termist and other-worldly, whereas Jesus' religion is immediate, short-termist, and focussed entirely upon this world and the present moment of ethical decision. Church-religion lays great emphasis upon correct doctrinal belief about various hidden realities, whereas Kingdom-religion is beliefless, laying all the emphasis upon action now.

It is very noticeable, by the way, that in his teaching about 'the Kingdom of God' Jesus provides no detailed account of God as King.[6] Just as in the New Jerusalem there is no Temple because God is dispersed everywhere, so in Jesus' Kingdom of God religion is immediate and God is not seen. God is hidden 'in the heart' in such a way that human impulse and divine inspiration are identical. The highest form of religion turns out to be one in which God has disappeared into the movement of life and into the human heart. The Church became a power-structure which instinctively objectifies God as the Being at the summit of the cosmic power-pyramid, but the Kingdom is not 'literally' theistic in quite that way.

Secondly, in Church-religion all value tends to become instrumental: every thing and every deed is good or bad only according as it does or does not contribute to your own ultimate salvation, whereas for Jesus all value tends to become intrinsic, because only the call of the present moment matters, and only the present moment is real. In Church-religion there is much emphasis upon introversion, inwardness, self-examination and the interior life of the soul, whereas Kingdom-religion is extravertive. We are expressly told to come out in public and put ourselves on show, like a city on a hill or a candle on its candlestick. Church religion is dominated by the consciousness of sin and the struggle to purify one's own soul, whereas Jesus' kingdom-religion has no theology of sin and redemption. He is not bothered about sin and personal purity, and he is not a systematic thinker. He does not take pains to avoid publicans and sinners, Samaritans and women of doubtful reputation. On the contrary, they are all welcome in his new moral world, his Kingdom.

This leads us to a third contrast: Church Christianity is sharply dualistic. It is always somewhat suspicious of this world and its pleas-

---

6. See Geza Vermes, *The Religion of Jesus the Jew*, pp. 135ff. Jesus does not speak of God as King, has a Kingdom that seems to lack a king, and describes the Kingdom as a hidden ethical reality that grows secretly.

ures, and draws clear lines between the permitted and the forbidden, the holy and the unclean, the Church and unbelievers and so forth; whereas Kingdom-religion is in the highest degree world-affirming and inclusive. Repeatedly, Jesus simply fails to make the sort of clear moral distinctions between different classes of people — male or female, high or low, Jew or gentile — that an observant Jew was expected to make; and in this respect he is clearly the ultimate source of the anti-discrimination theme in today's humanitarian ethics. Another corollary of his outlook is that for him there should not be a separate Church, drawn apart from the world, *at all* — and in fact he does not envisage one.

So Church Christianity, as it developed, created a Divine Saviour of the World and Incarnate God who was quite different from Jesus, and became a dogma-based, disciplinary religion of self-purification and other-worldly salvation that was in almost every way the opposite of the religion Jesus had taught. Despite the fact that it still prayed 'Thy Kingdom come *on earth*', the Church had forgotten the Kingdom. It forgot that it was itself originally intended to be only a transitional arrangement, and began to think of itself as absolute. It came to see itself as indefectible and infallible, and to see its own dogmas not as *temporary* representations but as immutable truths. By the end of the thirteenth century the Pope even claimed authority over the world of the dead, for he could free you from at least part of your time in Purgatory. So great does the Pope become that in fifteenth century and sixteenth century Christian art both God the Father and Christ Almighty borrow the papal tiara in order to show us what great figures they are.[7]

The Church thus over-reached itself horribly, and in the process quite forgot that its real task is only to prepare us for and to conduct us into a higher-order kind of religion, the Kingdom-religion that Jesus had prophesied and taught. The relation between the Church and the Kingdom should be like that between the Baptist and Jesus.

Against this background we can now see what form the reformation and renewal of Christianity will have to take. We are *not* talking about bringing Christianity into line with today's values. We are talking about trying to formulate a Christianity that is consistent with itself. As we have received it, developed Church-Christianity is radi-

---

7. In the Van Eyck brothers' Ghent altarpiece, 'The Adoration of the Lamb', the enthroned central figure wearing the triple tiara is undoubtedly Christ.

cally inconsistent with Jesus: it rests upon an interpretation of him that he would not have recognized, and it teaches a type of religion the opposite of his own.

In order to reform Christianity and make it internally consistent we need to do two things. *First*, we need to restore the proper relationship between the Church and the Kingdom. The Church is not ultimate: it is only transitional. The Kingdom is ultimate, in the sense that Kingdom-religion is the final kind of religion. So we need to cut down the overweening pretensions of the Church's mediated kind of religion, which always tries to make an absolute of the apparatus of mediation and so becomes a system of religious tyranny, and we need to restore the priority of the beliefless and immediate — or 'solar' — kind of religion that Jesus was after.

At this point there is an intimate analogy between the history of theology and the history of philosophy, and between Jesus and Socrates. Socrates taught the highest kind of philosophy, which is non-metaphysical and endlessly interested and questioning, but his followers, led by Plato, had to go through a detour of twenty-odd centuries of metaphysics before we could all begin to catch up with Socrates himself. And in exactly the same way, Jesus taught the highest kind of religion, which is what I have elsewhere called 'ecstatic immanence' or 'solar ethics': it is an intense, highly-focussed and deliberately non-discriminating love of our transient life and ethical commitment to the neighbour, just in the present moment, and unburdened by thoughts either about the past or about the future. But, like Socrates, Jesus was much too far ahead of his time, and his followers, led by Paul, had to go through a detour of seventeen centuries or so of Church Christianity before they could begin to catch up with Jesus himself.

In defence of the Church, it can be pointed out that Jesus lived at a time when absolute monarchy and various forms of slavery, bondage and serfdom were normal. Any religion that hoped to become socially established would naturally portray all of human life as lived in unconditional and lifelong allegiance to an absolute Lord who had the power of life and death over you, and to whom you owed an infinite debt of service. If you were faithful to the end, after you died he might graciously exalt you to a place by his side in the blessed region where he dwells in glory for ever. In short, Church Christianity said — *and still says* — all the right things about the human condition for people who live in slave society or feudal society, and under conditions that lingered (for some) in parts of Europe and the USA until the nineteenth century.[8] But the Protestant Reformation already included, from as early as Thomas Münzer in the 1520s, a strand that dreamt of going beyond the Church to the Kingdom. Gradually, the dream clarifies: the Kingdom-world will be built by human beings themselves. So our *second* reformation-task is that of building a fully modern Kingdom-religion. It will be a radically free society, in which — for the first time ever — the religious ideal is realized immanently and in the here and now. Human beings will at last learn to love life, just *this* life, unconditionally. And when human history reaches this point, Church-Christianity is at last relativized, the Divine Saviour of the ecclesiastical faith can be pensioned off, and the message of the historical Jesus can at last be understood. He dies as a god, but he returns to us as a human teacher.

And what a teacher: just as in matters of doctrine Jesus not merely teaches no system but is actively *anti*-dogmatic, so also in ethics, Jesus is not merely unsystematic but rather is actively anti-moralistic and anti-authoritarian.[9] He ridicules our impulse to make an authority-figure of him and to systematize his teaching. 'Neither will I tell you by what authority I do these things', he says: 'Why do you call me good?'. It is highly appropriate that perhaps the first thinker in the Christian tradition to understand him on this point was Friedrich Nietzsche, some nineteen centuries later, who takes care to denounce in advance those who will try to idolize him, and whose Zarathustra tries to get rid of his disciples: 'Don't follow me: follow yourselves!', he says.

This deliberate disruptiveness of Jesus clearly indicates that in his new moral world there will be no place for any ideological and coercive religious institution. In the old feudal world it was compulsory to assent to your monarch's creed, and if you obdurately refused, you would be put to death. So it was from about 400–1700 C.E. Human community was thought to be possible only on the basis of common and unconditional subjection to absolute patriarchal power. But during the Reformation period people begin to contemplate moving on from Church to Kingdom, and from credal religion to creedless,

8. It is worth asking why, in a country as committed to republicanism and liberal democracy as is the USA, most Christians remain insistent that the cosmos is an absolute monarchy. How does this happen?

9. John D. Caputo, *Against Ethics*, raises the question of an anti-ethics, but doesn't discuss Jesus. A. N. Wilson, *Jesus,* is good on the anti-systematic disruptiveness of Jesus. See, for example, his c. XI, esp. pp. 252f.

immediate religion. What holds people together in a world where all ideology is dead? The answer, in matters of doctrine, is mutual respect for each other's spiritual freedom. This really *can* generate unexpectedly strong mutual loyalty — or so we claim, on the basis of our experience in Sea of Faith. The time has now come to try out the same line of thinking in ethics: we should test the limits of moral pluralism by asking first whether we shouldn't treat Kingdom-ethics as an anti-ethics. 'Who made me a judge?' says Jesus. 'Judge not!', he says, and he also says: 'Judge for yourselves!'. All of which invites me to ask whether a society based on an anti-ethics may not turn out to be morally stronger than a society based on a strict, systematic moral code that is enforced by a combination of the law and public opinion.

Let us put the point this way. Let us suppose that in a thorough-going 'Kingdom' society there is no common and compulsory doctrine or moral code at all, except a general love of life and commitment to world-affirmation. We would radicalize Quakerism, and be unlimitedly democratic and pluralistic. Would such a society be morally cohesive enough to survive? I say, Yes. I'd like to test the limits. In the teaching of Jesus it is not suggested that the Kingdom-world will be a world without evil. On the contrary, he clearly envisages the continuance of suffering and tragedy. But the price to be paid is well worth paying, for the sake of having such a world: 'Turn the other cheek', he says: 'Resist not evil'.

In this whole discussion I am arguing that the right way to reform Christianity today is to be true to Christianity's own inner logic and to make the long-awaited move from church-religion to kingdom-religion. The time has come when we should abandon the old ecclesiastical theology of the kind that ran from St Paul to Karl Barth, and we should be developing a contemporary kingdom theology. This will enable the Christian tradition, after a 2000-year detour, at last to come circling back to Jesus himself.

Various objections will be raised to my thesis, and I must deal briefly with two of them. The first will come from New Testament scholars who will say that we do not know enough about Jesus with sufficient confidence and general agreement to be able even to *think* about using him as the basis for a reformation and renewal of Christianity.

I agree with much of this criticism. I agree that we have no access to any unchanging and pure essence of Christianity, either in the form of the faith of the primitive church or in the form of the teaching of Jesus, that we might urge people to return to, or use as a foundation for future theological construction. And I also agree that we must give up the old myths about 'Holy Tradition', about the 'Apostolic Succession' and about 'Jesus Christ, the same yesterday, today and forever'. My argument need not invoke such ideas. I need only argue that the old eschatological hope of the Israelite prophets, the hope for a renewed and liberated humanity at the end of historical time, has greatly influenced human beings for over two millennia, and has been specially influential in Western culture since the Reformation. It has inspired every sort of movement for social and political progress, whether on the part of Enlightenment liberals, socialists or anarchists. It has been the driving ideal that has animated Western culture, to such an extent that we should perhaps see the Christian movement as having begun like a coiled-up spring, and as passing through three main stages during its development. It began as immediate religion, in the teaching of Jesus: it passed out almost at once into a long detour through mediation or 'reflection'; and now since the Reformation it has been slowly coming back into this world, into 'life', and into immediacy regained.

An excellent sign of the return into immediacy and what it means is given by Tolstoy, in some famous lines from *War and Peace*:

> Life is everything. Life is God. Everything changes and moves to and fro, and that movement is God. And while there is life there is joy in consciousness of the Godhead. To love life is to love God.[10]

Perhaps it was at some point in the mid-nineteenth century that people realized that the sacred world of religion and the world of everyday life were no longer two distinct worlds, but had become one. So, to repeat an earlier comparison, just as philosophy, after the long detour through metaphysics that began with Plato, is content at last to return into the world of everyday life and becomes endlessly conversational, questioning and interpretative; so Christian thought, after the long detour through supernatural belief and dogmatic theology that began with Paul, is content at last also to return into the world of everyday human life. In committing ourselves ethically to

---

10. Cited from Bk 14, c. 3 in the old Louise and Aylmer Maude translation. See also my *The New Religion of Life in Everyday Speech*.

finite, temporal Be-ing, we find a new and better version of the happiness that our forebears found in contemplating God. So in a certain sense philosophy moves out in a great circle, and returns in the end to Socrates; and so too Christianity moves out in a great circle and returns in the end to the human Jesus. But as I say this I am of course no more claiming that a fully-reformed and modern Christianity can be deduced from a scholarly reconstruction of the teaching of Jesus than I am claiming that a modern philosophy can and should be deduced from the historical Socrates. All I am pointing out is that after the work of figures like Wittgenstein, Heidegger and the neo-pragmatists we increasingly accept that Plato is dead. We increasingly clearly acknowledge that there is only one world, and it is *this* world, the human world, *our* world. As we become philosophically and religiously acclimatized into this new world, we become content with it, and recognize that we have come back to Socrates and to Jesus after a long detour. In this realization there is hope of a new beginning.

The second objection that will be raised to my procedure comes also from New Testament scholars. Following in the tradition of Albert Schweitzer as it was commonly understood for most of the twentieth century, they will say that the whole of Jesus' teaching — his humanitarian ethics, his urgency, his intense focus upon the present moment of decision — all of it was conditioned by his expectation that God would very soon bring the world to an end. But he turned out to have been mistaken — which explains why the Church is right to have largely disregarded the historical Jesus.

In reply to this very common objection it is worth pointing out that (as I have said already) Jesus' view of God is subtler than he gets credit for. Much of the more lurid apocalyptic language attributed to him is nowadays thought to be secondary. His customary style of teaching, in parables and in his use of the 'divine passive' construction, shows that his god-talk was very veiled. He tends to hide God in the heart. In addition to this very obvious point I also say that the language of eschatology is not by any means completely remote from our present-day concerns. For there is a sense in which *we* also live in the last world, the world at the end of the world. After the end of metaphysical realism, we haven't got a cosmos in quite the old sense any more. We have only our own humanly-constructed world. And after the end of belief in progress, the end of political ideology, and the end of belief in life after death, we no longer foresee any better world beyond this world of ours. I am getting old now: my death will be my extinction, and in my death my world will also end. So, if I am ever to taste the blessedness of which religion speaks, I must choose it and enter it *now*. There will never have been a better moment than the present, and I will never have a better chance than I have now. I must get a move on, before it's too late.

Do you see an interesting paradox here? During the twentieth century our culture became at last completely secular — and as that happened it brought with it a certain return of the old eschatological urgency. The teaching and the world-view of Jesus are not in fact quite so remote and inapplicable to us as has often been said (and indeed it is arguable that in the English-speaking world Schweitzer has been much misheard on this point).

So the complete secularization of culture and world-view in our time may itself be experienced as a great religious event, out of which may come a purging and a renewal of our religious tradition.

In summary, I have argued that the historical moment has come for us to reduce our emotional investment in the Church and to abandon the traditional ecclesiastical theology and its typically dualistic ways of thinking. Instead we should develop a contemporary version of what I am calling 'Kingdom religion'. Doing this, we will formulate a new version of Christianity that is at last in harmony both with the original Jesus and with the needs of our own time.

Works Cited

Caputo, John D. *Against Ethics*. Bloomington-Indianapolis: Indiana University Press, 1993.
Cupitt, Don. *The New Religion of Life in Everyday Speech*. London: SCM Press, 1999.
Robinson, John A. T. *The New Reformation*. London: SCM Press, 1965.
Schweitzer, Albert. *The Quest of the Historical Jesus*. 1st complete ed. London: SCM Press, 2000.
Vermes, Geza. *The Religion of Jesus the Jew*. London: SCM Press, 1993.
Wilson, A. N. *Jesus*. London: Sinclair-Stevenson, 1992.

A Christianity for Tomorrow

The Vision of a New Reformation

John Shelby Spong

I speak today in a critical and yet I trust a hopeful mode, about something I treasure profoundly. I am an unashamed, deeply convinced, practicing Christian. I have no hesitancy in calling Jesus, my Lord. I see him as a "God Presence," a human doorway through which I have been able to walk into that God experience which I regard as ultimately holy and ultimately real. I think of myself as a god-intoxicated person bordering on being a mystic. I am not an uncommitted, objective or dispassionate observer of Christianity. I am a believer. I am unable to recall a time when this Christ figure was not part of my consciousness. I was even born in the church's arms, inside an Episcopal hospital named St. Peter's. I was baptized as an infant. I was confirmed in adolescence. The church was a central institution to me, almost a second home. I touched its life in myriads of ways. I attended Sunday school regularly. I was a soprano in its boys' choir. I was an acolyte serving in a bright red vestment at its altar. I was an active participant in its youth group in high school and its Canterbury Club while a university student. This church defined me to myself. I have no conscious sense of ever wanting to be anything but a priest. So single minded was I in the pursuit of this ambition that I could hardly wait to get through such preliminary things as high school, university, and theological seminary, so that I could get on with this compelling life vocation.

I was ordained into the church's priesthood at age 24 and served four churches in North Carolina and Virginia for a period of 21 years. I clearly served them well for this church elected me at age 44 to be one of its bishops. I fulfilled that role for 24 years. I loved my ordained career and, if given the opportunity to live my life a second time knowing all that I now know, I would still without hesitation choose this same path. So I ask you to recognize that I do not address the issues before this conference as an outsider.

The tension that informs this address for me comes from the fact that while I revel in the faith that has long nurtured me, I also live in a world in which both the church as I have known it and Christianity, as it has been traditionally defined, are clearly dying. Even though I believe myself to be a Christian I cannot for the life of me identify with much that Christianity has become. I find myself repelled, for example, when a bookstore is defined as a Christian bookstore because I know it will contain material that is intellectually embarrassing, highly prejudiced against women, advocating child rearing techniques that border on child abuse, and repeating the distorted ignorance of the past about the causes of homosexuality. If that were not bad enough the word Christian has also entered the political arena. When a commentator speaks of the Christian vote in an American election, he or she is describing a group of people who seem to me to be fearful, perhaps neurotic and not infrequently filled with both hatred and bigotry. I do not want to be identified with that perspective.

If those things are what the word Christian has come to mean then the present demise of the Christian Church seems almost deserved. I see the church today as primarily motivated by its own institutional survival needs. In the service of that goal, I find it fearful of new truth, unable or unwilling to engage the thought forms of the emerging world, hardening its message in the patterns of the past, becoming brittle, defensive and as a direct consequence becoming significantly marginalized. When this institution seeks to influence this nation's public policy in a specific way, it is not the plight of the poor or the dismantling of a killing prejudice that is its agenda, despite the overwhelming biblical mandate to address these human concerns. Rather the church's public face has become identified with its opposition to abortion, reflecting as it does a continuing ecclesiastical hostility toward women, and its almost obsessive negativity toward the homosexual minority of the world, revealing in that process both its prejudice and its ignorance.

I find myself no longer eager to rush to this institution's support no matter how much I love what I believe the church can become. I am not interested in engaging hysterical debates on issues of outdated authority. I do not believe that the church possesses revealed truth, an infallible pope, an inerrant Bible or an unchanging tradition. I regard all of those as irrational expressions of a radical insecurity on the part of an institution that can no longer cope with its own fragility.

The majority of the leaders of this institution appear to me to be defensive, to spend their time looking for someone to blame for the church's current dismal plight. Candidates are regularly suggested to fill this highly scapegoated role. Their names float before us: the secular humanists, the religious liberals, the Jesus Seminar, godless communism, the decline of true believers, modern education, Charles Darwin, Sigmund Freud, feminism, the gay lobby or all of the above.

Inside the Protestant wing of the church the main line traditions are declining at a rapid rate. The only protestant growth comes in its evangelical and fundamentalist side and that brand of Christianity has developed a veritable siege mentality which expresses itself in overt rudeness, killing hostility, character assassination and rejection that reaches the fever pitch of death threats. It grows only by claiming to possess a certainty and a security it can never deliver as it curries the favor of the frightened and insecure.

Inside the Catholic wing of the church where, because of its size and history, the illusion of power and influence still exists, we see an enormous clergy shortage coupled with an institutional retrenchment that seeks to reassert the mentality of the Inquisition. Some may think that language to be too strong but those who do simply have not read an official Vatican document released in the year 2000, signed off on by John Paul II himself, entitled IESUS DOMINUS. In that document the assertion was made that there is only one true religion, Christianity; and there is only one true church within that true religion, the Roman Catholic Church. This document went so far as to caution Roman Catholics against referring to other Christian bodies as sister churches for fear of implying that they might possess some note of legitimacy. It was an expression of tribal religion at its medieval worst.

I cringe at the realization that in the mind of the public, these are the only recognized contemporary voices of the Christian Church. Those who speak of a different approach, no matter how deeply committed they are to a Christian future, are frequently dismissed by these true believers as simply no longer Christian.

Most of my friends who share with me a Christian conviction and who see what I see have cut or at least significantly weakened their ties with organized Christianity. Many of those of you who attend this conference and who will address it, know that you fall into this category. Yet I find that, for reasons that I cannot fully understand rationally, I cannot and will not give up on the Christian church. Part of the reason is that I have a different vision of what the church can be and do that still drives me. That vision enables me to contemplate a church radically reformed, theologically literate, courageously confronting those dark places in life where humanity is diminished. To help the church enter this reformation has been my passion for years.

This reformation must begin in what is for me the first principle of all theological speculation. I cannot and will not move away from this conviction though it will obviously set me at odds with some of you. I believe that God is real and that the insatiable human quest for meaning is found in that reality. This means that in the last analysis I do not accept the premise that there is nothing to religious systems except human constructs built only on human need. I do not believe that the religious yearnings of human beings are simply the infantile projections of a frightened, dependent creature. I rather am convinced that something within human life always drives us beyond our limits into otherness, into the experience of transcendence, into the core of being itself that I still use the word God to describe. I experience this God as the depth dimension of my humanity, and I believe that this dimension is not an illusion, but a reality which I trust.

My second and equally vital theological principle that must guide the reformation is that the distinction must be grasped between an experience of God which I regard as both real and timeless and any subsequent human explanation of that God experience which is always compromised, and transitory. In our generation it is our God explanations that have become bankrupt, not the primary experience which called these explanations into being. Every human explanation is always and inevitably time bound and thus warped by the particularity of the one doing the explaining. So it is that all human explanations are finite and thus doomed to die. Please hear this so that semantics will not be the issue the divides us. I consign to the world of explanation — our scriptures, our creeds, our liturgies, our doctrines, our dogmas and all aspects of our theological systems. I regard none of them as eternal and I am convinced that all of them are capable of being abandoned by believers, at least in any literal sense, without abandoning the reality of the experience of God, even the God experience in Christ. To that degree I might be called by some of my critics a non realist.[1] But my commitment to non-realism ceases when

1. Non-realism is the word popularly used by the Sea of Faith Movement born in the United Kingdom and identified most prominently with the work of Don Cupitt of

I move beyond the explanations to the experience on which the explanation rests. For the God I meet experientially, the God who cannot be described intellectually, the God whose name cannot even be uttered without distorting the reality to which that name points, that God I am convinced is real. So inside this tension of dismissing all the explanations of our faith history yet defending the reality of the experience which created those explanations, my theological task as a Christian is to separate surgically the experience from the explanation. That separation becomes for me the key to the possibility of enabling a new reformation to be unleashed that will be so total that it might even be able to break the current death cycle that grips the Christian church and introduce the birth of something incredibly new, yet eternally real. In this presentation my task is to find a way to open this doorway into a Christian future.

I begin by documenting the fact that even in the gospels there are a variety of competing explanations for whatever the experience was that caused Christianity to be born. To the degree that we can recreate this experience, it lies in the realization that somehow or in some manner that which is truly holy, eternally timeless and ultimately real has been met in the human encounter with Jesus of Nazareth. It is the validity of this experience and not the way it has been explained that is, I believe, the irreducible basis upon which the future of Christianity rests.

A religious experience is either a perception of reality beyond the boundaries of our typical limits or it is a delusion created as a coping device by those who cannot tolerate, as that which is ultimate, a vision of meaninglessness. My conviction is that the former is true. At the beginning a God experience is almost always wordless. It has about it the marks of ecstasy. The person in the grip of such an experience stands outside or beyond the sense of self. In the freshness of that experience no rational explanations are sought and none are needed. That, it seems to me, is exactly where Paul is, when in writing to the Corinthians he simply says "in Christ, God was reconciling."[2] It was an ecstatic utterance about an experience he was both unable and unwilling to explain. Each of the primary words in that utterance "Christ," "God" and "reconciling" is quite clearly a cul-

Emmanuel College, Cambridge. I agree that all god talk is a human construct. But I believe that we have god talk because there is a reality to which the word God points and that reality is more than a human construct.
2. 2 Cor 5:19 RSV

turally conditioned word possessing a presumed common definition, but that content does not, at the moment of the ecstatic utterance, enter Paul's mind. He simply seeks to give voice to what was for him a transforming moment, so he says "In Christ, God was reconciling."

But ecstatic articulations do not remain unexplained for long. By the time Paul wrote his Epistle to the Romans in the mid to late fifties, he has shifted quite naturally into an explanatory mode. The Christians in the city of Rome were a community of believers he had never met. He wanted to impress them so that they might assist his future missionary plans, so he sought to explain to them just how it was that the holy God had been seen as present in the life of the human Jesus. Here Paul's time in history which shaped his assumptions and his definition of God, both colored and distorted his explanation. The God portrayed in Paul's Jewish scriptures was defined as a being supernatural in power, external to life and periodically invading the world in miraculous ways, a clear theistic definition. So the God of the Bible was said to have walked in the garden with Adam and Eve in the cool of the evening. This God warned Noah of the coming flood and ordered him to build an ark before sending the deluge. This God chose Abraham, spoke to Moses through a burning bush, split the Red Sea, raised up prophets and was even said to have predicted future occurrences in human history. It was this God, Paul asserted, that he had met and engaged in some manner in the life of Jesus. How this external God and this human life Paul called the Christ, became so bound together that to meet one was to experience the other, was what Paul tried to explain in the first four verses of the Epistle to the Romans. His explanation was fascinating.

"God," he said, "declared Jesus to be the Son of God." God did it through something Paul called "the spirit of holiness" and this action was accomplished for Paul at the time "of the resurrection." It was a remarkable early Christian explanatory statement and by the standards of later Christian orthodoxy was totally heretical. Listen to what Paul was asserting. God, presumably the supernatural creator beyond the sky, made the declaration about Jesus' divine sonship. God was the designator. Jesus was the one designated. This is hardly the language of co-equality. This declaration, Paul asserted, was accomplished through a vague entity called "the spirit of holiness." The Holy Spirit, as we speak of this aspect of God today, had not yet achieved specific form in Paul's mind, nor had the Trinity, as the church would later define that concept. Finally, this declaration occurred, Paul said, in that moment Christians began to call resurrection. Indeed this was the ultimate meaning of Easter for Paul, who had clearly never heard of such traditions as the empty tomb, the angelic visitors or the resuscitated body. So this first Pauline attempt to make sense of this profound and life changing experience was by later tests of orthodoxy quite inadequate. But, please note, the inadequacy of the explanation does not invalidate the reality of the experience. Paul, like everyone who dares to speak of God, discovered that there is no such thing as a god language with which to process a God experience. The language we use is human, culturally conditioned, and incapable of doing more than pointing to that which it can never fully embrace. To attribute ultimate reality to the constructs of our language, to make religious claims for the human explanations of the God experience is to become idolatrous, and foolish. No explanation will ever be eternal and Paul's explanation in Romans was destined to be changed quickly.

In the early 70's the first gospel, called Mark, appeared with the opening words "The Gospel of Jesus Christ the Son of God." This author could, therefore, hardly wait for God to confirm in the final episode of Jesus' life, what was being proclaimed in verse one. Yet Mark was clearly leaning on the content of Paul's words from Romans even as he changed them. In Mark's opening story, the account of Jesus' baptism, God still declared Jesus to be the Son of God, just as Paul had said. Mark even placed the actual words of this declaration onto God's lips. Following the public baptism, Mark had the heavenly voice heard offstage say: "This is my beloved son in whom I am well pleased."[3] God made this declaration, Mark said, still following Paul's lead, by the action of the spirit. In Mark's story, however, this vague entity was more specifically defined. The spirit could actually descend out of the sky and embrace Jesus as a sign that the divine and human had come together. Mark's crucial change was to move God's declaration from the resurrection, where it was located by Paul, to the baptism. Though the two accounts varied in this detail, both were attempts to explain how external divine power came to be experienced in the human Jesus.

---

3. Mark 1:11. These words, while not a direct quotation, are certainly shaped by the words of Isaiah 42:1 which the prophet said were the words by which God designated the "suffering servant" when this Isaiah creation emerged in the prophet's writing.

In the next ten to twenty years of Christian history two other gospels, Matthew and Luke, came into being. Both of them were dependent on Mark as well as on other sources. In these two later gospels the explanations of how God had come to be present in this Jesus continued to grow. Yet Paul's original concepts were still shaping the development. In both Matthew and Luke, God still declared Jesus to be the Son of God. In Matthew this declaration was made by an unnamed angel in a dream to Joseph.[4] In Luke it was made by a specific angel, named Gabriel, to Mary in person.[5] This union between Jesus and God was still achieved through the operation of the Holy Spirit who was now so specific as to play the male role in the act of conception. So at this stage of theological explanation Jesus was said to be the Son of God, not by God's action in raising him from the dead as it was for Paul, and not by God's action in pouring the Spirit upon him in baptism as it was for Mark, but by the action of God, as Spirit, in creating this divine life out of the substance of a virgin. This was the moment in which the virgin tradition entered Christianity, a ninth decade phenomenon. As supernatural and miraculous as that story was, please note it was not to be the end of this ongoing, developing, explanatory process.

In the middle years of the tenth decade the final canonical gospel called John came into being. John's explanation of the God presence in Jesus was not dependent on a virgin birth. Rather the pre-existing divine logos or Word of God, had simply become enfleshed in Jesus. There was, therefore, for this author, no time when Jesus and God were not united. If Jesus was identified with the logos which spoke in the act of creation, saying "let there be light," then Jesus was preexistent with God and of the very essence of God. This late developing Johannine understanding was to become the ultimate affirmation on which the Christian church's future doctrinal development would rest.

What I want us to note is that the explanations vary widely even in the New Testament. God brought the divine and human together in Jesus when God declared Jesus to be the Son of God at the time of the resurrection, was Paul's explanation when he wrote to the Romans in the late 50s. God declared Jesus to be Son of God in the act of his baptism by pouring the Holy Spirit on him, was Mark's

4. Matt 1:20–23.
5. Luke 1:26–35.

explanation in the early 70s. God actually conceived this Jesus by the operation of the Holy Spirit on a virgin, became the explanation of Matthew in the early 80s and Luke in the late 80s or early 90s. Jesus was part of who God is from the dawn of creation, said John, writing in the mid 90s. Note the variety of ways the God presence in Jesus was explained. No explanation is either eternally valid or eternally true. But also note that underneath this wide variety of biblical explanations there is still the absolute consistency of the experience. Somehow, in some way, God had been met, engaged and confronted in the humanity of Jesus, through whom God was said to be reconciling the world to God.

My contention is that the God experience is real. The divine does permeate the human. This is what Jesus means. The explanations, however, that seek to give rational form to that ecstatic experience are never eternal since they inevitably are expressed in the concepts of the day in which the explanations are formed and limited by the available knowledge. So if the church is interested in a reformation sufficiently radical to create a new vision of what Christianity is, it must develop the ability to lay aside all the theological explanations of antiquity as inevitably inadequate. This means that the church must recognize that its first century biblical explanations, its fourth and fifth century creedal explanations and its later developing system of doctrines and dogmas are human creations, not divine revelations and none of them is either finally true or eternally valid. The only thing that cannot be jettisoned is the experience that in some way the holy God was met in the human Jesus and lives were transformed by that encounter. The ultimate heresy of Christianity lies not in its inability to explain adequately the Christ experience. It lies in the claim uttered through the ages that human words could not only define for all time something called orthodoxy, but that the ultimate and saving truth of the God experience could actually reside in the theological explanations. In Christ God was reconciling. Scriptures and creeds point to the experience. That is all they can do. They can never capture or finally embody it. If they claim to do so they become idols that eventually will die. That death is now upon us.

Over the years a theological consensus developed, based upon these various biblical explanations about how the external God had entered the life of Jesus of Nazareth. That consensus combined some deeply incompatible concepts. It was said that in Jesus, the pre-existent logos in John's Gospel, had been enfleshed through the virginal conception portrayed in Matthew and Luke. It was a strange combination, but it won the day. By the fourth and fifth centuries of the common era this consensus was developed against the background of the Greek thinking Mediterranean world and the result was a series of convoluted creeds that sought to create conformity by closing every theological loophole, and the development of doctrines and theological systems that were invested with infallibility. This was when doctrines like Incarnation were formed, and that is when people began to claim that the doctrine of the Holy Trinity actually defined God. All trinitarian language could ever do was to define the way human beings believed they had experienced God. Between the Trinitiarian claim and the Trinitarian reality, there is a vast difference. When the church, seeking to secure its power, began to literalize these explanations, the demise and the ultimate death of what we call "traditional Christianity," became inevitable.

In the orthodox consensus Jesus was the invasion of the supernatural God into human history. The virgin birth was God's point of entry, the divine landing field if you will. The scriptural stories of Jesus' ability to do godlike things – such as stilling the storm, walking on water, healing the sick, raising the dead and even his own ability to reverse the death imposed on him at the time of the crucifixion were interpreted as the literary tales that demonstrated his nature as God in human form. The exit stories of his gravity defying ascension beyond the sky to where the theistic God was presumed to live completed the divine round trip, at least based on first century assumptions about the shape of reality. Christianity has been theologically identified with this explanatory process since the fourth century. Even the Reformation in the sixteenth century was primarily about power and control, not about making sense out of what were even by that time ancient and dated explanations.

But as the world of knowledge about how things worked in the universe began to explode into human awareness, the ability on the part of people either to believe those ancient explanations or the ecclesiastical leaders competence to defend these biblical and creedal propositions became less and less possible. When the existence of the egg cell was discovered in the eighteenth century, making the female an equal co-creator of each new child, all virgin birth stories died as literal biology. So the traditional Christian understanding of how the external God was said to have entered the human Jesus was obliterated by modern genetic discoveries about reproduction.

When Copernicus, Kepler and Galileo had completed their work and human beings began to understand the vastness of the universe, the story of Jesus' cosmic ascension as the way he had returned to the God above the sky also became nonsensical. We know that if Jesus literally ascended into the sky he did not get to heaven he got into orbit. So both the entry and the exit stories of Jesus were reduced to being literal impossibilities.

When Isaac Newton began to explain the relationship between cause and effect the bulk of the traditional way the Jesus story was told became inoperative. Newton closed the doors to those phenomena heretofore attributed to divine intervention. He shrank dramatically the places in which magic and miracle were said to occur. He made all of the supernatural tales in which the theistic God invaded the world less and less believable. That process continues at full speed to this very moment. So the explanation of the God experience in Jesus that provided the content for the doctrine of the Incarnation shriveled into a bit of ill informed piety. Christianity, as the system based on the experience that the holy God was somehow met in the human Jesus, could clearly no longer rest on the entry and exit stories found in the scriptures, nor in the fanciful tales of the miraculous acts that God in human form might do. So the first task of the coming reformation must be to declare the explanations of yesterday to be bankrupt for today. Does that then signal the end of classical Christianity? Not if there is still the reality of the experience which inspired these now inept explanations.

File that for a moment and move with me to that other great word in the Pauline phrase, "reconciling." The purpose of God's presence in Christ was said to be that of accomplishing the task of reconciling. What was it that needed to be reconciled? How was that word to be understood?

The biblical tradition explained the human sense of alienation by defining human life as sinful, fallen, unable to save itself and in need of rescue. Our liturgies are full of references to that definition. "We have left undone those things which we ought to have done. We have done those things we ought not to have done." "Without you we can do nothing that is good," for "there is no health in us."

The Jesus story was told against this understanding of human life. It was buttressed by the biblical tradition which was developed to explain how this state of life had come about. The original creation, it was said, was good, complete and finished. The human creatures, male and female, were placed into that perfect world to be its stewards. However, in a primal act of disobedience these human creatures broke the perfection of God's creation, fell into sin and were corrupted beyond their ability to overcome their self-imposed distortion. In turn, these now sinful creatures passed this fallen humanity down from generation to generation. All of the divine efforts to reconcile God with these fallen human beings failed. After the flood, when God sought to destroy evil and start over, God discovered that God's servant Noah still possessed a humanity that was distorted.[6] Neither did the call of Abraham bring the perfection God was believed to be seeking.[7] Even the Exodus followed by the gift of the Torah failed to lead the chosen people to righteousness. The prophets were unable to recall the people to their original created glory. So according to the traditional explanation Jesus became God's final almost desperate act to reclaim the world from the power of evil. Again first century Jewish images shaped the explanation. Like the lamb of Yom Kippur, the day of the Atonement, Jesus was said to be the perfect offering which the theistic God both required and accepted, and the blood from that sacrifice also cleansed the people from their sins. Like the scapegoat of Yom Kippur Jesus was thought of as the sin bearer. Upon his head and back the sins of the world were laid and he purged human life of the fall by taking those sins away. Like the paschal lamb of Passover, Jesus' death was the sacrifice required to break the power of death itself. The fallen distorted human family could thus be made whole simply by entering symbolically into the life of Jesus, who was, said this explanation, God incarnate, paying the price we could not pay. He was said to have overcome human sin and thus to be the doorway into the reconciliation that would restore human life to the perfection known in the Garden of Eden. Around these themes the church organized its liturgical life. Baptism reenacted the moment in which the fall into sin was washed away and the Eucharist reenacted the sacrifice of the cross whereby our salvation was procured.

This became the content of the church's doctrine of the Atonement and thus the frame of reference upon which the power

---

6. See Gen 9:20ff. in which Noah gets drunk right after the flood and was looked upon by Ham, his son and the father of Canaan. This text was used to justify the later subjugation of the people of Canaan.

7. In this story Abraham lied about his wife and, claiming that she was his sister, then offered Sarah as a sexual partner to the Pharaoh, hardly the behavior of the purified.

claims of the Christian church were built. The church was to be the place where the salvation Jesus affected became available. Outside the church all human beings were still lost in their original sin. Since baptism and the Eucharist were the sacraments, said to be necessary to salvation, and since the only people who could validly perform these sacraments were the church's ordained priests, the church's grip on salvation was complete. "There is no salvation outside the church" became the cry that was repeated in every generation as fragile people claimed that they had the only, the infallible, the inerrant key to salvation.

But the world in which these explanations were developed has died and so have these explanations. Bemoaning it does not make it less so. Charles Darwin in 1859 challenged the view of reality on which this particular telling of the Jesus story was based. There was no finished and perfect creation, said Darwin. Creation is still ongoing. There was no perfect human life that at the dawn of creation fell into the state of sin from which Jesus was forced to deliver us. Instead human life has emerged from a single cell in the sea perhaps four billion years ago until it evolved into a creature who knows what it means to be separated from the natural world by the emergence of a self-consciousness that developed perhaps as recently as 50,000–100,000 years ago. This self-conscious creature has organized life to serve the primary evolutionary need to survive making his or her continued existence the highest human value. This has resulted in the emergence of a radically self-centered humanity whose will to survive, no matter what the cost, is the source of most of what we now call evil. There was no fall, no original sin and thus no need for a divine rescue, no sacrifice of Jesus, no saving blood. The whole explanatory story collapses. It cannot be patched or revised.

Evil, that was born in human incompleteness and shaped by the struggle to survive our evolutionary history, is not something that can be overcome by the sacrificial death of the Son of God. So the primary Christian myth becomes inoperative. There is no way that people can be restored to something they have never been. Thus the doctrine of the Atonement goes the way of the doctrine of the Incarnation, the doctrine of the Trinity, the doctrine of the validity of the Sacraments and the power on which the institution called the church based its claim to be the sole possessor and dispenser of salvation. These explanations die not because the truth they sought to convey is wrong, but rather because that truth was conveyed in a way that our expanded knowledge has shown to be unbelievable. A Christian church clinging to these doctrinal explanations in the twenty-first century is doomed to die. But my contention is that the destiny of all human explanations even theological ones is to die. But the death of the explanation does not mean that the experience which required the explanation in the first place is either invalid or unreal.

That issue does, however, raise the final question that represents what many seem to think is the traditional believer's last stand: Can Christianity continue in any sense, when it is stripped of all that historically seemed to define it? Is there any alternative? To cling to unbelievable symbols, to shout them loudly, to buttress them with claims of infallibility or inerrancy, is not to serve truth but to reveal hysteria. But that does not mean that we have to abandon the experience which these symbols sought to explain. The new Reformation must, I believe, begin with the dismissal of all of the traditional explanations, but it must still cling to the reality of the experience that those explanations were designed to communicate.

What would a Christianity where the principal experience was separated from the traditional explanations, look like? Time does not allow me to do more than hint at an answer. At the very least we would have to say that in the Christianity of tomorrow God can no longer be thought of as a Being external to life who must invade our world to accomplish the divine purpose. So the theistic God will surely die. But the death of theism does not mean that there is no divine presence. The question becomes, "can this divine presence be perceived apart from the vocabulary of theism?" I think it can. Paul Tillich has suggested that God must be perceived not as a being — not even the supreme being or the supernatural being but rather as the ground of all being. The Ground of Being is not external to life. It is rather present in the being of all things. Perhaps the Ground of Being can be engaged and even worshiped by those who as self-conscious creatures believe that in the depths of our humanity we can experience transcendence, otherness, the Holy, a reality I call God. God can no longer be perceived as a miracle working deity, but as the source of life and love permeating the whole creation and capable of being engaged consciously in the human experience when wholeness, healing, and full humanity are experienced.

If it is the experience of God that is real not the explanations of that God experience, then can we not suggest that it is the God who is the source of life, the source of love and the ground of being who was met in the life, love and being of the human Jesus of Nazareth? Can he not thus still be, for some like me, a defining life in the divine human encounter? We no longer have to be bound by the theistic explanations. That was the way first century people explained their experience in terms of the only God concept they knew. But could it not have been that in his expanded life, Jesus revealed the God, who is the source of life? Could it not be that in the love he shared so wastefully, he revealed the God who is the source of love? Could it not be that in the fullness of being that he manifested in both his life and death that he revealed the God who is the ground of being? Could it not be that in the depths of human consciousness humanity flows into divinity? Is that the experience that caused people to state ecstatically that in some way, the Holy God was present in this Christ? Jesus did not come to live and die in order to rescue the fallen. He, a human being, became rather an empowering God presence calling people to step beyond the boundaries of their fears to grasp a new humanity, a humanity not divided by the security systems of tribe, prejudice, gender, or even religion. Each of these security systems was designed to aid in the quest for human survival. They are the protective layers wrapped around, not the fallen but the unfinished, the incomplete, the self-conscious creature called homo sapiens.

The God presence in Jesus was an empowering call to us all to step beyond the boundaries of our incompleteness into a more complete humanity. To journey into that new humanity is, I believe, to journey into the holy God. To experience the meaning of this Jesus is to touch the dimensions of transcendence, otherness and holiness. The church that will continue to live in this world must shed the literalism of its explanations, surrender its excessive claims to be the sole source of salvation, the only reservoir of divine grace and begin the task of being the community dedicated to calling human beings to step beyond the barriers erected to enable them to survive the rigors of evolution, into a barrier free humanity — a humanity that is not fallen but is only unfinished, a humanity waiting yearning to be made whole.

In that experience lies what I now call "A New Christianity for a New World." I will spell out that vision in far greater detail in a book by that title which will appear in the fall of 2001. In that volume I will propose a God who is beyond such explanations as theism but not beyond the experience of that which is real, holy, other and eternal; a Christ who is beyond the explanations of incarnational thinking, but not beyond the experience of a timeless divinity erupting in human life; a church, not as the doorway to salvation but as the community created to deepen life and enhance humanity, liturgies designed not to pay homage or to flatter an external deity, but to increase our God consciousness, expand the boundaries of human community, and to break down the barriers that divide the human family. Prayer will no longer be adult letters to a Santa Claus God requesting what only an intervening power not bound by the laws of our world could accomplish, but a way to live into and share the God presence that surrounds us. Ethics will be not a code of conduct, dictated by a theistic God and written in a book or on tablets of stone but will rather be grounded in the principle that since God is met as the source of life, the source of love and the ground of being, any action which enhances life, increases love, and heightens being is both godlike and good. Any action which diminishes life, depresses love and shrinks being is evil. Finally I will propose a view of eternal life, not as a place where goodness is rewarded and evil punished, but where eternity is a present reality that we enter in the process of living fully, loving wastefully and being all that we can be and from that eternity, I maintain, we can never depart.

The Christian church born in this Reformation, designed to live out these values will have to give up conversion efforts and missionary enterprises, for both are based on the premise that ultimate truth can ever be a human possession. Human beings will always see God as a dimension of our own life and thus through a glass darkly. That is a human inevitability. But our Christian vocation, corporately and individually, will be to remove the defensive barriers present in all of life so that everyone can meet the God who is the source of life by living fully, engage the God who is the source of love by loving wastefully, and worship the God who is the Ground of being by having the courage to be all that every person can be.

That is my vision of the church of the future. So let the Reformation begin.

Incredible Creed, Credible Faith

Problem and Promise

Roy W. Hoover

Introduction

It was after church one Sunday morning while members of the congregation were lingering in the lounge for coffee and cookies and conversation that a longtime member approached me and asked, "Why is it that when so much has changed in the way we understand ourselves and our world that the church insists on clinging to its old traditional language of faith?" Doing my best to offer instant, comprehensible expertise at the touch of an unanticipated question, I suggested a couple of possible reasons. One might be that traditional language carries with it a sense of connection with the past, a sense of participating in a community with a long and venerable history that many do not want to lose. It is probably also true, I suggested, that the church continues to use its traditional language because it is afraid not to, afraid of offending and losing some of its constituents. It's difficult and risky to introduce change, so the church continues to use the traditional language. "Yes" she said, "and no one believes it anymore."

In that brief and fleeting after-worship exchange something of the dilemma and disappointment of our religious situation was briefly encapsulated — a moment in time that has no doubt had analogous encapsulations in the experience of many of those who will read these lines. It is anecdotal evidence of the reality on the ground of what theologian Edward Farley has called "the collapse of the house of authority" — the house of surety in which the church has lived since the early centuries of its history.[1] This mighty fortress of faith was built upon the authority of scripture as the inspired word of God, upon the authority of the leaders of the church as the divinely appointed successors of the divinely appointed apostles, and upon the authority of the creed as the divinely authorized work of the

1. Farley, *Reflection*, p. 165.

81

divinely appointed leaders of the church. But this great and venerable house of authority has collapsed, not because anyone has deliberately set out to destroy it, but because it has become incredible. This house of authority began and has been sustained not principally by money and power, however much of each the church came to acquire, but by what its people believed. But as that one worshiper said with such simple clarity on that Sunday morning not long ago, "nobody believes it any more."

There is a problem with that worshiper's simple clarity, however: it is both true and not true at the same time. It is true that the traditional forms of faith enshrined in the house of authority no longer command the assent of a multitide of moderns. The church alumni association is large and growing. The number of those who assume that the church has nothing of significance or consequence to offer is large also. For all of them the house of authority is at best only a majestic ruin, the relic of an era that ended some time ago. But to say that "no one believes it any more," or that the house of authority has collapsed is also, sociologically and even religiously, not true. Everyone can see that in much of the Christian world "the house of authority is still standing and crammed full of both eager and reluctant occupants," says theologian Farley, and he describes them well:

> They are many types. Most widespread is the persistence of Catholic and Protestant folk religion where religious realities are understood in literal and cosmological terms. These occupants are either untouched by historical consciousness or are so successful in compartmentalizing the psyche and areas of experience (like fundamentalist physicists) that the house of authority and whatever might count against it are kept on opposite poles of the psyche's planet, a virtual Arctic and Antartica. And there are the theological occupants, some of whom recognize the radical results of the collapse of the house, the effect of an earthquake on faith's self-interpreted content, and who attempt to live in the house as antiquarians. The house of authority and Christianity are the same so they apologetically defend the house. So goes Catholic textbook theology and modern Protestant orthodoxy. Others of the theological occupants are full participants in historical consciousness and are fully knowledgeable about the uses and implications of critical methods. But they may not be as savvy

as their conservative colleagues about the destructive effect these things have on the house of authority. Some have actually moved out but retain a verbal house of authority in their ways of talking about Scripture. They sound as if they were occupants. Others live in the house as renovators, thinking that what is needed is a bit of repair work, a new hermeneutical picture window in the living room, some new historical tiles on the roof. Such are the so-called Protestant and Catholic neoorthodox theologians.

[The house of authority continues to have another kind of occupant, the one for whom it is the very house of God. For this occupant] it not only carries the predicates of God (absoluteness, certainty, purity, eternality); it communicates them to the occupant who then becomes certain, pure, eternal, and impregnable. The way of authority itself tends to evoke such a response for . . . it extends a divine act (of meaning, willing) to a non-divine event which is a multiplicity of historical-natural events . . . [This raises the spector of idolatry]: that the house of authority, like any created entity, *can* function as the ersatz god. History testifies that it has functioned in that way. It therefore attracts into its occupancy those (which can be any and every human being) who respond to the insecurity and anxiety, the fragility and threats of finitude, by securing themselves in an absolute system, institution, writing, or leadership.[2]

Tradition and Scholarship

Neither quarreling with those who continue to occupy the house of authority, nor tracing the history of the awful things the church has been willing to do in the name of such claims to authority is my purpose here. Those who know that the house of authority has collapsed under the weight of its own incredibility do not need to be persuaded to abandon it or to flee from its dehumanizing pretensions. But insofar as we are unwilling to surrender the Christian tradition to the house of authority as if that were its only possible home, it may be of use to take note of some things that Yale historian Jaroslav Pelikan has had to say about tradition. The collapse of the house of authority

2. Farley, *Reflections*, pp. 166–67.

may not require us to suppose that it must necessarily be accompanied by the termination of tradition.

For example, Pelikan says that "tradition becomes an idol. . . when it makes the preservation and the repetition of the past an end in itself; it claims to have the transcendent reality captive and encapsulated in that past, and it requires an idolatrous submission to the authority of tradition, since truth would not dare to appear outside it." An "authentic and living tradition," on the other hand, always "points beyond itself" and "does not present itself as coextensive with the truth it teaches." A living tradition also has "the capacity to develop while still maintaining its identity and continuity," and is able to appropriate persuasive criticism. Such "healthy development . . . keeps a tradition both out of the cancer ward and out of the fossil museum." "Ultimately," Pelikan suggests, "tradition will be vindicated, for each of us as an individual and for us as communities, by how it manages to accord with our own deepest intuitions and highest aspirations."[3] In other words, a tradition lives if its founding insights and aspirations about our common humanity continue to be validated in our own experience.

With such openness to criticism and development tradition offers us invaluable resources for continuity and renewal; without such openness and development it offers us only the tyranny of the dead. On the one hand, as Pelikan sagely observes, "during much of our history, and down to our own time, tradition has provided the perennial themes and the key metaphors by which creative expression has been preserved from the banality and the trivialization to which a total immersion in the here and now could have subjected it."[4] On the other hand, and just as sagely, Pelikan notes that "the reformers of every age . . . have protested against the tyranny of the dead, and in doing so have called for innovation and insight in place of tradition." It cannot be denied, Pelikan acknowledges, that the human spirit is endowed with an inherent capacity for insight that must not be held in bondage to an authoritarian past. Furthermore, "the recognition of the tension between tradition and insight is . . . an ineradicable element of the tradition itself, which must therefore not be identified with a traditionalism that seeks to preserve it by embalming it."[5]

3. Pelikan, *Vindication*, pp. 54–60.
4. Pelikan, *Vindication*, p. 78.
5. Pelikan, *Vindication*, pp. 65, 72–73.

If the Christian tradition hopes to survive as "the living faith of the dead" rather than to suffer the fate of being "the dead faith of the living,"[6] it cannot do without the resources offered to it by historical-critical scholarship. There are many, not only in fundamentalist circles and in the Offices of the Congregation for the Doctrine of the Faith in the Vatican, but also among mainline Protestant clergy and laity who currently hold a contrary view: that historical-critical scholarship has the effect of destroying Christian faith. In my view, they could not be more mistaken. Historical-critical scholarship offers the church an indispensable resource for doing what Jaroslav Pelikan says that a living tradition always does: it is able to appropriate persuasive criticism; it has the capacity to change without losing its sense of identity and continuity; and it recognizes how its founding insights and aspirations continue to be validated in our own experience. A tradition that stays alive in this way is the one that will keep itself "both out of the cancer ward and out of the fossil museum."

Realistically, it is simply too late now to reject the light that historical scholarship has thrown on Christian origins and on the whole history of the Christian tradition. Pelikan has characterized our situation with trenchant clarity:

> None of us can go back — and, I suppose, none of us would, except in an occasional wistful moment, want to go back — to a method of reading the traditions of our heritage that did not do justice to their historical character. Or, to put it more directly, none of us can ever again establish some sort of sanctuary into which the historical-critical study of "sacred tradition" may not enter. The history of thought, the history of science, and the history of faith are all filled with the "bare, ruin'd choirs" of such sanctuaries.
>
> Our task is, rather, to face the issue directly, and to do so as scholars and thinkers and citizens and believers (or, at any rate, as some of the above) who accept, gratefully or at least gracefully, all the historical disclosures that have come out of historicism and its research. And the unavoidable question is: How, then, may we acknowledge the human, all-too-human nature of the traditions that are our intellectual, moral, political, and spiritual heritage, and nevertheless (or perhaps even

---

6. These phrases are drawn from Pelikan, *Tradition*, p. 65.

therefore?) affirm those traditions . . . and go so far as to call them, in some meaningful sense, sacred?[7]

Truth is, as moderns we can no more shed our historical consciousness than we can rid ourselves of the knowledge that the earth is round and circles the sun. The church should have learned from its experience with Galileo that it cannot succeed in suppressing what cannot be denied, and the new historical understanding of Christian origins that is the fruit of historical-critical scholarship cannot be denied.

Pelikan's astute observations about a living tradition encourage us to think that while challenges to traditionalism might (and perhaps should) be fatal, challenges to a tradition need not be. They can, in fact, be a source of revitalizing a tradition; and anyone who is interested in coming to terms with historical scholarship on the Jesus tradition should have reason to think that it could help to effect an historic renewal, even a new reformation.

Paradigm Shifts and the History of Science

In his notable book, *The Structure of Scientific Revolutions,* Thomas Kuhn traces the process by which science has advanced in the course of its history. Kuhn shows that the history of science has not been simply a smooth, incremental accumulation of knowledge. Rather, when the discovery of new scientific data is found to be inexplicable by traditional scientific theory, it eventually induces some scientist or scientists to construct a new theory that is able to account for both the old and the new data. The old conceptual world which was unable to make sense of the new data is replaced by a new theory by which both the old and the new data are found to make sense. In accepting the new theory a scientist learns to look at all the data from a new perspective. It is by a series of such paradigm schifts that scientfic knowledge has advanced. New explanatory theory that involved looking at the data from a new perspective was required, not merely new information. Such a "reconstruction of prior theory and . . . re-evaluation of prior fact [is] an intrinsically revolutionary process that is seldom completed by a single man," Kuhn remarks,

7. Pelikan, *Vindication*, pp. 50–51.

"and never overnight."[8] We should be neither surprised nor discouraged, if an analogous process in the field of religion takes some time.

The Need for a New Theological Paradigm

For quite some time now many of those who have read recent scholarship on the historical Jesus seem to have been looking for new historical information that can be used to embellish and burnish the traditional theological paradigm by which they have interpreted the claims and meaning of Christian faith. Not long ago, for example, a very capable UCC pastor told me that he had been interested in the Jesus Seminar's research on the historical Jesus when he first heard about it in the late 1980's. He had thought the Seminar would turn up new information that would fill in Jesus' historical background, and that would be useful to him. But when the Seminar began to report that the Jesus who emerged from the best historical data we could find in the ancient sources did not look like the Jesus of his theological persuasion, he lost interest and has since disregarded the Seminar's work as not merely useless, but as harmful — destructive of Christian faith. Borrowing Thomas Kuhn's work as a metaphor, I respectfully suggest that this pastor is in a situation like that of a scientist who is confronting new and puzzling, perhaps even disconcerting data without the new theory needed for it to make sense. He is not alone.

The fact is, I think, that the new data that historical scholarship has turned up on the historical Jesus and on Christian origins more generally has pointed to the need for a new theological paradigm and will make sense only from the perspective that a new paradigm will offer. That need has been created by our modern knowledge of the world and human existence in general, of course, and not only by historical scholarship. One of the modern theologians who has recognized this most clearly is Gordon Kaufman. Here are a couple of brief examples of how he has expressed such a view:

> Theologians today must take full responsibility for all the concepts they use and all the claims they advance. They may no longer evade accountability by advocating positions simply

8. Kuhn, *Scientific Revolutions*, p. 7.

because they seem well grounded in tradition or in what earlier generations regarded as divine revelation.

. . . Since much about the world (as we presently understand it) was completely unknown to our religious traditions, and this significantly affects the way in which God had been conceived, theologians dare not simply take over traditional ideas; we must be prepared to criticize every use and interpretation of the symbol "God" that has appeared to date.[9]

What we know (or think that we know) about the world in which we live suggests a picture very different from the one purveyed in Christian tradition; indeed, it makes the traditional picture, I suggest, literally unthinkable by us, unintelligible (though of course we can still *assert* it). To try to think the idea of a divine super-Self *outside of* or beyond the universe (which is hundreds of millions of light years across) boggles the mind; moreover, trying to resolve this problem by thinking in terms of a divine Spirit or Self moving immanently *within* the universe (obviously a considerable transformation of the traditional mythic picture) is no easier. So other metaphors for God, supposedly more compatible with modern notions of the world, may be proposed in the attempt to save something of the original meaning: ground of being, first cause, creative event, power, life, a vague "cosmic love." All of these present watered-down versions of the meaning carried by the picture of the creator/lord/father; they are masks for this great conception on which they secretly draw and which gives them their religious power. What is needed today is not one more camouflage of the old mythic notion but rather a new conception of God, one that resonates more directly with our modern experience and understanding of the world.[10]

Not only do we see and understand the world differently than did those who created the now traditional forms of Christian faith, we see ourselves differently also. In the ancient creeds humans are viewed as embodied souls, temporarily resident on earth, but bound for eter-

9. Kaufman, *Mystery*, pp. 28, 29.
10. Kaufman, *Mystery*, pp. 305–306.

nity. The great issue of our lives, therefore, is the assurance of safe passage to that ultimate destination. The ancient creeds thus assume that the larger context of human life is the eternity that we will directly enter at our death or at the end of the world, whichever comes first. But this is not the way thinking people see their lives today.

How might we characterize the view of human beings that is most widely held by educated people in the West today? Here is how Gordon Kaufman has framed an answer to that question:

[The idea that human beings are "immortal souls"] does not provide us with a good place to begin our interpretation of the human today. The phrase "immortal soul" no longer conveys clear or agreed meaning, and to many it seems not only archaic and obscure but nonsensical; it certainly does not express a common starting point that we can all take for granted as we begin our thinking together. Rather, I suggest, we will come much closer to articulating the fundamental assumptions about the nature of the human which are widely accepted today if we speak of our interconnectedness and interdependence with all other forms of life (on the one hand), and of our cultural creativity in history, producing a thoroughly cultural form of existence (on the other) — if we speak of ourselves, that is to say, as what I shall call "biohistorical" beings. We are given our life by — and we continue to be sustained by — the great evolving ecosystem of life on planet Earth; but we humans have ourselves transformed that life into diverse forms of historical existence, and it is this our historicity which, above all gives our existence its distinctively human character.

It is this complex developmental reality which (for most educated westerners) the word "human" commonly designates today. If we look backward and downward through the biological foundations or our being, and through the various tiers of life and complex crystaline forms from which they evolved, we come ultimately to the fundamental structures of energy and matter underlying and composing our universe; if we look outward and upward through the historical realities of our culture and consciousness and creativity, which have evolved out of and become superimposed on those foundations and

which make our existence distinctively *human*, we find ourselves immersed in and aspiring toward realms of value and
meaning — Truth, Beauty, Goodness. Any religious or theological interpretation of our humanity, if it is to be intelligible
to us today, must make sense of this complex open-ended
developing process that we are — rooted in the earth, but
aspiring to the heavens above — and of the qualities of life
and being that we have in and through this process. For this is
the way we who live this biohistorical process, and who are
aware of ourselves as moments within this biohistorical
process, today experience and understand ourselves.[11]

In the last few lines of this excerpt Kaufman makes the important
point that the now widely held view of the nature of the human not
only furnishes the conceptual frame within which we understand our
secular life today — as if that could be compartmentalized and separated from our spiritual experience — but furnishes the conceptual
frame within which any intelligible affirmations of religious or theological meaning must be made as well. It is just this biohistorical existence that must be a landscape open to religious meaning if there is
to be any such meaning at all.

The fact is, as I see it, religious language that conforms to the traditional theological paradigm of the ancient creeds in which humans
are seen as "immortal souls" does not speak to people who see themselves as biohistorical beings. Even to people who were born and
raised in the church such religious talk has become a foreign language. The various attempts to "translate" this archaic speech by
proposing that it should be read metaphorically or symbolically are
finally only half-way measures even after all of the arguments in support of such "solutions" have been made. The residual literal meaning of the original literal language weighs down the "symbolic" and
"metaphorical" interpretation and too often turns it into a form of
religious mush. This lends itself to the perception that when such
interpreters make a religious statement it is never quite clear whether
they really mean it or not. The attractiveness of this "solution"
appears to be that you can live in a state of blessed ambiguity: you
can believe almost anything you like and think that you are being

---

11. Kaufman, *Mystery*, p. 109. For another insightful discussion of a modern understanding of the human by a leading theologian, see Edward Farley, *Good and Evil*,
especially pp. 27–113.

both thoroughly modern and thoroughly traditional at the same time, when actually you are being neither. It is proclaimed as good news that "you can have your historical Jesus and your spiritual Christ too." Perfect. Now we don't have to bite that menacing bullet after all. We can turn it into a jelly bean. We should not be surprised if some who hear this line do not quite believe it. It leaves them in the limbo of too many blurred distinctions between fact and fiction, history and symbol. Such is the price imposed by those who would have us try to live our religious lives in two disparate historical and cultural eras at the same time. There is a better way to proceed and a better outcome to look forward to.

The Historical Orientation of Christian Faith

As a first step in such a better procedure it would be useful to remind ourselves that in certain crucial respects biblical faith has its origin in historical events — not in sacred scriptures, authoritative creeds, or apostolic institutions. Ancient Israel saw their exodus from Egypt as an act of God by which they were liberated from bondage and called into a new form of community. As G. Ernest Wright once famously put it, [Israel's] "knowledge of God was an *inference* from what actually had happened in human history."[12] Analogously, the life and teachings of Jesus in first century Roman Palestine was the event in history in which his followers saw God at work for their redemption. Given the authority that has come to be invested in Christian scriptures, creeds, and institutions, it is not unimportant to be reminded that these are all derivatives of events in history that the founders of the biblical tradition saw as having compelling and creative significance. Indeed, without these historical events these scriptures, creeds, and institutions would never have come into being.

This reminder shows that biblical faith has always had to do with the question of the meaning of human experience in history; and that constitutes a point of connection with the tradition when Kaufman

---

12. G. Ernest Wright, *God Who Acts*, p. 44, emphasis added. Wright originally thought that in recognizing that ancient Israel confessed its faith by reciting "the mighty acts of God," the foremost of which was the Exodus, he had found the source and center of biblical faith as a whole. That proved to be too sweeping a claim, as numerous critics have since pointed out. But Wright was not completely wrong. The meanings that ancient Israel attributed to the Exodus and that the early church attributed to the life and teachings of Jesus of Nazareth were indeed formative for each community.

and others make the claim that a contemporary Christian theology must meet the challenge of making sense of our own historicity, as we have come to understand it in the modern world. Thus in pointing to our historicity as the locus of religious meaning for moderns, we are re-appropriating a motif embedded in our tradition, even with the considerable changes in conceptuality this involves, not introducing a concern that is alien to it.

The Historical Jesus Rather Than the Mythical Jesus

The second step in the better procedure advocated here is to embrace the idea of thinking and speaking about Jesus as a figure of history rather than as the second person of the Trinity, as the creeds crafted at Nicea in 325 C.E. and at Chalcedon in 451 C.E. do. If Jesus of Nazareth is going to be regarded as a figure who may have religious significance for moderns, rather than only as the principal icon of the Christian tradition (and as such a figure of the religious past, but not of the religious present and future), then he will have to be seen in terms of his historicity rather than in terms of his scriptural and creedal authority. The Jesus who might matter to moderns is the Jesus who was involved in the same basic conditions of human life that we are and had to deal with them without benefit of a divine nature that was clearly superior to every earthly circumstance and limitation, as well as to every opponent. The latter figure can only be the fictional Jesus of ancient mythical imagination, not the flesh and blood young man who grew up in northern Israel. Jesus of Nazareth met the conditions of life in his place and time not as one who was resigned to the way things were, but as one who was moved and enlightened by a vision of the way things ought to be.[13] That made him a threat to the privileged, the established, the powerful and those who benefitted from being in their employ, but a liberator to many who were bound by those in power and their servants, and by their own weak and dull resignations. He was no doubt a threat to traditionalists down as well as up the social scale too. The challenge this Jesus may pose for us is not so much to follow in his footsteps as to catch a glimpse, even a critical glimpse, of his vision of "the good life" = life ruled by

13. Matthew 5:38–48 and 6:24–33 offer lucid expressions of Jesus' point of view regarding the reign of God. See *The Five Gospels*, pp. 144–45, pp. 152–53 for brief analysis and comment on these passages.

God's generosity and goodness as light for paths he never walked, but we do: the pathways of the modern world.

Will people in and out of the church today be interested in such a Jesus? "I saw Jesus tonight as a three-dimensional person for the first time in my life," I heard a middle-aged woman say in a Seattle church one evening near the close of an adult education session. "I've waited forty years for this class," is what on another occasion a man in a Bellevue, Washington church said. The day after a Jesus Seminar on the Road in Rock Hill, South Carolina last November a man who had driven there from Atlanta e-mailed Westar Institute to say, "It was the first time [in my experience] people associated with Christianity had spoken my language!" I take these sample bites of anecdotal evidence as a sign of the times. They speak for others "out there" who are waiting to hear a believable word.

In the introduction to this paper I made reference to Edward Farley's apt characterization of our religious situation as one in which we are confronted with the collapse of the house of authority. I suggest that the house of authority had collapsed for the Jesus of history also, and that in this respect there is something particularly analagous between our historical moment and his that would not resonate in the same way for those who lived in an era in which the house of authority stood intact. What prompts this suggestion is the activity of John the Baptist and the fact that Jesus was initially drawn to it. John summoned people to baptism in the Jordan River. Why the Jordan? There was plenty of water available closer to population centers elsewhere in the land that would have made John's baptism more accessible to people. The most likely explanation, I think, is that John was playing on the appeal of the wilderness and the Jordan as symbols of Israel's origins when from the banks of the Jordan they first took possession of the Promised Land, according to the biblical story. That he offered baptism as a cleansing from sin in that location implies that in his view the house of authority, the Temple establishment in Jerusalem, had collapsed. It had become religiously bankrupt, incapable of mediating the spiritual cleansing and moral renewal the nation needed. To gain access to that cleansing and new beginning, Israel would have to return to the ideals of its origins, if it wanted to regain the genuineness it had lost, and to escape the fire of coming judgment. John not only was preaching this, he was also dramatizing his message by staging a bit of religious and political theatre in a location that symbolized the genuineness and purity of

Israel's religious ideals. Very probably, John thought that the political house of authority had no genuine authority either. Herod Antipas certainly heard him that way. Jesus accepted the baptism John offered, but did not repeat his fiery message of judgment to come nor did he continue his baptizing practice. Jesus and John agreed about the collapse of the house of religious authority, it seems, but disagreed about what to say and do about it. What the idea of the reign of God meant to Jesus was not impending judgment, but a vision of the way things ought to be, life as ruled by God's generosity and goodness. Jesus did not follow John's script; he called it as he saw it.

Preaching the Gospel Rather Than Preaching the Bible

A third step in the better procedure suggested here follows from the first two sketched above: a reconsideration of the way we understand and read from the Bible in worship and of the way we typically go about the task of preaching. The understanding and use of the Bible that is typical in Protestant worship and preaching is driven by notions about the authority and truth of scripture and tradition that are ill-suited to the task of exposing and articulating the meaning of Christian faith in the modern era. They are both full time residents of the house of authority, that once venerable structure that is now in a state of collapse. That this claim is not just a matter of academic speculation is indicated by a couple of examples of disconcerted testimony that come out of the experience of weekly worship. One is an observation that I heard the late Joseph Sittler, well known Professor of Theology at Lutheran Shool of Theology at Chicago, make at a conference for clergy at USC years ago. Sittler recalled the frequency with which on Sunday mornings his good Lutheran pastor would earnestly admonish his parishioners that *the just shall live by faith and not by works of righteousness.* "I look around the sanctuary at my fellow-Lutherans, and I don't see anyone trying it," Sittler said. In his view, his fellow-Lutherans had learned this classically Lutheran lesson well. So far as he could see none of them was trying to gain salvation by piling up credits from works of righteousness. It was no longer an issue for them. But, as Sittler saw it, matters that were or ought to be at issue for them were not being identified and addressed from the pulpit of his home church. If the gospel is a word that brings the meaning of a past event to bear on the present in such a way as to enable one to see possibilities for a redemptive future,[14] then one might say that Sittler's pastor was preaching the tradition rather than preaching the gospel.

A second testimonial arrived in my e-mail last October from a good friend in Seattle:

> This question has weighed heavily in my mind for some time and I can't seem to let it go. I am uncomfortable on a Sunday morning when I go to church and hear a preacher painstakingly (and sometimes eloquently) attempt to unravel the words written 2000 years ago. It seems like much of the preacher's effort — and ours as listeners — is spent trying to translate and make meaningful words set in a foreign culture and hidden in parable and myth. . . . The question I am raising is whether we are religiously a backward-looking people? Should we not be looking for the revelations of God in our present time and culture and civilization? Should our religious questing not be focusing on listening for the voice of God in the now? . . . So the question troubling me that will not go away is: why do I spend a major portion of my time focusing on an outmoded Christianity? Why do I go to a church that insists on adherence to a biblical lectionary approach which each Sunday attempts to look for the truth laid down in scriptures long ago? Why does much of mainline Christianity, including my own church, seemingly turn a dull ear to any new gospel? If one of the central teachings of Jesus concerned our need to discover the realm of God all around us, why are we digging in ancient scriptural beds? If, as I believe, God is speaking through new prophets about a new peril facing the world [the threat posed to the global ecosystem by reckless exploitation of the earth] why am I not paying more attention to the present than the past? [15]

It should not be assumed that what was lacking in the preaching referred to by theologian Sittler and by my church-going friend in Seattle is due to a lack of homiletical effort and talent. On the contrary, the real problem, in the view of theologian Edward Farley, is that "a notion of preaching prevails in Christendom that poses to the

---

14. These phrases revise those of Farley, "Preaching," p. 102.
15. These e-mail excerpts are cited with the permission of their sender, Bob Burkhart.

preacher a task impossible to carry out, a problem impossible to solve."[16] The problem is embedded in the dominant paradigm of preaching: the preacher is supposed to preach the Bible or the biblical message; the way one does this is to base the sermon on a scriptural passage; the presumption is that each such biblical passage contains a truth of God and that the faithful and resourceful preacher will find a way to connect that truth with the present situation of the hearers. The task of the preacher, thus, is to construct a rhetorical bridge between the biblical passage and his or her hearers.[17]

For a fundamentalist preacher any problem posed by this paradigm will only be homiletical; it will never be theological. The doctrine of the verbal inerrancy of scripture assures the fundamentalist preacher that every word in scripture is God's word to us and that the preacher who "rightly explains the word of truth" (2 Tim 2:15) will succeed in finding in any passage what God intended for us to hear. On the other hand, the preacher who is convinced that the idea of the inerrancy of scripture is untenable and whose understanding of scripture is informed by historical-critical scholarship will know that breaking the biblical writings up into short passages often does violence to the character and meaning of those writings as theological argument, or narrative, or poetic vision, or as an attempt to address problems or resolve controversies. It also pays little heed to their historicity. The truth is that "the whole paradigm of necessarily true passages breaks on the rocks of historical consciousness and requires a fundamentalist element to make it work."[18] The lectionary preacher is thus ineluctably working with a broken paradigm.

That "fundamentalist element" presents another problem for all preachers who have abandoned or rejected the notion of inerrancy as the doctrine of scriptural authority, but retained the rhetoric about the Bible as, in some fashion, the word of God and follow the dominant paradigm of preaching on a biblical passage whether self-selected or prescribed by the creators of the common lectionary: it almost inevitably results in introducing a note of ambivalence in the way scripture is presented and read in worship as well as in the rhetoric of preaching: it leaves the hearer with some doubt about whether the preacher really means it or the hearer can really believe it. It

---

16. Farley, "Preaching," p. 90.
17. This is a very abbreviated summary of what Farley lays out in some detail in "Preaching," pp. 91–98.
18. Farley, "Preaching," p. 95.

makes one a resident in what Edward Farley calls a verbal house of authority: you sound like a resident of the house of authority, but you don't really live there. If we have decided to move out of the theological and ecclesiastical house of authority, we should reject such rhetorical ambivalence and move out of the verbal house of authority also. More than consistency is involved here; our credibility is at stake. If theological fundamentalism is untenable, then the vestiges of fundamentalism that survive in our rhetoric are untenable also.

Thus the dominant paradigm of preaching too often traps the preacher into seeming to perpetuate an element of fundamentalism that he or she is convinced is indefensible. It also burdens her or him with an impossible task. According to the principal paradigm, the lectionary preacher is supposed to find a preachable truth in a biblical passage. Absent the notion of scripture as inspired by God and verbally inerrant, however, there may be nothing specifically preachable in the passage. In some cases one may even find unpreachable elements in a passage: something problematically patriarchal, or ethnocentric, or culture-bound , or scientifically or historically mistaken. One can then resort to the hunt for *something* in the passage as the basis of the sermon: a word, a phrase, an act, or one may read the text as a metaphor or story. Something must be found that can be turned into a lesson for life today. Although it was not the intention of most biblical authors to provide such passage-sized lessons, that is what the preacher is supposed to find there (while perhaps paying only a little attention to what the author did intend). Inevitably it often happens that the text only serves as a pretext, a point of departure for the sermon, not its theme or substance.[19] The notion that by using such tactics one is nevertheless being a biblical preacher becomes pretty thin.

It may be suggestive to compare the assumptions and practices embedded in this dominant paradigm for preaching with what we can gather about Jesus' assumptions and practices. For instance, as far as we can tell, Jesus was not what we would call a biblical preacher: it was not his habit to appeal to the authority of scripture as the basis of his teaching.[20] Rather, his habit was to make frequent

19. This characterization of how the attempt to carry out the impossible task assigned to the preacher is often resolved I owe mostly to Farley's remarks in "Preaching," pp. 96–97.

20. I accept the finding of scholarship that appeals to scripture as the basis of Jesus' teaching in the Gospels or as the script for the unfolding of his life and destiny are the

use of parables and aphorisms, forms of rhetoric that expect their hearers to think for themselves and that seek to persuade them to accept his teaching because they recognize its truth, not because it is based on the authority of scripture. In short, Jesus offered his contemporaries what might be called "a religion of insight" as an alternative to the religion of authority represented in his day by a priestly hierarchy, Temple ritual, and sacred texts.

(This reference to Jesus' rhetorical preferences is intended only to call attention to the fact that the preaching of the gospel originated outside the then house of authority and in forms other than the dominant teaching paradigm of the scribes — commentary on scripture — not to propose that Jesus furnishes us with the only legitimate model of Christian rhetoric. Parable and aphorism no doubt can still proclaim the gospel; but they need not be regarded as the only language of the gospel.)

What would preaching be if it were not expected to conform to the dominant paradigm? If preaching were not supposed to find truth in a text and connect it to the present, what should it be supposed to do? A response to that question that would be as helpful as it ought to be requires more substance than can be offered in a few comments near the end of a brief paper. But a few comments might point us in a fruitful direction. Taking one cue from Jesus, one might say that to preach the gospel is to cultivate the imagination and wisdom to see our lives as under the rule of God's unfailing generosity and enduring goodness, which means among other things, as not necessarily confined or conformed to the way things arranged by the culture and the ruling powers at the present are; or, as Reinhold Niebuhr put it in a modern and critical form, to see "the relevance of an impossible ethical ideal."[21] Other cues can be taken from interpreters of the gospel both early and late in the history of the Christian tradition who have come to see, through the life and teaching of Jesus, what Paul Tillich once called "the experience of the holy as what ought to be."[22] In proposing an alternative to the still dominant even though broken paradigm of biblical preaching, theologian Farley suggests that

---

work of Gospel authors or the early Christian communities, not what was typical of Jesus. For example, the antitheses found in Matt 5:21–44 are the construction of Matthew, not the words of Jesus; and both the text cited and the sermon preached on the occasion of Jesus' return to the synagogue in Nazareth in Luke 4:16–30 are not a report of what Jesus actually said at the time, but are furnished by Luke.

21. Niebuhr, *Interpretation,* chapter 4.
22. Tillich, *Encounter,* p. 58.

[the] gospel is not simply given all at once like a gift-wrapped package. It is something to be proclaimed, but the summons to proclaim it is a summons to struggle with the mystery of God's salvific action and how that transforms the world. To proclaim the gospel then is to enter the world of the gospel, struggling with questions of suffering, evil, idolatry, hope and freedom.

The world of the gospel does have certain recurring themes, even a certain structure. This structure is partly temporal, a bringing of a past event to bear on the present so as to open the future to redemption. It is centrally about the future, what can be, what historical evils and fates do not have to be. Looked at another way, the gospel is — and this is its prophetic element — a disruption, an exposure of corporate oppression and individual collusion, and, at the same time, an uncovering of redemptive possibilities. To say it is the good news of the kingdom of God is to say both of these things. And those who find themselves proclaiming these good tidings will surely be drawn to understanding the reality and power of the deep symbols in the world of the gospel. This is why preaching the gospel summons the preacher to biblical and theological study and reflection. For we enter the world of the gospel by way of the world of the Bible and the world of the interpretation of the Christian faith. To understand the gospel and the world of the gospel is to struggle critically with the truth and reality of these things.[23]

In his recently published book, *Eyewitness to Power*, presidential advisor and journalist David Gergen refers to G. K. Chesteron's observation that America is the only nation in the world that is founded on what it believes, especially as classically expressed in the preamble to the Declaration of Independence. "It was not intended to be a statement of who we are," Gergen says, "but of what we dream of becoming, realizing that the journey never ends. It is our

23. Farley, "Preaching," p. 102. Compare Gordon Kaufman's remark that "as the principal collection of primary documents reporting the alleged acts of God, the Bible can never be surpassed or replaced; it is an indispensable source of faith and the principal resource for theological work." From "What Shall We Do With the Bible?" p. 104. By "deep symbols" Farley means "the values by which a community understands itself, from which it takes its aims, and to which it appeals as canons of cultural criticism." This definition is from his volume, *Deep Symbols*, p. 3.

communal vision. That's why a president . . . need not reinvent the national vision upon taking office. He should instead give fresh life to the one we have, applying it to the context of the times, leading the nation forward to its greater fulfillment."[24] In a similar vein one can refer to the gospel as the founding and communal vision of Christian faith. The preacher who seeks to relate it to the context of the times and to summon his or her hearers to a new measure of its fulfillment will find it to be an infinitely renewable resource for discovering the wisdom, grace, and courage we need "for the living of these days."[25]

24. Gergen, *Eyewitness*, p. 348.
25. From the hymn written by Harry Emerson Fosdick, "God of Grace and God of Glory."

Works Consulted

Farley, Edward. *Deep Symbols. Their Postmodern Effacement and Reclamation.* Trinity Press International, 1996.
_____. *Ecclesial Reflection. An Anatomy of Theological Method.* Fortress Press, 1982.
_____. *Good and Evil. Interpreting a Human Condition.* Augsburg Fortress, 1990.
_____. "Preaching the Bible and Preaching the Gospel." *Theology Today* 51,1 (April, 1994), pp. 90–103.
Funk, Robert W. and Roy W. Hoover. *The Five Gospels. The Search for the Authentic Words of Jesus.* Macmillan, 1993.
Gergen, David. *Eyewitness to Power.* Simon & Schuster, 2000.
Hayes, John H. and Frederick Prussner. *Old Testament Theology: Its History and Development.* John Knox Press, 1985.
Kaufman, Gordon D. *In Face of Mystery. A Constructive Theology.* Harvard University Press, 1993.
_____. "What Shall We Do With the Bible?" *Interpretation* 25,1 (January, 1971), pp. 95–112.
Kuhn, Thomas S. *The Structure of Scientific Revolutions.* Second Edition. University of Chicago Press, 1970.
Niebuhr, Reinhold. *An Interpretation of Christian Ethics.* Harper and Row, 1935, 1963.
Pelikan, Jaroslav. *The Vindication of Tradition. The 1983 Jefferson Lecture in the Humanities.* Yale University Press, 1984.
Tillich, Paul. *Christianity and the Encounter of the World Religions.* Columbia University Press, 1963.
Wright, G. Ernest. *God Who Acts. Biblical Theology as Recital.* Alec R. Allenson, Inc., 1952.

Is the Apocalyptic Jesus History?

Robert J. Miller

The debate over whether the historical Jesus was an apocalyptic prophet is at the heart of the "Jesus wars." The answer one gives to this question, and how one goes about answering it, shapes the way one understands much of the gospel evidence. This particular question may well be the single most important one about the historical Jesus, for it goes directly to the character of his message and mission. Let me warn the reader that I am a participant in this debate, not a neutral observer of it. I maintain that Jesus was not an apocalyptic prophet.

In this essay I offer some reflections on what is at stake in this debate: how it affects both our understanding of Jesus and the prospects for a viable faith true to his name. My purpose is not so much to argue for a position, though there is some of that, but more to analyze the debate and to press a few key issues in the hope of sparking productive discussion. Some of the discussion I invite is consciously self-critical, a task we neglect to our intellectual peril.

Theological Investments in the Apocalyptic Jesus

Albert Schweitzer's milestone work, *The Quest of the Historical Jesus* (1906), put twentieth-century scholarship on notice about letting theological preferences set the agenda for constructions of the historical Jesus. We all look back in dismay at the bad old days when the Protestant Jesus battled empty ritualism and the Catholic Jesus had no siblings, established Petrine primacy, and instituted the Eucharist. Even so, is it still not the ultimate (if unspoken) hope of anyone who identifies with the Christian tradition to "discover" that the historical Jesus espoused ideas and values that support one's own? As for those who maintain that Christian life and thought should ignore the Jesus of history in favor of the Christ of faith, can there be any doubt that they will abandon this stance if the historical Jesus turns out to be at home in their theology?

Heeding Schweitzer's lesson has sensitized us to the various ways our social, religious, and political location can influence our reading of the historical evidence. Among biblical scholars this helped to clinch the argument that pure objectivity in the study of history is a mythic ideal. Probably the greatest benefit of Schweitzer's analysis has been the inculcation of a healthy circumspection about and steady refinement of historical method. Probably its most baneful effect is that it has armed scholars with a rhetorical weapon of mass destruction. To accuse an opponent of coming up with a Jesus after his or her own image is singularly satisfying. Not only does it let you discredit your opponent's position without having to engage any of his or her evidence or arguments; it is also impossible to refute.

From this vantage point let me offer an observation on how this plays out in the debate over whether Jesus was an apocalyptic prophet.

Schweitzer read Jesus against the the background of a thoroughly apocalyptic first-century Judaism. In Schweitzer' mind, Jesus' apocalypticism "on the one hand, underscored the *commonalities* between Jesus and his environment, and the profound *distance* between Jesus and early twentieth-century Christian theology, on the other."[1] As Stephen Patterson explains in an incisive analysis of the cultural context of twentieth-century gospel scholarship,[2] the European optimism of the late nineteenth and very early twentieth century gave way to foreboding and then to profound disillusionment in the wake of two World Wars, the Holocaust, the Cold War, and the nuclear threat. In this cultural environment the apocalyptic Jesus no longer seemed such a stranger.

More than anyone else, it was Bultmann who made the apocalyptic Jesus safe for liberal Protestantism. In his treatment of the gospels and their traditions, the adjective "eschatological" served to *distinguish* Jesus from his environment. "For Bultmann . . . the term 'eschatological' stands for the novelty of Christianity, its incomparable superiority, the uniqueness of its victorious religion, deservedly victorious."[3] A paradigm case of this appropriation of eschatology is *The*

---

1. Kloppenborg Verbin, *Excavating Q*, 438, emphasis original.
2. Patterson, *God of Jesus*, pp.164–69
3. Georgi, Dieter, quoted in Kloppenborg Verbin, *Excavating Q*, p. 438, n.52

Charismatic Leader and His Followers (1981) by Martin Hengel, which "uses the category of 'eschatological charismatic' in order to render Jesus incommensurable and unique within Judaism and the Hellenistic world."[4] Theologians such as Moltmann and Pannenberg found convergence between their reading of Jesus' eschatology and the heart of Christian theology. In this intellectual matrix eschatology became a cipher for uniqueness and ultimacy.[5] This reversed the polarity that Schweitzer emphasized: the eschatological Jesus was now set over against his ancient contemporaries, but was congenial to modern Christianity.

From the perspective of this analysis we can notice some high irony in the proclivity of defenders of the apocalyptic Jesus to beat their opponents (all of whom seem to be present or past members of the Jesus Seminar) with the Schweitzer stick. "They" readily accuse "us" of refashioning Jesus to conform to our elite academic sensibilities. They claim (or usually imply) that we intuitively picked the Jesus we liked and then cooked the evidence to get what we wanted. Nastier critics impugn our integrity by asserting that we did this in bad faith. More polite, and hence more condescending, critics allow that we may have done this unconsciously. The irony here is that those critics sometimes brandish the apocalypticism of Jesus as if it were their certificate of immunization against the nearly irresistible tendency to modernize him. They are either unaware or unconcerned with how easily the eschatological Jesus can accommodate contemporary christological interests.

A second irony takes us into more ominous territory. Advocates of a non-apocalyptic Jesus are sometimes charged with reconstructing a "non-Jewish" Jesus, as if first-century Judaism was a substance and apocalypticism an essential element of it. While the disingenuousness of the accusation makes refuting it unnecessary, I bring it up because of the (usually) implicit accusation of anti-Semitism that seems to lurk below the surface of the "non-Jewish" charge. It is not the vacuousness of the innuendo that interests me here,[6] but the anxious self-consciousness with which it seems to be made.[7] Since the Holocaust, Christian intellectuals have become acutely sensitive to the insidious ways in which anti-Semitism can infect their work. It is

4. Kloppenborg Verbin, *Excavating Q*, p. 438.
5. Kloppenborg Verbin, *Excavating Q*, p. 439.
6. On this see Miller, *The Jesus Seminar and its Critics*, pp. 74–75.
7. See also King, "Back to the Future," pp. 89–90.

as if our critics believe that an insistence on Jesus' apocalypticism so completely certifies his Jewishness that it repels any lingering whiff of the stench of anti-Semitism. The irony here is that the "eschatological" Jesus has been co-opted as code for the "unique" Jesus, a uniqueness invariably understood as superiority. The eschatological Jesus is thus implicated in supercessionism, which is fraught with anti-Jewish overtones. By contrast, a non-apocalyptic Jesus cannot easily be folded into claims for or assumptions about the unique superiority of Christianity.

The Apocalyptic Jesus was Wrong

Another interesting aspect of the scholarly construct of the eschatological Jesus is the issue of Jesus' error. If the historical Jesus predicted the imminent End,[8] then, obviously, he was wrong. The genius of Bultmann's program was that he was able to build a viable theology on the apocalyptic Jesus without it making any difference that this Jesus was mistaken about the central theme of his message. Bultmann could pull this off for two reasons. 1) For him the contents of Jesus' teaching are irrelevant to Christian theology because they exist in an outmoded mythological worldview. So it doesn't matter that Jesus was wrong about what he preached. 2) After the eschatological message of Jesus was processed through Bultmann's Heideggarian existentialist hermeneutic, all that was left of it was an urgent but vague "call to decision." The eschatology of this Jesus has to do with the challenge of individual human authenticity, not with an imminent divine intervention into the human history of the first century. Bultmann's eschatological Jesus was thus amenable to the projects of liberal Protestantism. Moltmann and Pannenberg worked out systematic theologies inspired by the eschatological Jesus. Since this eschatology is abstracted from its historical concreteness in first-century Judaism, it is reduced to an "annoucement of an imminent and decisive transformation of human reality."[9] Here too the fact that the specific apocalyptic predictions in the gospels are false is irrelevant. The issue never arises.

The Catholic church has sanctioned critical biblical scholarship only since the middle of the twentieth century. Except for Crossan and Schillebeeckx, Catholic scholars showed little interest in the his-

---

8. Most explicitly in Mark 1:15, 9:1, 13:30, and Matt 10:23, but elsewhere as well.
9. Kloppenborg Verbin, *Excavating Q*, p. 438.

torical Jesus until the last two decades and even now it is an area of minor concern. The most important Catholic advocate for the apocalyptic Jesus, John Meier, sticks closely to his historical task and shows no interest in reinterpreting ancient apocalypticism for modern use. Catholic scholars whose historical Jesus is apocalyptic should have no anxiety about admitting that Jesus was wrong in his predictions, for Catholic theology has no need for an inerrant Jesus.

The problem is acute, however, for evangelical scholars because they need to defend both a strong sense of the historicity of the gospels and the supernatural status of Jesus. The evangelical approach to the gospels acknowledges that early Christians embellished and interpreted (correctly of course) the words of Jesus, but it denies (on moral grounds) that they created sayings and attributed them to Jesus. Though evangelicals allow that Jesus' human knowledge was limited (about scientific matters, for instance) they are not willing to grant that he may have been wrong about what they consider to be matters of revelation. This puts them in the unenviable position of upholding Jesus' theological inerrancy *and* his apocalyptic predictions. Since this position is clearly untenable, it should not surprise us that most evangelical scholars take the prudent course of ducking the question. For example, Charles Holman, in a brief excursus on the "Historical Jesus,"[10] attributes Mark 9:1, 13:30, and Matt 10:23 to Jesus. He notes that their non-fulfillment was an embarrassment to early Christians, but somehow avoids raising the question of Jesus' error.

The few evangelical scholars who do face the question try to paper over the problem, but the paper is thin. Scot McKnight asks "Was Jesus Mistaken?" and answers "no."

> Jesus prophesied that God would wrap things up within one generation. However, instead of saying that Jesus was mistaken, that he was either a false prophet or a misguided fanatic, we ought to admit that his knowledge of the future was limited.[11]

Apparently, false predictions do not constitute error: "he was not wrong" (138); "Jesus was not mistaken" (139).

Ben Witherington takes a different approach. He poses the prob-

10. *Till Jesus Comes*, pp. 134–37. The quotes around "Historical Jesus" are his — one wonders why.
11. McKnight, *New Vision*, p. 138.

lem of how Jesus could have both predicted the End as he did in the sayings about the Coming Son of Man sayings and declared that he did not know "the day or the hour" of its arrival (Mark 13:32). Since Witherington does not have the option of judging any saying of Jesus in the canonical gospels to be inauthentic, he concludes that "Jesus did not proclaim that the end was *necessarily* imminent. At most he could only have spoken of its possible imminence."[12] On this basis the question of whether Jesus was wrong does not come up. You can never be wrong if you stick to predicting what *might* happen.

Finally, we need to note Dale Allison's disarming honesty on this matter. "Jesus the millenarian prophet, like all millenarian prophets, was wrong."[13] Allison neither resorts to special pleading nor looks for some deeper sense in which Jesus was right. Nevertheless, Allison commends Jesus' false apocalyptic hopes in the face of a nihilism which he sees as its only alternative. The final paragraph in Allison's book is a remarkable manifesto and deserves to be quoted in full.

> And yet, despite everything, for those who have ears to hear, Jesus, the millenarian herald of judgment and salvation, says the only things worth saying, for his dream is the only one worth dreaming. If our wounds never heal, if the outrageous spectacle of a history filled with cataclysmic sadness is never undone, if there is nothing more for those who were slaughtered in the death camps or for six-year olds devoured by cancer, then let us eat and drink, for tomorrow we die. If in the end there is no good God to calm this sea of troubles, to raise the dead, and to give good news to the poor, then this is indeed a tale told by an idiot, signifying nothing.[14]

Whether the conscious embrace of a falsified fantasy can be a viable basis for Christian theology remains to be seen.

How Much was the Apocalyptic Jesus Wrong About?

Since the apocalyptic Jesus made concrete predictions, his message and mission was, at least to some extent, falsified by subsequent

12. *The Jesus Quest*, p. 96, emphasis original. See my critique in *Jesus Seminar and its Critics*, pp. 115–18.
13. Allison, *Jesus*, p. 218.
14. Allison, *Jesus*, p. 219.

events. What does this error mean about the truth of the rest of his teaching? His conviction that the End was imminent is not just one item among others. It is foundational. How much of his message and mission stands or falls with its apocalyptic foundation?

To frame the question this way entails that if Jesus was an apocalyptic prophet, the Christian theological project has to be a salvage job. If theology is to have any meaningful connection to the apocalyptic Jesus, the theological task must start by assessing the wreckage of his message and mission and deciding how much is usable, how much can be repaired, and how much is lost for good.

Even if Jesus' perspective was not apocalyptic, Christian theology still involves a critical sifting of his legacy, not because it collided with historical reality, but simply because his world was so different from ours. The issue of the truth of Jesus' teaching shakes down very differently for a non-apocalyptic Jesus. Since his message is not falsifiable historically, the specifically theological dimension of the issue comes into sharper focus. The question is not whether Jesus was right or wrong about the future. It is whether he was right or wrong about God.

For the sake of the discussion, let me offer brief observations on how judgments about the viability of Jesus' message can be affected by the decision about whether he was an apocalyptic prophet. I address four topics as test cases.

1. *Social Deviance.* A good bit of Jesus' "ethics" recommend behaviors and attitudes aberrant to the business-as-usual of his society. Interpreters of New Testament eschatology commonly understand teachings like this to constitute an "interim ethic," a way of living necessitated by the eschatological crisis and intended only for the short time until the End. A case in point is Paul's advice on sex and marriage in 1 Corinthians 7. If Jesus taught an apocalyptic message, how much of his teaching should be considered an interim ethic?

For example, consider Jesus' extraordinary demands to renounce family ties (Q 14:26), to walk away from home and family (Mark 10:29-30), and not to bury one's dead parents (Q 9:59-60). Coming from an apocalyptic Jesus these sayings seem to be meant literally, in the belief that the social structures of the world-as-we-know-it would soon be irrelevant in the new world that God was about to create. Since Jesus was wrong about the future, was he, in hindsight, wrong to subvert these family bonds? On the other hand, coming from a non-apocalyptic Jesus, these radical directives seem less literal and more aphoristic. They challenge people to re-examine all their priorities, even the most intimate and sacred, in light of the demands of God's present kingdom.

2. *Beatitudes.* When an apocalyptic Jesus congratulates the poor, the hungry, and the sorrowing, he does so out of his conviction that their circumstances would soon be reversed when God imposed his rule on the earth. Since this kingdom did not come as expected, the apocalyptic Jesus was mistaken to congratulate these unfortunates. Worse yet, he may have been unwittingly cruel in giving them false hope.

If Jesus was not apocalyptic, the beatitudes mean that the poor, the hungry, and the sorrowing enjoy God's favor in their present lives, in light of who they are now, not in light of what might happen to them later. Whether it is true or false that such people are divinely favored cannot be settled by empirical events. In a non-apocalyptic framework our decision about the truth of the beatitudes does not involve an assessment of the living conditions of the poor, the hungry, and the sorrowing. It is a theological decision in which we ask ourselves how we imagine God.

3. *Exorcisms.* An apocalyptic Jesus understands his battles with demons to be the opening skirmishes in the final conflict between Good and Evil. For him the restoration of the possessed to wholeness was a preview of the *shalom* of the imminent kingdom which would come after God wrested control of this world from the satanic forces currently running it. Does the failure of Jesus' apocalyptic hopes vitiate the message of his exorcisms?

On the other hand, the exorcisms of a non-apocalyptic Jesus are meant to show, one person at a time, that God is always and everywhere opposed to all manner of evil and oppression, physical as well as social, economic, and religious.

4. *God.* Surely the most important question is whether Jesus was right about God. The God of apocalypticism is a Deity who intervenes from outside our world to set things right, to do for us what we cannot do for ourselves. He is a Deity able and willing to use coercive power to effect his will, even if, mysteriously, he always seems to

hold that power in reserve for future use. When he finally exercises that power, however, it will be overwhelming and he will triumph against otherwise invincible earthly and demonic forces.

The apocalyptic Jesus was proven wrong about God's plan for human history. Was the apocalyptic Jesus also wrong about God? And if so, is there any real point to the theological salvage operation?

Apocalypticism and Divine Violence

Jesus did not live in violent times, at least by ancient standards. Assuming he lived his whole life in Galilee, Jesus never witnessed warfare, fled from an approaching army, or saw a city destroyed. It was probably rare for him even to see troops. He lived during the Pax Romana. But this Pax was the epitome of Peace Through Strength. It was enforced by the Roman legions in Syria, ready to snuff out any organized resistance to the Empire. Around the time of Jesus' birth, the Roman army had destroyed Sepphoris and enslaved its population in reprisal for its protesting Roman appointment of another Herodian king. This display of Rome's ability to crush those who might oppose its will was surely fresh in the Galilean memory. From Rome's perspective such reminders were useful in reinforcing the lesson that resisting the Empire was futile.

There is no evidence that Jesus endorsed or even considered a military solution to the predatory injustice of Roman rule. We may be inclined to think that Jesus rejected military resistance because he was a realist, because he realized that Rome would pay any price to hold onto its rule and so it was impossible to defeat Rome and suicidal to try. We tend to view the Zealots as fanatics and want to think that Jesus would have too, had they been around in his lifetime.

Zealotry was not irrational fanaticism. It was rooted in a particular theology, a view of God; specifically, an apocalyptic view. The Zealots knew they could never defeat Rome on their own, but they believed they weren't on their own. God was on their side and would fight with them and no earthly power could defeat God. Josephus tells us that the Zealots held out to the end expecting legions of angels to intervene. The War Scroll from Qumran gave detailed battlefield instructions to the sons of light for the Final Conflict. They too believed that God would send supernatural military assistance. They were mistaken. No angels appeared and both the Zealots in Jerusalem and the Essenes at Qumran were slaughtered by the Romans. Because their hopes proved to be delusions, we are tempted to think that the Zealots and the Essenes were irrational. Yet their hopes were entirely reasonable, given their apocalyptic image of God. (The same goes for today's Muslim suicide bombers. Given their theological beliefs, they are trading their mortal lives for eternal life in Paradise. This is a rational choice under any circumstance, all the more so considering how stunted their earthly futures are. Writing them off as irrational fanatics allows us to miss the hard questions about the political and historical processes that make such beliefs so inviting.)

I want to explore the hypothesis that Jesus' rejection of violence was not tactical, but theological. He ruled out the option of armed resistance, not because of a hard-headed assessment of the military situation, but because he rejected apocalypticism and the image of God it entails. He rejected the belief that God will solve the problem of human evil by killing all the evil humans. Jesus rejected the image of a God who accomplishes justice through violence. Let's not under-estimate the price tag for this thesis. It means that Jesus rejected the God of the Exodus, the Yahweh whom the Israelites praised as a war-rior (*ish milchamah*, Exod 15:3). This puts Jesus at a critical distance from his tradition.

The cost of this thesis is high, but so are its benefits, for it enables us to account for the central irony in Jesus' notion of the kingdom of God: God has a kingdom, but does not act like a king. Despite the centrality of God's kingdom in Jesus' teaching, God is never repre-sented by a king in the authentic parables and aphorisms. Instead he is a benevolent parent, addressed as father, but acting at times like a mother, not insisting on patriarchal prerogatives nor even showing concern for male honor (see the Prodigal Son). His kingdom is imag-ined, not as the majestic cedar of Lebanon that dominates the land-scape, but as the scruffy mustard bush that makes the best of wherever it happens to gain a foothold.

The God of Jesus makes no promise to protect his subjects from their enemies. Instead he directs them to love their enemies and bless their tormentors. He sends sun and rain equally on those who obey him and those who defy him. Such a God is an un-king, a pathetic weakling to those who measure the power of gods by their ability to enforce their will, punish their enemies, and protect their subjects. To an apocalyptic mind, the God of the authentic parables and apho-risms is not a king at all, for a kingdom that cannot be imposed on the unwilling is a contradiction in terms.

Imagining a Jesus who rejects the God of violence opens the door to the charge that such a Jesus is non-Jewish. By now we should be immune to the rhetorical sting of such caricature. But underneath the caricature, and ignoring the cheap polemic, there is a legitimate concern. The Yahweh of the Torah and the Prophets is a God of coercive violence. To be sure, that is not the only way Yahweh is imagined in the scriptures, but there is no point arguing that that is not the dominant image of the Deity in those traditions. Special pleading won't work. In Genesis Yahweh annihilates "all flesh" because (ironically) "the earth is filled with violence" (Gen 6:13). In Exodus Yahweh liberates the oppressed by killing the oppressors' babies and destroying their army. In Joshua Yahweh mandates campaigns of ethnic cleansing. In Joshua through Kings, Yahweh protects and rewards Israel by going to war against its enemies. In the Prophets Yahweh punishes sinful Israel by going to war against his own people. Throughout the Law and the Prophets Yahweh works his will through armies and his purpose is manifested in the army of the victor, be it Israelite or Gentile.

At the time of Jesus a Jewish view grounded in scripture would thus accept that God was on the side of Rome, just as Jeremiah had proclaimed that God was on the side of Babylon. In rejecting this understanding of God, Jesus threw off the belief that Rome was serving God's will, that Israel's oppression was a just punishment for its sin. There seems to be no other way to make sense of Jesus' message and mission than to posit at its heart a certitude that God was on the side of Rome's victims, that their condition was contrary to God's will, and that God's power was manifested, not in the sweep of marching armies, but in the attempts by the nobodies of this world to treat each other with dignity and to see themselves as the deserving children of a benevolent heavenly Father.

So we have to face the question of the Jewishness of a Jesus who believes in a non-violent God, a God who is an anti-king. Characterizing this Jesus as non-Jewish is obviously absurd. But there is a real issue behind it: what kind of Jew was Jesus? From which aspects of his Israelite heritage did he draw his inspiration and from which did he dissent? Which aspects of the Jewish tradition were non-negotiable in the first century? Many scholars, conservative and liberal, believe that Jesus was loose with purity standards, was deliberately lax about sabbath observance, and openly associated with the unclean. No one calls this Jesus non-Jewish. Evangelical scholars argue for a historical Jesus who believed himself to be the unique Son of God, or Wisdom personified, or even Yahweh in person. How Jewish is this Jesus? N.T. Wright maintains that Jesus believed that his Roman crucifixion would be a definitive expiation for Israel's sin. How Jewish is this Jesus?

Amos radically relativizes Israel's election and prophesied the end of Israel as a people (Amos 9:7–8a). Jeremiah calls the Davidic Covenant and its temple theology a lie (Jer 7:1–15), even though that covenant and theology had been vigorously promoted by Isaiah. The Book of Ruth asserts the sanctity of mixed marriages, probably in rebuttal to Ezra's condemnation of them. Third Isaiah condemns animal sacrifice *per se* (Isa 66:3). Job rails against the deuteronomic principle and Qoheleth calmly considers it to be self-evidently false. The Wisdom of Solomon adopts some patently Greek philosophy to legitimate the martyrs who died resisting Hellenism.[15] And so on. The Jewish tradition is peppered with Jews who reject apparently core elements of their theological heritage.

Consider one more reflection on the rhetoric of the "non-Jewish Jesus" accusation. This accusation carries the unmistakable innuendo of anti-Judaism and is a thinly-veiled attempt to seize the moral high ground. But let's ask who honors Judaism more. Is it one who insists that its God is a Deity of coercive violence, whose will is expressed in every military victory, and that only a non-Jew could think otherwise? Or is it one who sees in Jesus' words and deeds a Jewish experiment in imagining a non-violent God? I wonder.

Parables and the (Non-)Apocalyptic Jesus

The decision about whether Jesus was an apocalyptic prophet influences our understanding of his teaching. A number of Jesus' words and deeds can be taken in either an apocalyptic or a non-apocalyptic sense. This is evident, for example, in the cases of the beatitudes and the exorcisms discussed above. Both readings are legitimate and the differences in meaning come not from the material itself but from the larger context one uses to interpret it. Since the parables are both the most distinctive way in which Jesus expressed himself and unusually

15. See Miller, "Immortality."

open-ended in their meaning, it behooves us to consider how parables fare in the two opposing interpretive frameworks.

I suggest we focus on two kingdom parables as test cases, The
Mustard and The Leaven. In each case we can track the contrasting
interpretations of these miniature stories that follow from an understanding of the kingdom as either apocalyptic or non-apocalyptic.

If the kingdom of God is apocalyptic, these parables are read as
growth stories. This is how the Christian tradition has understood
them; indeed, the synoptic gospels seem to take them that way. As
growth stories, however, The Mustard and The Leaven are rather
banal. A tiny seed grows into the largest of garden plants (Mark) or
a tree (Q). A pinch of leaven causes the rising of a large mass of
dough. The referents of "mustard" and "leaven" are the literal things
denoted by the nouns. They have no connotative value and do not
function as symbols. Mustard and leaven are used as comparisons
for the kingdom only because they start small and end big. Other
examples could have served just as well. After all, every plant starts
from a seed. The mustard is actually an uninspiring example for a
lesson about growth. If the object is to contrast inconspicuous origins with impressive results, why single out the lowly mustard bush?
Why not a tree: the rugged olive, or the stately palm? Better yet, why
not the strong and lofty cedar of Lebanon, a tree that symbolizes
world empires in Ezekiel and Daniel? The Q parable actually has the
mustard growing into a tree, which is botanically impossible. Since
Jesus' audience knew that mustard cannot become a tree, the parable, as an illustration of the triumphant final state of the kingdom,
undercuts itself because it implies the *futility* of such a hope. Since
the Q parable ends up with a tree, why not use a real one? As an
illustration of a glorious apocalyptic kingdom, the mustard is an inept
choice.

As parables of an apocalyptic kingdom, The Mustard and The
Leaven celebrate the contrast of humble beginning and grand finale
as a manifestation of divine power. In this respect the kingdom of
God embodies the same values as the kingdom of Rome, which grew
from a small town into a worldwide empire. As growth stories these
parables reaffirm that God is on the side of the victor, exactly the lesson Rome wanted to teach its subjects.

On the other hand, as parables of a non-apocalyptic kingdom The
Mustard and The Leaven are wickedly clever satires of imperial values and religious respectability. The mustard takes aim at the cedar

of Lebanon. The allusion is established by "the birds of the air nesting in its branches," a nearly verbatim echo of passages in which the cedar is a metaphor for the empires of Egypt, Assyria, Babylon, and the restored Israel (Ezek 17:23, 31:6; Dan 4:12). The lowliness and un-awe-inspiring character of the mustard bush, qualities that reduce the effectiveness of the story as an illustration of eschatological growth, are exactly the point in a parable of the non-apocalyptic kingdom: God's domain does not look majestic, stable, secure, enduring, domineering. The mustard thus subverts the standard markers of imperial power. For the imperial cedar, "all the birds of the air" who "nest in its branches" (Ezek 31:6) represent the conquered peoples living under the "protection" of empires like Assyria. But in a mustard bush in a garden (Luke 13:19) or a field (Matt 13:31), roosting birds are a nuisance, as are the kind of people Jesus elsewhere declares to be citizens of the kingdom of God.

Furthermore, a non-apocalyptic reading of the parable gives full rein to the symbolic value of mustard. This hardy and aggressive bush is well known for its tendency to spread beyond its allotted place and upset the order of a well-managed garden. The Mishnah (Kilayim 3.2) forbids its cultivation in a garden, lest it lead to a violation of the law of like kinds (Lev 19:19). The mustard-kingdom is thus prone to transgress boundaries of religious purity and social respectability. It blooms where it was not planted, bringing along its unwelcome inhabitants.

Leaven symbolizes the profane, the unholy (Exodus 12). Leavening symbolizes the process of corruption. Paul twice quotes a proverb, "A little leaven leavens the whole batch of dough" (1 Cor 5:6; Gal 5:8), both times to warn his congregation that it risks moral infection by tolerating the presence of certain corrupting individuals. The parable of the leaven therefore likens the growth of the kingdom of God to the spread of moral corruption. It associates the sphere of divine influence with the unholy. We should not underestimate how offensive this parable must have sounded to Jews. (Imagine a rabbi at a congregational Seder teaching that God's rule works on us like leaven.)

If the parable is about an apocalyptic kingdom, leaven can function only as an agent of growth. It cannot have any symbolic resonance because that would undermine the apocalyptic scenario. God's purpose in the apocalyptic intervention is to impose the hegemony of the holy on the present world imagined as hopelessly unholy and corrupt. The apocalyptic reading of this parable thus must sever the image of leaven from its symbolic value in the Jewish world of meaning. (Which Jesus looks non-Jewish now?)

If mustard and leaven are allowed to be symbols that resonate with the Hebrew scriptures, both of these parables subvert apocalyptic assumptions. They can rightly be considered *anti*-apocalyptic.

If this is true for The Mustard and The Leaven, we should investigate other parables for similar qualities. Two more parables come to mind in this regard, and there may well be others like them. 1) If the father in The Two Sons is meant to represent God, he is a sorry excuse for an apocalyptic Deity. He gives no special reward for his elder son's perseverant obedience (an essential element of apocalypticism). The father shamelessly fawns over his younger son, in utter disregard for his own honor,[16] behavior most unbefitting the apocalyptic king of the cosmos to whom all who defy his authority will be forced to submit. 2) The Good Samaritan promotes an attitude toward the enemy that is antithetical to the apocalyptic dualism of the sons of light and the sons of darkness. My point is not only that these two parables insinuate notions incompatible with apocalypticism. My point is stronger: if the image of God and the attitude toward the enemy in these parables are allowed to burrow into the symbolic world of the listener, they can disable the apocalyptic imagination.

I have no grounds for thinking that scholars with an apocalyptic Jesus read these four parables the way I do. Here I am only guessing, but perhaps scholars who have immersed themselves in the symbolism of ancient Judaism can intuit the anti-apocalyptic tendencies in these parables, just as I imagine Jesus' listeners doing. Perhaps these parables are so well crafted that they can have this effect on the imagination of perceptive listeners without their being fully aware of it. Admittedly, this is wishful thinking. I indulge in it here only because it cannot be a coincidence that scholarly reconstructions of the apocalyptic Jesus give such short shrift to the parables. Flipping through the four apocalyptic Jesus books on the ready-reference shelf above my desk, here's what I see. The parables are virtually absent in Sanders' *The Historical Figure of Jesus*. Fredriksen seems to make no

16. Scott, *Hear Then the Parable*, p. 117.

use of them at all in her *Jesus of Nazareth*. Meier's *Marginal Jew* programmatically marginalizes the parables.[17] Allison's *Jesus of Nazareth* seems to relegate parables to the footnotes, where they serve only to document themes Jesus taught more clearly elsewhere. It is up to these scholars to explain why we should largely ignore Jesus' most distinctive and most original contribution to humanity's treasury of religious teaching. For whatever reason, the parables have been unhelpful in making the case for the apocalyptic Jesus.

17. "Some readers may be surprised to see that very few parables are used in the main part of my argument" [that Jesus was an apocalyptic prophet]. *Marginal Jew*, vol. 2, p. 290.

Works Consulted

Allison, Dale. *Jesus of Nazareth, Millenarian Prophet*. Minneapolis: Fortress, 1998.
Fredriksen, Paula. *Jesus of Nazareth, King of the Jews*. New York: Knopf, 2000.
Holman, Charles. *Till Jesus Comes*. Peabody, MA: Hendrickson, 1996.
King, Karen. "Back to the Future." Pp. 77–107 in *The Once and Future Jesus*. The Jesus Seminar. Santa Rosa: Polebridge, 2000.
Kloppenborg Verbin, John. *Excavating Q*. Minneapolis: Fortress, 2000.
McKnight, Scot. *A New Vision for Israel*. Grand Rapids: Eerdmans, 1999.
Meier, John. *A Marginal Jew*. Volume 2: Mentor, Message, and Miracles. New York: Doubleday, 1994.
Miller, Robert J. *The Jesus Seminar and its Critics*. Santa Rosa: Polebridge, 1999.
_____. "Immortality and Religious Identity in Wisdom 2–5." In *Reimagining Christian Origins*. Ed. Elizabeth Castelli and Hal Taussig. Valley Forge, PA: Trinity, 1996. Pp. 199-213.
Patterson, Stephen. *The God of Jesus*. Harrisburg, PA: Trinity, 1998.
Sanders, E.P. *The Historical Figure of Jesus*. London: Penguin, 1993.
Scott, Bernard Brandon. *Hear Then the Parable*. Minneapolis: Fortress, 1989.
Witherington, Ben. *The Jesus Quest*. Downers Grove, IL: InterVarsity, 1995.

From Parable to Ethics

Bernard Brandon Scott

Despite the renaissance in historical Jesus research, studies on Jesus' ethics have been few and far between. Several reasons account for this. No theological position dominates among New Testament scholars, certainly no debate like that between Bultmannians and Barthians that dominated the 50–70s. In those days of the Biblical Theology movement studies on the ethics of Jesus were common. Richard Hiers in *Jesus and Ethics: Four Interpretations* published in 1968 summarized a lively debate that has now largely fallen silent. Now issues of historical reliability and social construction, not the abstract issues of ethics, have dominated the current debate.

Perhaps another reason for this apparent lack of interest in Jesus' ethics is that the Sermon on the Mount no longer provides a clear mode for such a discussion. Despite Hans Deiter Betz's efforts to prove the non-Matthean character of the Sermon,[1] Matthean scholarship has demonstrated that it is more the product of the author of that Gospel than the creation of Jesus.[2] While the Sermon certainly contains Jesus material, the Sermon itself is clearly redactional in character.

Yet three recent studies of Jesus have paid careful attention to the ethics of Jesus without naming it as such. John Dominic Crossan argues that Jesus' strategy "was the combination of *free healing and common eating*, a religious and economic egalitarianism that negated alike and at once the hierarchical and patronal normalcies of Jewish religion and Roman power."[3] This marks out the beginning of an ethical system, but Crossan has not pursued its inter-connections to ask what generates this system or what are its logical connections.

1. *The Sermon on the Mount.*
2. Graham N. Stanton, *A Gospel for a New People,* pp. 310–18, has convincingly argued against Betz's proposal.
3. *The Historical Jesus,* p. 422.

Marcus Borg, beginning with his Oxford dissertation,[4] has proposed a contrast between what he calls a politics of holiness representing the standard Jewish position and a politics of compassion representing the position of Jesus.[5] But there are several problems with this proposal. A.-J. Levine has pointed out, even phrasing the question in this way prejudices the case against Judaism.[6] If one had to choose between holiness defined as separation or compassion, who would not choose compassion? What is appealing about Borg's argument is his recognition that these two positions imply a politics, a way life that is lived with others, both within and outside the group. What Borg has accented is that the issue for Jesus is the status of the purity code as the definer of what it means to be with God, to be a part of God's people.

Walter Wink has pursued *The Powers* through many volumes and so has offered a sustained investigation of New Testament ethics in regard to what he terms the Domination System.[7] Wink sees as "Jesus' total project: the overcoming of the Domination System itself."[8] Jesus is "an egalitarian prophet who repudiates the very premises on which domination is based: the right of some to lord it over others by means of power, wealth, shaming, or titles."[9]

Wink shares much in common with Crossan, but he has worked it out in a more systematic and comprehensive fashion. For Wink, overcoming the Domination System constitutes the essence of the Gospel and is the hermeneutical lens through which he reads the New Testament, later Christianity, and the world. This is both a strength and weakness of his program. While there is no inherent problem with his using the Domination System as a hermeneutical lens, the question arises whether that lens derives from his study of the Jesus material or does he use the Domination System to determine what is from Jesus? His less than rigorous use of criteria of authenticity at times leads to this suspicion. The strength of the Domination System as hermeneutical lens is its tight fit with the social situation of the Roman Empire.

---

4. *Conflict, Holiness & Politics.*
5. *Jesus, a New Vision*, pp. 86–93, 131–40.
6. "Putting Jesus Where He Belongs," esp. footnote 5.
7. *Naming the Powers; Unmasking the Powers: The Invisible Forces That Determine Human Existence; Engaging the Powers.*
8. Wink, *Engaging the Powers*, p. 11.
9. Walter Wink, *When the Powers Fall*, p. 7.

Ethics

Perhaps the obvious needs stating. Jesus had no conscious ethical system. He was a peasant and functioned within orality. People who think orally think concretely, not abstractly in conscious ethical systems. As Walter Ong famously observed, in oral cultures folks must "think memorable thoughts."[10] Jesus thinks in parables and aphorisms. To discuss Jesus' ethical system is to discuss something that we must first construct. He himself does not discuss ethics. Jesus' ethical system is implied, not stated. It was never conscious with him.

Within Judaism Torah stands as the ultimate foundation and source of an ethical system.[11] Unlike any other ancient document it seeks to account for the everyday life of the nation of Israel. It specifies both the life of the nation, the family, and the individual. One of the primary ways in which that ethical control was exercised was through the purity code. Purity was and is an issue in all Mediterranean culture — it is not the exclusive domain of Judaism. Within second temple Judaisms, the application of the purity code was an especially debated issue. This is clear whether one looks at Qumran with its priestly program of purification or the Pharisees with their concern to make Torah and its purity code applicable to all, even women.

What is the purity code? Fundamental to the purity code is the putting of things in the right order. The first creation story is a classic example of the purity code. God goes about setting the cosmos in order, putting everything in its proper place — separating chaos from order, light from darkness, pronouncing it all good. This story is a classic myth of the purity code. God straightens up the world, puts it in right order. The relation between external impurity and internal moral fault (sin) is complex and inconsistent. One should not assume a direct line of connection. One does not necessarily imply the other. Sin appears to be a concern of the prophets, while purity is a concern of the priestly writers. Impurity is an external disordering, an out-of-placeness. The purity code attempts to restore things to the proper order of creation.

10. Walter J. Ong, *Orality and Literacy,* p. 34.
11. Jacob Neusner, *The Way of Torah,* p. 51. But Neusner has always insisted that Torah is larger than the written Torah; see Jacob Neusner, *The Oral Torah.*

Legal Sayings

When we try to fit Jesus within the social world of first century Judaisms, we quickly observe several factors. First as a peasant, his concerns with the purity code are quite different than those of the upper classes. As a member of the lower classes and perhaps even of the disposables, his class would not have had the wherewithal to observe the purity code. His group would have risked almost perpetual impurity.

Second, Jesus does not quote Torah frequently. The gospel traditions quote Torah much more frequently on his behalf. In the Sermon on the Mount, the formulaic beginnings, "You have heard . . . , but I say to you," are not from Jesus but from the oral tradition, as Bultmann long ago argued.[12] Jesus' engagement with Torah is more indirect. I would suggest that it lies in the background as the unquestioned foundation. For example, the saying concerning turning the other cheek (Matt 5:38:42) as found in the Sermon on the Mount or Q serves to demonstrate Jesus' position over and against the Torah. But the introduction is redactional, an addition of the oral tradition. As Walter Wink has shown, "Turning the other cheek to a 'superior' who has backhanded an 'inferior' is an act of defiance, not submission; stripping naked when a creditor demands one's outer garment brings down shame on the head of the creditor for causing the poor debtor's nakedness; carrying a soldier's pack a second mile would put him in violation of military law."[13] This is not a new Torah much less a rejection of Torah, but as Robert Tannehill has argued, a concrete focalization of Torah.[14] It is an example of what Ong terms, concrete thinking, thinking memorable thoughts. Torah here lies in the deep background, underwriting and supporting the thinking.

So to begin thinking about Jesus' ethical system we should not begin by setting it in contrast to Torah. Such is both unhelpful and more importantly wrong. In the end, it would be most surprising to find out that Jesus rejected or set aside Torah. The saying "Don't imagine that I have come to annul the Law or the Prophets," (Mt 5:17) certainly does not come from Jesus, although I am sure it summarizes a sentiment with which he would agree.

---

12. Rudolf Bultmann, *The History of the Synoptic Tradition*, pp. 135–36.
13. Wink, *When the Powers Fall*, p. 9.
14. Robert C. Tannehill, *The Sword of His Mouth*.

From Parable to Ethics

To initially sketch the outline of Jesus' ethical system I want to use three of Jesus' parables as archetypes to elaborate the coordinates of an ethical system. The three parables — Leaven, the Samaritan, and the Prodigals — are authentic, although the second part of the Prodigals has been challenged on occasion. But within recent historical Jesus scholarship these three parables have been unchallenged, even though they have also been ignored.[15] These three parables will provide examples of Jesus' concrete thinking from which we will attempt to sketch out the coordinates of an implied ethical system.

A preliminary observation about the behavior of the characters in the parables is in order. Frequently the characters of the major narrative parables engage in unethical behavior, behavior that has often scandalized the piety of the later tradition and its interpreters, calling for comment, misdirection, or emendation. The dishonest steward cheats the master; the master of the vineyard pays all laborers the same subsistent wage. The judge who respects neither God nor man and the widow are engaged in a battering contest; the rich farmer is an Epicurean. The three slaves in the Talents are all problematic. Two earn exorbitant and usurious returns on investment, the third is an overly cautious custodian, and the master is hard hearted, reaping where he does not sow. The tenants of the vineyard engage in a murderous riot. And these are only the obvious examples. At the level of characterization, the characters in Jesus' parables frequently are models of unethical comportment, much to the tradition's chagrin. This provides us with an important initial observation. Jesus' concrete ethical thinking is not much interested in ethics as good manners. His ethics are after something that requires a deeper reflection.

Leaven

The Leaven exhibits in a confined exegetical space an excellent example of Jesus' concrete ethical thinking. "The kingdom of heaven

---

15. John Meier, *A Marginal Jew*, vol. 2, p. 290, has even argued that the parables are not the place to begin to understand Jesus because their meaning needs to be determined from outside. This seems to me to be perverse thinking, actually taking Mark 4:11–12 as a true definition of parables. "To those outside everything is presented in parables (or riddles as Jeremias suggested), so that they may look with eyes wide open but never quite see." Jesus told parables as a concrete thinker to clarify, not to obscure. Meier rejects the parables as the starting point because they refute his understanding of the kingdom.

is like leaven which a woman took and hid in three measures of flour, until it was all leavened" (Matt 13:33, my translation). At the syntagmatic level, the sentence level, so to speak, this is almost a common sense observation, with only a few items to disturb its apparent placid surface. The New American Bible translation almost totally blands out any possible resonance in this parable. "The reign of God is like yeast which a woman took and kneaded into three measures of flour. Eventually the whole mass of dough began to rise."

Three measures, the one resonance the New American Bible does not eliminate, can provide a convenient starting point. Three measures is about 40 pounds of flour, a very large baking session. But the real excitement is at the paradigmatic or deep level. The story of the prophecy of the birth of Isaac, when the three angels visit Abraham at the Oaks of Mamre (Gen 18), provides the most famous example of three measures in the Hebrew Bible. Sarah prepares for the visitors three measures of cakes. This type of allusive reference is typical of how Torah would be referred to in an oral performance and how Torah undergirds Jesus' concrete thinking. The oral performer creates a performance arena that operates by metonymy. A simple reference metonymically conjures up a whole depth of reference by means of the part standing for the whole.[16] At the paradigmatic level the reference to three measures suggests that in parable something like the events at the Oaks of Mamre is happening.

The parable's other terms are more problematic at the paradigmatic level. There is a rumbling below the surface. Leaven in the ancient world is a universal sign of moral corruption.[17] Paul quotes the aphorism, "Do you not know that a little leaven leavens to the whole lump (1 Cor 5:6; Gals 5:9) to emphasize how a little evil corrupts the whole. Mark has Jesus warn the disciples about the leaven of the Pharisees (Mark 8:15), in a context where leaven refers to the Pharisees's request for a sign. The metaphor suggests that such a question, while on the surface innocuous, will corrupt everything. The symbolism of the leaven is comparable to the aphorism of the rotten apple in American folklore — one rotten apple spoils the whole barrel.

Furthermore, in Hebrew symbolism unleavened is the appropriate marker for the holy. This is made very clear in the institution of the

---

16. John Miles Foley, *The Singer of Tales in Performance*, pp. 46–49.
17. See my *Hear Then the Parable,* pp. 324–25.

feast of Passover. "For seven days you are to eat unleavened bread. On the very first day you must rid your houses of leaven; from the first day to the seventh anyone who eats leavened bread is to be expelled from Israel. On the first day there is to be a sacred assembly" (Exod 12:15–16). The association of unleavened with the sacred and leavened with the impure could not be clearer.

The other terms in the parable — the woman, hiding, until everything is leaven — are also problematic from a paradigmatic perspective.[18] But the initial term makes the essential point. The kingdom of God and leaven are incompatible and incomparable terms. They do not belong together. The kingdom of God is NOT like leavened but UNleavened bread. Precisely for this reason the tradition has fought and ignored the obvious implications of this parable, turning it into an proverb that from a small beginning comes great event. This move is first clearly made in the Gospel of Thomas 96. "The kingdom of the father is like a certain woman. She took a little leaven, [concealed] it in some dough, and made it into large loaves." Thomas inserts the metaphorical overtone "from small beginning to large outcome," thus distracting from the parable's more odious overtones.[19]

Coordinates

What are the ethical implications of this parable? The parable proposes a radically new definition of the experience of God, of God's activity, and by implication of God. The kingdom (the sacred, the clean, the good) does not convert the leaven (the unclean) into the sacred and the clean. Rather it is the reverse.[20] The kingdom becomes leaven. The sacred and clean become unclean. Theologically this involves God's uncleanness. Jesus' ethical system has an apparently logical contradiction at its heart. It envisions God as unclean; it does not envision God making the unclean clean. The parable does not say "until all is make into leaven." Such would be a real miracle. Rather the parable says "until everything is leavened."

Literally this parable makes no sense. God by definition cannot be unclean. So radical is the assumption that God is unclean, so

18. See my *Hear Then the Parable*.

19. Q is moving in a similar direction by pairing the Leaven with the Mustard Seed, which is frequently in the ancient world a metaphor for the smallest.

20. The direction of metaphor is from A to B. Most reverse it in the case of parables. Is the kingdom disclosed by the parable or the parable by the kingdom? This is an essential methodological issue that determines how one interprets the parables.

counter-intuitive to the normal religious thinking, even offensive, that in order to demonstrate its correctness I must show how it makes sense of items in the Jesus tradition, how it can serve as a unifying insight into Jesus' ethical thinking. This allows further expansion and explanation of the insight as well as producing what I hope is a convincing arrangement or configuration of the data. To employ a mathematical metaphor, I hope this will allow us to deduce the coordinates of Jesus' implied ethical system.

This insight that God becomes unclean goes a long way toward explaining the frequent references to Jesus' association with the outcast, lepers, sinners and the special place of women in his activity. These people find themselves accepted as they are without the need to become clean or honorable. The Beatitudes also form part of this pattern, for they bless people who are not obviously to be congratulated. The poor are blessed (Luke 6:20) because they are poor and to them belongs the kingdom of God now, not because they will be rich. This overturns the assumption that underlies the books from Deuteronomy to 2 Kings that poverty and disease are God's punishment for sins (Deut 28).

The saying that it is not what goes into the mouth that defiles a person, but what comes out, excretion (Mark 7:14; Thom 14:5), frustrates the ability of the food laws to define what is clean and holy. Jesus appears to have carried out this aphorism literally in his eating habits by not washing his hands and eating with unclean people. The function of food laws is to codify the divine so one can know where the divine is. But if foods can no longer represent and replicate the divine by marking the line between clean and unclean, then people can no longer be divided into clean and unclean.

This same rejection of the line between the clean and unclean finds expression in several parables. In the Mustard Seed (Mark 4:30–32; Q13:18–19; Thom 20:2–4) the planting of mustard seed, a weed like plant, pollutes the garden, making it unclean.[21] Various revisions of the parable have obscured this aspect, though it is clearly in the Q (Lukan) version. Likewise, Crossan has shown in his analysis of the Treasure that the treasure, a gift, becomes a seduction for the man, who in his joy at finding the treasure, rushes out to do an

---

21. *Hear Then the Parable*, pp. 381–82. Like the Leaven, the tradition tried at an early stage to avoid the implications of this parable by distracting the attention to the metaphor of small to great. In Mark the shrub becomes a tree, a true miracle, and in Matthew it becomes a shrub and then a tree!

immoral thing.[22] He buries the treasure and goes and buys the field, thus signaling that the treasure is not his. He steals it from its rightful owner. This parable is a counterpoint to the Leaven. What is good, a treasure, seduces the man into doing evil. Belonging to this same configuration is the Eye of a Needle (Mark 10:24). The rich man is like treasure, one who should be blessed according to Deuteronomy, but it will be more difficult for him to enter the kingdom of God than for a camel to pass through the eye of needle. Likewise the warning against the scribes, "who like to parade around in long robes"(Mark 12:38–39) belongs here. Scribes know what is clean and unclean and who can thus represent the divine. But they should not be imitated for the basis on which their scholarship rests has been undermined. The complex of sayings dealing with the the healthy and sick clearly indicate that God is on the side of the sick. It is they who need a physican (Mark 2:17). God identifies not with the honorable and righteous, but the shamed and sinners.

Finally, into this configuration I would place those parables that exhibit characters who do not quite seem to conform to the standard of behavior thought appropriate to the kingdom of God. For example, the violence of the assassin who tests his power by thrusting his sword through a wall shocks a hearer (Thom 98). Like the man who finds treasure, the wheeling and dealing of the shrewd manager (Luke 16:1–8a) has confounded various interpreters since before the parable was incorporated into the gospel tradition.[23] When dismissed from his job as steward, he goes to those who owe a debt to his master and drastically reduces their debt. The shamelessness of the man who delays in welcoming his guest in Two Friends at Midnight (Luke 11:5–8) and the corrupt judge who fears neither God nor people in dealing with the widow's request (Luke 18:2–5) both exhibit behavior that confounds an audience. The very amorality of the parables has proven problematic for most interpreters, to the point that the tradition has tried to explain it away. In the end, the toll collector, standing at the back of the temple begging for mercy and not the Pharisee who openly gives God thanks, goes home acquitted (Luke 18:10–14). The temple no longer sets the rules.

"No prophet is welcome on his home turf"(Mark 6:4) because there the rules are known. So one is homeless, unlike the foxes who

---

22. Crossan, *Finding Is the First Act.*

23. C.H. Dodd, *The Parables of the Kingdom,* p. 17, in reference to Luke 16:8a–15, "We can almost see here notes for three separate sermons on the parable as text."

have dens, the son of man has no place to lay his head (Luke 9:58). Jesus' probable conflict with his family and village belongs to this set of coordinates.

What is one to do in a situation where leaven represents the kingdom of God, when what goes into a person does not defile, where toll collectors go home acquitted, the poor are congratulated and home has disappeared? "You must be as sly as a snake and as simple as a dove" (Matt 10:16).

Samaritan

The parable of the Samaritan (Luke 10:30–35) extends the ethical assumptions of the Leaven, only in a narrative format. The traditional interpretation of this parable in which the Samaritan is a good Samaritan encourages common sense altruistic behavior, that we should love our neighbor as ourselves. While common sense, it is difficult. The Lucan example story is told against xenophobia, a common enough affliction of the human race, an affliction too often encouraged by the communities that regard this text as sacred.

As Robert Funk showed in his pioneering work on parables, such a traditional reading of the parable is a *goyim* reading for it ignores the literal significance of the helper being a Samaritan. The literalness of the Samaritan gives the parable its metaphorical kick.[24] Hugh Montefiore noticed almost a hundred years ago that to say in Hebrew, "priest, Levite, and Samaritan," make about as much sense as to say in English, "bishop, priest, and Frenchman."[25] In both cases it is the wrong triad. In parable the expected triad is priest, Levite, and Israelite, in which the Israelite is a layman. Thus the story plays upon the anticlericalism of the period.

In form the parable is a hero story and the audience of such a story expects to identify with the hero. Such is the form's common expectation. But in this narrative, the hero, a Samaritan, makes identification very difficult, if not impossible for a first century Jewish audience. So when the potential hero turns out to be unacceptable, an audience faces a number of options. First, an audience can decide that the story is stupid, would never happened this way in real life, and opt out of the narrative. For such a hearer, their moral world remains the same. To borrow a term from computer programming,

24. Robert W. Funk, *Language, Hermeneutic and Word of God*, p. 213.
25. Claude G. Montefiore, *The Synoptic Gospels*, p. 467.

this is the default moral world. In the parable's original audience I would assume most stayed in the default moral world and did not enter the world of the parable.

An audience can identify with the hero, the Samaritan, but for most this would be a practical impossibility. Nevertheless, those who could make such an identification are already in a different moral world than the default moral world and in no need of the parable.

Finally, an audience can identify with the man in the ditch. This involves a twofold step. One first must abandon the pretensions that the form of the story sets up which require an audience to adopt the role of hero. Instead one must accept as hero/savior a character whom the tradition has stigmatized as villain. Such an audience must construct a new moral world and begin the abandonment of the default moral world.

The Samaritan is the narrative equivalent of leaven. But as a coordinate in a moral world Samaritan functions differently. The Samaritan requires the construction of a moral world in which the map of human relations is reorganized. In the ancient world people operated with a map made up of concentric circles.[26] At the center of the map was the family, then the village, the tribe, the nation, and finally in the outside circle the foreigner. The further one got from the center of the circle, the more distrustful and problematic the relationship became. The Samaritan is not only a foreigner, but because of the religious enmity between Samaritans and Jews, the Samaritan is the unclean, half-blood, as it were, an anti-family.

Thus the new moral map is redrawn so that the outside circle is now placed in the center. One is to view the outside as the inside.

Prodigals

My final example to sketch out the coordinates of the moral map is the parable of the Prodigal Son (Luke 15:11–32) as the tradition has named it, indicating where it believes the emphasis should fall. The story of the younger son is the child's dream of daddy setting everything aright and as such it is a very popular fantasy. The parable's first act describes the default moral world.

In expectation the second part of this parable should ratify the first part. This narrative belongs to the genre of the two brothers.[27]

26. Bruce J. Malina, *The New Testament World*, p. 25, has accented the importance of mapping in human understanding.
27. See my *Hear Then The Parable*, p. 111–12.

The younger brother is a scapegrace and the elder brother is responsible. Normally the elder brother is rejected in favor of the younger. The making righteous of the younger is purchased at the price of the elder. The range of variation in this story runs from Cain and Abel to Esau and Jacob. Luke clearly reads the story in light of this tradition and sees it as told against the Pharisees and scribes. The Pharisees and scribes are the elder brother, who are to be rejected in favor of the younger brother, the gentiles. The parable so interpreted becomes a paradigm of the rejection of Israel in favor of the gentile church. But all is not lost for Israel, as Jeremias says, their rejection is not complete, all they must do is repent and believe in the Gospel.[28]

The parable's conclusion plays this reading false. When the father addresses the elder son with "You are always with me and all that is mine is yours," the default world constructed by the two brothers typology crumbles. Why should he repent and believe in the Gospel if he has everything? What is expected is that the elder son will be rejected and the inheritance given to the younger son as in the case of Esau and Jacob, the archetypical version of this story.

The father's response provokes review of what is going on in this parable and throws a new light on the interaction between the three characters. The parable employs the archetype of the two brothers and the implied family mode to reconfigure the meaning of " to rightwise," the use Kendrick Grobels felicitous translation of *dikaiein*.[29] In the default version of this story, the rightwising of the younger son is purchased at the expense of the elder. In fact, his story should serve to reinforce the rightwising of the younger. It is as though in order to demonstrate righteousness of one character there must be an unrighteous one. A hero, especially one as problematic as the younger son, demands a villain.

In parable, the father refuses to choose between his sons. There appears to be nothing they can do to push him away. He gladly divides his life (*bios*) between them and expectantly and exorbitantly receives back the younger son after he has squandered his inheritance. When the elder son castigates the father for his acceptance of "this son of yours . . . who has squandered your estate with prostitutes" the father does not respond as expected with at least a rebuke or even better a rejection, a banishment into the desert so this new Jacob can

28. Joachim Jeremias, *The Parables of Jesus*, p. 131.
29. Grobel employed the Middle English verb "rightwise" instead of the more normal translation of "justify." See his explanation in Rudolf Bultmann, *Theology of the New Testament*, vol. 1, p. 254.

claim his inheritance. Rather he affirms that everything belongs to the elder son and that he cannot be separated from the father. This father, as the parable's first line affirms, has two sons, not one who is accepted and the other rejected.

This parable implies a third act. Soon the father will die. Then the sons will face the decision which script to follow — theirs or their father's? Do they follow the default moral order determined by the genre of the two sons or a new moral order narrated by the parable? If they remain in the default moral world, they will probably kill each other. If they opt for the world of the parable, they will follow the father's example and accept each other.

Rightwising is not over-and-against, but both/and. Rightwising does not constitute some new group of the rightwised from which the unrightwised are excluded. If leaven is the fundamental metaphor, then all is leavened.

New Coordinates

Jesus' new moral map demands a new set of coordinates, three of which I have sketched out.

1) God is unclean. This is the most radical and most fundamental of the new coordinates. But this coheres with other evidence. Jesus' contemporaries thought he had a demon. It is because he identifies God with the unclean that he is perceived as demonic by the default moral world. Likewise Jesus' association with the unclean, the outcast, sinners, all coheres with this fundamental coordinate. Jesus' disrespect for the purity code finds its explanation here.

2) The relational map is redrawn so the outside is on the inside. This is what Crossan means by commonsality and unbrokered kingdom and Wink sees in Jesus' attack on the Domination System. With such a map of relationships the client-patron world of brokered relationships is destroyed. The hierarchical world arranged from emperor to disposable peasant is no longer the unquestioned way it is. A new world without the default map predicting and dictating relationships needs to be found.

3) Rightwising is no longer at the expense of another. As E.P. Sanders has argued, Jesus does not call for repentance.[30] Rather in his moral world shame and honor are no longer pivotal values arranging

---

30. *Jesus and Judaism*, p. 203; *The Historical Figure of Jesus* p. 230.

folks into a moral hierarchy. This explains Jesus' acceptance of the toll collectors without demanding that they take up another, acceptable occupation.

Why is this not moral relativism? Jesus is not interested in developing a moral system, although one is implied. He is initiating a community. His interest is who is in the kingdom of God. The next generation's task will be to elaborate the conditions for staying in.

In the effort to describe Jesus' ethical system I have relied upon two metaphorical models. From mathematics I have borrowed the image of coordinates and from computer science the notion of the default. It is important to see that Jesus' ethical system only makes sense in light of the default moral world. There is an over-againstness that is essential to Jesus' ethical vision. Seamus Heaney has argued that poetry too demands "a counter-reality in the scales." I take the liberty of quoting a passage to give a sense of Heaney's argument.

> And in the activity of poetry too, there is a tendency to place a counter-reality in the scales — a reality which may be only imagined but which nevertheless has weight because it is imagined within the gravitational pull of the actual and can therefore hold its own and balance out against the historical situation. This redressing effect of poetry comes from its being a glimpsed alternative, a revelation of potential that is denied or constantly threatened by circumstances. And sometimes, of course, it happens that such a revelation, once enshrined in the poem, remains as a standard for the poet, so that he or she must then submit to the strain of bearing witness in his or her own life to the place of consciousness established in the poem.[31]

Heaney brings out a number of points in his understanding of how poetry functions that are critical to understanding how Jesus' parables and aphorisms functioned. Jesus' parables and his implied ethical system is not an alternative to the default moral world in the sense that it is a replacement. It is a counterweight, a counter-reality, in Heaney's terms. Thus, it is always dialogically related to that default world. The default world will almost always win in the long run, because it is the default.

---

31. Seamus Heaney, *The Redress of Poetry*, pp. 3–4.

Jesus' parables are "a glimpsed alternative, a revelation of potential that is denied or constantly threatened by circumstance," or in my terms, constantly threatened by the default world. A glimpsed alternative is not a worked out program. It is always temporary, glimpsed. It is a possibility, not a reality.

Once enshrined in parable, it remains a standard for the poet, or in this case Jesus. Thus the kingdom of God does not drive Jesus, but the glimpse enshrined in the parable which is likened to the kingdom of God. It is an alternative reality only as a counter-balance to the real reality, whether the Roman empire or the Temple state. Thus the third stage of the quest which wants to put the deeds first has it exactly wrong. As Heaney remarks, the poet "must then submit to the strain of bearing witness in his or her own life to the place of consciousness established in the poem." In Jesus' parables his consciousness is established and his life bears witness to that. Thus the parables provide the coordinates for understanding Jesus' deeds.

Heaney has captured in his understanding of the redress of poetry an insight into how Jesus' language offered to his audience and himself an alternative to the world in which they were trapped. A world segregated by purity laws separating the unclean from the clean and into further degrees of purity or shame. A world where those on the bottom are imprisoned in unchangeable structures and await a divine solution. A world in which enemies threaten at every point. Jesus in his language offers a counter world, a vision, an openness to experience. It is a "glimpsed alternative, a revelation of potential that is denied or constantly threatened by circumstances." It may only be an imagined or re-imagined alternative, but it dervies its weight from its opposition to and careful observation of the historical world. Apart from the gravitational pull of that historical world, it is without meaning or open to whatever one wants it to mean. It will soon return to the default moral world, as the exegesis of the parables demonstrates. The traditional interpretation is the default moral world.

The problem with this view of Jesus is that it runs counter to the assumption that he is the founder of a new religion.[32] This demands something new and complete, not something in counter-balance, not just a glimpse. Such a view of Jesus appears too ephemeral for what came afterwards, Christianity, the church. With my view, Jesus

32. I find myself here in profound agreement with Burton Mack.

remains firmly attached to Judaism and is engaged in an argument within Judaism. He is part of a continuing debate. To put it too boldly, he is against the Deuteronomist and sides with Job and Qohelet.

To return to Heaney's argument, poetry is a redress because it envisions "a reality which may be only imagined but which nevertheless has weight because it is imagined within the gravitational pull of the actual and can therefore hold its own and balance out against the historical situation." The redress of the parable is hope and hope has power, not because it is a concrete program, a worked out plan or blueprint, but because it creates the counter-reality to the default moral world. It says things do not have to be this way.

Václav Havel was imprisoned for his poems and plays, led the velvet revolution, and became the first President of Czechoslovakia and then Czech. What Havel has to say about hope explains how the parables and kingdom of God functioned as a revolutionary symbol for Jesus and his followers. Hope, he says, is

> "a state of mind, not a state of the world . . . and it's not essentially dependent on some particular observation of the world or estimate of the situation . . . it transcends the world that is immediately experienced, and is anchored somewhere beyond its horizons . . . It is not the conviction that something will turn out well, but the certainty that something makes sense, regardless of how it turns out."[33]

It is not accident that those who espouse an apocalyptic Jesus avoid the parables. You cannot get from the parables to an apocalyptic Jesus, although you can get from an apocalyptic Jesus to an apocalyptic interpretation of the parables. But such an interpretation is the default moral world, because apocalyptic is the Deuteronomist's vision as the future divine fact. From an apocalyptic Jesus one does get to the founder of Christianity.

In this essay I have tried to follow the methodology outlined by Jonathan Z. Smith: description, comparison, redescription, rectification. The bulk of the essay has consisted of description. The comparison demands that one employ for comparison models, theories, etc., that propose a translation different from the data. As Smith argues,

33. Vaclav Havel, *Disturbing the Peace*, p. 181.

"To summarize: a theory, a model, a conceptual theory, *cannot be simply the data writ large.*"[34] For this reason I have employed metaphors from mathematics and computer science and the understanding of poetry. This has led to a redescription of Jesus' implied ethical system and a rectification of how we should understand both his ethics and his social situation.

34. Jonathan Z. Smith, "Bible and Religion," p. 91.

Works Cited

Betz, Hans Dieter. *The Sermon on the Mount.* Hermeneia Commentary Series. Minneapolis: Fortress Press, 1995.

Borg, Marcus J. *Conflict, Holiness & Politics in the Teachings of Jesus*, Studies in the Bible and Early Christianity 5. New York: Edwin Mellen Press, 1984.

_____. *Jesus, a New Vision: Spirit, Culture, and the Life of Discipleship.* San Francisco: Harper and Row, 1987.

Bultmann, Rudolf. *The History of the Synoptic Tradition.* Trans. John Marsh. New York: Harper & Row, 1963.

_____. *Theology of the New Testament.* Trans. Kendrick Grobel, 2 vols. New York: New Charles Scribner's Sons, 1951, 1955.

Crossan, John Dominic. *Finding Is the First Act.* Semeia Supplements. Philadelphia: Fortress Press, 1979.

_____. *The Historical Jesus: The Life of a Mediterranean Jewish Peasant.* San Francisco: HarperSanFrancisco, 1991.

Dodd, C. H. *The Parables of the Kingdom.* New York: Charles Scribner's Sons, 1935, 1961.

Foley, John Miles. *The Singer of Tales in Performance.* Bloomington: Indiana University Press, 1995.

Funk, Robert W. *Language, Hermeneutic and Word of God.* New York: Harper and Row, 1966.

Havel, Vaclav. *Disturbing the Peace*, trans. Paul Wilson. London: Faber and Faber, 1990.

Heaney, Seamus. *The Redress of Poetry.* London: Faber and Faber, 1995.

Hiers, Richard. *Jesus and Ethics: Four Interpretations.* Philadelphia: Westminster Press, 1968.

Jeremias, Joachim. *The Parables of Jesus.* Trans. S.H. Hooke. New York: Charles Scribner's Sons, 1972.

Levine, A.-J. "Putting Jesus Where He Belongs: The Man from Nazareth in His Jewish World," *Perspectives in Religious Studies*, forthcoming.

Malina, Bruce J. *The New Testament World, Insights from Cultural Anthropology.* Atlanta: John Knox, 1981.

Meier, John P. *A Marginal Jew: Rethinking the Historical Jesus.* The Anchor Bible Reference Library. Garden City: Doubleday, 1994.

Montefiore, Claude G. *The Synoptic Gospels.* 2nd ed., vol. 1. New York: KTAV Publishing House, 1968.

Neusner, Jacob. *The Oral Torah: The Sacred Books of Judaism.* San Francisco: Harper & Row, 1986.

_____. *The Way of Torah: An Introduction to Judaism: Religious Life of Man.* North Scituate, MA: Duxbury Press, 1979.

Ong, Walter J. *Orality and Literacy, the Technologizing of the Word*, ed. Terence
        Hawkes, *New Accents*. London and New York: Methuen, 1982.
Sanders, E. P. *Jesus and Judaism*. Philadelphia: Fortress Press, 1985.
_____. *The Historical Figure of Jesus*. New York: Allen Lane, The Penguin Press, 1993.
Scott, Bernard Brandon. *Hear Then the Parable: A Commentary on the Parables of
        Jesus*. Minneapolis: Fortress Press, 1989.
Smith, Jonathan Z. "Bible and Religion," *Bulletin of the Council of Societies for the
        Study of Religion* 29, no. 4 (2000).
Stanton, Graham N. *A Gospel for a New People: Studies in Matthew*. Edinburgh:
        T.&T. Clark, 1992.
Tannehill, Robert C. *The Sword of His Mouth*. Semeia Supplements. Philadelphia:
        Fortress Press; Missoula, MT: Scholars Press, 1975.
Wink, Walter. *Engaging the Powers*. Minneapolis: Fortress Press, 1992.
_____. *Naming the Powers*. Philadelphia: Fortress Press, 1984.
_____. *Unmasking the Powers: The Invisible Forces That Determine Human Existence*.
        Philadelphia: Fortress Press, 1986.
_____. *When the Powers Fall: Reconciliation in the Healing of Nations*. Minneapolis:
        Fortress Press, 1998.

Can We Let Jesus Die?

Arthur J. Dewey

Would the crucifixion have had any sublimity or meaning if Jesus had seen himself crowned with the halo of martyrdom? What we have later added was not there for him. And we must forget all about it if we are to hear his commands.
— Dag Hammarskjold

No statement, theological or otherwise, should be made that would not be credible in the presence of burning children.
— Irving Greenberg

The Matter of Perspective

For nearly two millennia the death of Jesus of Nazareth has conspicuously concentrated the Christian imagination. From the Alexamenos Graffito in Rome to the *Ten Punching Bags* of Andy Warhol and Jean-Michel Basquiat,[1] from early gospel confabulations to *Jesus Christ Superstar*, from the grotesque death scenes mirroring the Black Death of the late Middle Ages to the gnarled crucifixes carved in contemporary Latin American base communities, the passion of Jesus has haunted the Western imagination.

Since the eighteenth century the historical imagination has introduced a novel perspective on the death of Jesus. Critical scholars have removed the death of Jesus from ecclesial wraps and have attempted to place the question of Jesus' fate within a public forum. This, however, has not stopped many in the churches from dismissing such

1. Dillenberger, *Religious Art*, pp. 95–97

135

enterprise. The death of Jesus, embedded in primordial images and emotional overlays, speaks volumes to them. Unfortunately such uncritical acceptance of the "traditional" story of the death of Jesus has had tragic ramifications. Many churchgoers have been pressed into guilt complexes unwittingly. Most horribly the very telling of the death story of Jesus has become the occasion for generating anti-Semitism in the West. Salvation by the blood of the Lamb has had its price, a very human price.

Most recently the public debate over the question of the historical Jesus has resumed the Enlightenment's agenda. The Jesus Seminar has gone on record, publishing their attempts to detect the historicity of the death of Jesus. What is clear from the present debate is that many, both scholars and believers, share still a common understanding of the tradition of the death of Jesus. They assume that the tradition delivers a report of what actually happened. Such a position is found not only among most conservative scholars. While admitting that the gospel evidence is more complicated than what a literalist would allow, even liberal scholars assume that one can plausibly suppose that some history lies behind the later communities' constructions. This position, which I would call *underlying realism,* is both metaphysical and religious. It not only supports the claim to historical fact but also, albeit covertly, is underpinned by religious conviction.

For most bible readers their understanding of the traditions of the death of Jesus is largely ahistorical. The overarching narrative (from Genesis to Armageddon) defines the conditions of imagining. There is no sense of the consequences of living within the historical imagination. There is little or no regard for the ways in which the stories of the death of Jesus were fabricated. The readers show little awareness of being distinct from the storyline, no sense that a different cultural background is in play in what appears a common foreground. Certainly there is no concern to detect the groping developments that emerged from the various Jesus traditions.

This ahistorical understanding is coupled with an ahistorical self-understanding. The bible readers (and scholars) do not suspect that they are engaged in redescribing the fate of Jesus, effectively extending and transmuting the present moving tradition. Rather, they look upon the gospels as fixed scripts. Their task becomes one of simple, neutral transmission. Such an assumption allows the readers to evade the obvious: the rank contingency of those who convey and are concerned about the tradition. They try to avoid at all costs that such storytelling cannot prevent their own demise. The story tradition serves as a firewall to the obscene incursions of history.

Such traditional reading stances permit the maintenance of past and present power plays. There is no consideration given to who are defining the terms of the discourse or what the discourse permits to be heard. No one would want to admit that within the very metaphors of the text there might be embedded a *servile conscious-ness*. Instead, the texts are read as innocent reports of what happened.

I would propose to re-read the traditions of the death of Jesus in a non-realist way. I take the arguments and conclusions of the Jesus Seminar as a starting point for discussion. The Seminar has resisted the usual reading of the passion narratives as factual reports by main-taining that the burden of proof rests upon those who claim authen-ticity for the words and deeds of Jesus. The Seminar has ever been vigilant against a "congenial Jesus." Another way of saying this is that the death of Jesus is not a simple invention of one's desires. In fact, a critical reading of the death traditions of Jesus may well help us view the death of Jesus in human terms – perhaps for the first time. We may gain some appreciation of the human effort that went into the construction of these stories. We may even begin to approach the death of Jesus in a non-apologetic fashion. Could it be that we might finally let Jesus die a human death?

As we shall see, a historical reconsideration of the traditions of the death of Jesus dislocates any hard and fast understanding of Jesus' fate. Rather than serving as reliable reports, the passion narratives express the creative registers of each historical community. What can be gleaned from the earliest layers of the traditions will surprise the conventional appraisal of the death of Jesus. Not all followers of Jesus were preoccupied with his death. At least twenty years went by before we have any indication that there was a need to construct an overarching narrative to Jesus' fate. Even then, it was still not a uni-versal concern in the developing traditions. We shall further see that the death story of Jesus is eventually constructed along the mythic lines of a well-known Jewish narrative frame and that this construc-tion arises out of a concern for the destiny of those in the later com-munities rather than simply for the fate of Jesus.

Today we cannot presume that the death story of Jesus has any currency for the global community. Such a presumption would come from a neo-colonial employment of the tradition. Indeed, the tendency still is to use the story of Jesus' death in an exclusivist fashion that would preclude understanding the story tradition within a liberating perspective. Instead of such presumption the post-modern interpreter must risk the chance there is no meaning whatsoever. It might well be that the hope of setting the tradition free will come only by patiently listening to hear if others around the globe can retell the tale in a radically different setting.

Historical Observations

The starting point for reflection on the death of Jesus is history. No longer can we begin with dogmatic assertions or creedal formulations. For these too are embedded in the movement of history. One's own "faith stance" is no longer a viable sanctuary from the historical press. We know too well that we are historical beings through and through. Thus, however we begin the investigation, it is with the full recognition of the historical reality of our investigation. Not only do we see our limits and language games but we also perceive the historical difference from those who preceded us.

Precisely because we are embedded in history it is crucial to admit the fragments, the gaps, and the uncertainties. The temptation to draw straight lines from one discovered point to another is quite strong for any bible reader, especially for the historian. This tendency is the basis for the argument from plausibility. Although plausibility alone never gets beyond the possible, readers and scholars alike are wont to assume that what is seen in the text connects to an unseen "fact." There is little concern that the texture of the text might well be a multi-layered palimpsest that bears much in terms of the history of a developing fictional tradition. In our rush to judgment, to get the facts straight, we often miss the historical clues scattered along the margins of the page.

The Historical Jesus and Death

In publishing its sometime provocative findings, the Jesus Seminar concluded that Jesus was an itinerant wordsmith who invited his audience into his experimental vision of the Empire of God. But the question of death was another matter. The usual sayings that would furnish Jesus' anticipation of death were not included in the database. The Seminar did not find the so-called Passion Predictions (Mark 8:31; 9:30–32; 10:32–34) to be authentic. Even Mark 14:25 so overlaid with later community elements was considered doubtful. None of the extravagant utterances of the Johannine Jesus were voted red or pink. The monumental Farewell Address of the Last Supper in John was seen as a later construction. Moreover, the Seminar found that Jesus was not an apocalyptic seer. Subsequent writers placed Mark 13 and the various other scripts of imminent doom on Jesus' lips.

Nevertheless, if we hunt through the sayings of Jesus voted red or pink we find a remarkable assortment. What is most interesting is how vital and fresh the sayings sound. There is no anguish or self-conscious martyrdom to be noted. In short, Jesus did not anticipate his death in sacrificial terms. Some might attribute this to a youthful enthusiasm or idealism, yet the story of the rich man (Luke 12:16–20) cautions this consideration. Death was part of Jesus' world. But neither it nor its customs held him evidently at bay (Q Luke 9:59–60). He lived out of a fundamental trust of Reality (Q Luke 12:22–28). Now this sense of trust allowed him to see the critical choices which living entailed (Q Luke 14:26; Q Luke 17:33). In the very midst of human contingency (Q Luke 9:58) and need (Q Matt 6:11) stood the opportunity of experiencing God's Empire (Q Luke 9:59–60). We do not see some heroic pose, anticipating a traumatic incident and fiery conclusion. Nor do we see some overarching mythic narrative that attempts to make sense of his impending death.

There are some scholars (even among the Seminar) who understandably argue that Jesus must have known the political score. He would have known that what he said and did would eventually meet political resistance. Yet such speculation is precisely that. It is built once again on the argument of plausibility. I would contend that it is used to support a position assumed rather than arrived at. The words of the historical Jesus would appear to give a lie to their "political realism." The peasant wordsmith may have had other things in mind. I would contend Jesus envisioned a Reality much more immediate (and with greater social consequences) than the ordinary politico. It would not be surprising for the Romans to sniff something was amiss. But Pilate did not need certain evidence to liquidate a perceived threat, albeit a fly on the Roman elbow. The "carelessness" of Jesus for his fate may well be a consequence of his trusting vision of God's effective presence. We further cannot dismiss outright another version of Jesus' end: his death caught everyone off guard, including Jesus.

Non-Gospel Evidence for the Death of Jesus

Regarding the "facts" of the death of Jesus from non-Christian evidence we can say that both Tacitus (*Annals* 15.44) and Josephus (*Antiquities* 18.63–64) independently attest to the execution of Jesus by crucifixion through the agency of Pontius Pilate. There is nothing else that can be confirmed through the agreement of independent sources. The Talmudic material (*Babylonian Talmud* b Sanhedrin 43a.) presents a late, tendentious interpretation of the fate of Jesus.

This is all the evidence that there is concerning the death of Jesus from non-Christian sources. The modern reader might be startled by the meager amount of evidence. However, one should recall that the death of Jesus, the Jew, was hardly a world-shaking event for the Roman world. From the imperial perspective Jesus' death was one of the many thousands of non-entities liquidated to maintain the status quo. Only in retrospect, from the later experience of the early Jesus movement, did the death agony of Jesus gradually become important. It is precisely because the followers of Jesus continued on after his death and had an affect upon their world that we have even this fragmentary evidence from "outsiders." Both Tacitus and Josephus point to the survival of the Jesus sect, while the Babylonian Talmud indirectly responds to the competition between the emerging Rabbinic Judaism and fledgling Christianity.

Early Roman Creedal Formulae: late 2nd century — early 3rd century C.E.

When we turn to any possible Christian witness outside of the gospel material, we find that the early Christian creeds give us little more than the stark simplicity of their creedal skeletons. We know only that Jesus was: *crucified under Pontius Pilate and buried.* Hippolytus, in his *Apostolic Tradition* (215 C.E.) inserts *"and died"* after *"Pontius Pilate."*

It should be pointed out that the creedal formulae do not implicate the leaders of the Jews, nor do they elaborate on the circumstances of his death. Even later creedal formulae, which mention a "descent into the underworld" upon Jesus' burial, do not embellish the actual passion sequence.

The Death of Jesus in Q

The Sayings Gospel (Q) understands Jesus as a prophet and man of wisdom. In transmitting in subsequent redactions the wise sayings of Jesus, the Sayings Gospel characterizes Jesus as one of the children of Wisdom (Q Luke 7:34–35). His death is alluded to as one of the many teachers and prophets killed by a faithless people (Q Luke 11:49–50, 51b; 13:34). The death of Jesus in the Sayings Gospel is not a focal point for the community. The words of Jesus form the atmosphere of this early community. One wonders if this emphasis carried forward the tone of the historical Jesus. If the historical Jesus was more attentive to his provocative envisioning, as I have suggested above, then we might see in the Sayings Gospel a continuation of this imaginative enterprise. The assimilation of Jesus under Lady Wisdom's banner may well have been an attempt by the community not only to locate this wise teacher within Israel's traditions but also to make sense of the community's rejection by their own people (Q Luke11:49, 51b). Jesus' death does not seem to have been a major issue for the Sayings Gospel Community. It does receive some explanation, but this may well be due to the community's later experience (Q Luke11:30; 22:28). Evidently the effect of Jesus' words still had strength and currency after his death.

The Gospel of Thomas follows in the Sayings Gospel's momentum. Not only is there no emphasis on the death of Jesus, but there is not even any mention of it. Real life can be attained through insight into the words delivered by the Living One.

Pre-Pauline Traditions

When we turn to the writings of Paul, we become acutely aware that we are in a different historical location. Paul has joined a Hellenized form of the Jesus movement *that had already developed into a Christ cult*. A quantum leap was made from the Jesus movements to the Christ cult. Jesus the itinerant sage had been transformed into a divine figure whose death and resurrection the Hellenistic communities viewed as a saving event. Bultmann's formula that the proclaimer has become the proclaimed does little to assist us in determining how this transition occurred. The mythic language employed by the Christ cult reflects the social formation of a Hellenized Jewish-Gentile mix.

The writings of Paul present us with most of the fragmentary evidence out of which the pre-Pauline situation can be constructed.

The pre-Pauline formulation behind Rom 3:21–26 presupposes a focus upon the death of Jesus as a saving event. The sacrificial language of martyrdom underlies this material. Sam K. Williams argues that the martyr proves his faithfulness to his cause by undergoing trial and death. The "fidelity" (*pistis*) of Jesus in Rom 3:25 refers to the hero's endurance, while the "expiation" refers to the effectiveness of the hero's death. David Seeley, in contrast, would place the emphasis upon the noble death of the martyr rather than on the sacrifice. Essentially Jesus has been cast as one who nobly meets his death for a cause. Pushing these insights further, Burton Mack argues that Jesus' death was seen as a demonstration of Jesus' *pistis* and that all who share such *pistis* were also accepted by God. Jesus dies then for a new cause: for the community of God's justice. The Jewish concern for the justice of God is recast under the image of the noble one who dies for a cause. The story allows all to see how God acknowledges this event as an authentic manifestation of justice. The social experience of the Jesus people provides the basis for this interpretation of the death of Jesus. His death becomes the symbolic linchpin for a mixed association of Jews and Gentiles, enabling this community to bring forward the Jewish traditions without losing the Gentile insertion.

Another example of a pre-Pauline "Anointed" cult is found in Phil 2:6–11. Due to the non-Pauline language found in vv. 6–11, the introductory remark of v. 5, and the concluding connection of v. 12 ("Therefore, my beloved,"), one can easily remove this material from the surrounding exhortatory remarks (vv. 5, 12–13). Yet, although vv. 6–11 can be isolated as a pre-Pauline hymn [vv. 10, 11 ("every knee should bend," "every tongue confess" suggest liturgical actions) numerous debates have been launched over the source, background, structure, redaction, and meaning of the piece. Space does not permit an exposition of the various backgrounds argued for the hymn. The Jewish Wisdom tradition (e.g., Prov. 8–9) may well be the crucible for this material. Indeed, others have suggested more specifically that the suffering servant theme from Second Isaiah or that of the vindication of the suffering righteous one (Wis. Sol. 2–5) may afford the basis for this hymn. Finally, the redeemer myth found throughout the ancient world is also a candidate for providing the imaginative matrix for this piece.

What has often been overlooked in searching for the imaginative realm of this hymn is the propaganda surrounding the character of Alexander the Great. In Plutarch's *On the Fortune of Alexander* 1.8 (330D), Alexander is described as a conqueror quite distinct from all others. "He did not overrun Asia like a thief . . . nor did he consider it something to plunder. . . . " "Because he wanted to show that all things on earth were subject to one principle and one government, that all humans were one people, he conformed himself in such a way." Only his untimely death prevented this utopian vision from becoming a reality. Three points should be made. First, there are telling linguistic similarities between the Philippian hymn and Plutarch's treatment of Alexander. Second, one cannot overlook the historical background of Philippi. Originally named after the father of Alexander the Great, the city was settled by Roman veterans of the Civil Wars and rebuilt in the splendors of Roman fashion. Third, this dream of a civilized society, brought about through the agency of a divine man, remained alive in the Roman propaganda machine. The emperors exploited this lingering hope. The legendary drive of Alexander the Great, refined for the Imperial propaganda machine, has taken another turn through the wisdom speculation of the early Jesus believers.

Analysis of 1 Cor 15:3–5 has led to the conclusion that this material predates Paul. Moreover, the statements about the death of Christ (1 Cor 15:3–4a) are distinct from those about the resurrection/apparitions (1 Cor 15:4b–5). Mack noted that the death statements deliver significance for the community whereas the resurrection/apparition statements refer to Jesus' fate.[2] The fragmentary pre-Pauline material already bears mythic features. 1 Cor 15:3–5 presumes the entitling of Jesus as the Anointed One who dies "according to the writings." Mack has shrewdly noted that, despite a multitude of scholars discerning the probable use of such scriptural citations, allusions, and themes, there is a decided reluctance on the part of many scholars to conclude that the passion narrative was a fictional composition.[3] What few have done is to see that the various scriptural citations and allusions emerging from the developing tradition were formatted into a basic narrative of the tale of the vindicated suffering one.

2. *Myth of Innocence,* p. 104.
3. *Myth of Innocence,* p. 257.

The Tradition of Scriptural Citation: Prophecy historicized

1Corinthians 15:3 furnishes one instance of another tradition arising after the death of Jesus. In this tradition Jewish scriptures are applied to gesture at the fate of Jesus. Besides 1 Cor 15:3, one can point to Mark 14:21, 49; Matt 26:56; Luke 24:26–27; John 19:36; Acts 2:22–36 as indications that the early communities were in the habit of using specific scriptural citations in an attempt to come to grips with the meaning of Jesus' death. The distinction by John Dominic Crossan becomes extremely helpful in reconstructing the historical activity. The early communities were not recalling the "facts" of the death of Jesus. They were about the business of making sense of it. It is not a question of history remembered but of prophecy historicized.

As some of Jesus' followers reflected on the events of the past, they asked themselves why these things had to happen. They became convinced that God had foreordained the events. They began looking for prophecies that would help them understand the social disgrace of the death of Jesus. The use of scriptural citations [Psalms (Pss 2:1,7; 16:8–11; 22:1, 18, 22; 69:21, 30; 110:1; 132:11) and Prophets (Amos 8:9; Isa 50:6, 7; Zech 12:10)] became a shorthand way of dealing with the meaning of Jesus' death. It is important to note that each citation was a creative connection by an anonymous member of the Jesus communities. The death of Jesus was provocative enough to call for a ransacking of the religious memories. In a fashion typical of first century Judaism the unknown followers returned to their basic repertoire: the Jewish Writings. We have seen a comparable activity at Qumran in the Hodayot and Pesharim. The Psalms' staple rhythmic components furnish the themes of persecution (Pss 2:1–2; 22:1–8; 69:20–21) and vindication (Pss 2:7–8; 22:22–24; 69:30–33) for citation. However, it should be understood that there is not as yet a fully developed narrative such as we find later in Peter, Mark, Matthew, Luke and John. An example of how much of the later gospel narrative is indebted to the building blocks of scriptural citations can be found in Mark 14–15, where extensive citation, allusion and characterization through scriptural reference abound.

So far we have seen a number of ways of interpreting the death of Jesus. The Sayings Gospel does not make much of the death of Jesus. There is a different emphasis — words of life. This direction is maintained in the Gospel of Thomas.

In the pre-Pauline material we find the death of Jesus interpreted as the noble death of a martyr, who sacrifices himself for a cause.

In the pre-Pauline hymn of Philippians 2 we can detect the death of Jesus interpreted within the mythic format of a divine figure descending to earth to bring benefits.

The citations of Scripture already in play before the composition of the narrative gospel draw upon the themes of the vindication of a persecuted one as intimated in the Psalms and Prophets.

The Death of Jesus in Paul

Because of the enormous amount of research on Paul's understanding of the death of Jesus it is actually surprising to find out that when one counts the actual number of times Paul mentions the death of Jesus the percentage is strangely quite low. This finding may be surprising on account of the centuries of Christian theological overlay on the authentic letters of Paul. 46 verses refer to death of Jesus in authentic Pauline letters (46 verses out of 1475 vv. — 3.1%).[4] Certainly the death of Jesus was important to Paul. But we must take off our Reformation glasses to perceive what the historical Paul was about when he mentioned or referred to the death of Jesus.

From the actual material in Paul we can say the following. Jesus actually died. This is a given for Paul. Paul takes pains to make sure this is the point in Phil 2:8. Second, Jesus was crucified. But there is nothing beyond the mere mention of crucifixion. The only exception seems to be 1 Cor 2:8, where the "rulers of this age crucified" Jesus. The mythic description points to a theological intent. It does not help identify those responsible. If Paul assumes a Roman execution, then the Roman officials would be understood as "of this age." 1 Thess 2:15 would link the Judeans with the death of Jesus. However, this verse is probably part of an insertion (1 Thess 2:13–16).

Paul used traditions about the death of Jesus, which, as mentioned above, already had been interpreted theologically. Paul continued this

4. Thessalonians 4 vv. out of 85 vv. (4.7%) 1:10; 2:15; 4:14; 5:10. Galatians 7 vv. out of 149 vv. (4.6%) 1:4; 2:19; 2:21; 3:1; 3:13; 6:12; 6:14. 1 Corinthians 11 vv. out of 434 vv. (2.5%) 1:13; 1:17; 1:18; 1:23; 2:2; 2:8; 5:8; 8:11; 11:23; 11:26; 15:3. Philippians 3 vv. out of 104 vv. (2.8%) 2:8; 3:10; 3:18. 2 Corinthians 4 vv. out of 250 vv. (1.6%) 4:10; 5:14; 5:15; 13:4. Philemon 0 v. out of 25 vv. (0%). Romans 17 vv. out of 428 vv. (3.9%) 3:14; 3:25; 5:6–8; 5:10; 6:3; 6:5; 6:6–8; 6:10; 8:32; 8:34; 10:7; 14:9; 15:3.

interpretive tradition, using the earlier images (e.g., Jesus' death as that of a martyr, Rom 3:24–26; Jesus' death as the decisive turning point in a divine descent, Phil 2:6–11). Paul was not interested in any extensive narrative about the death of Jesus. He used earlier terms and images in a rhetorical fashion. The manner of the death of Jesus took on metaphoric and symbolic significance for Paul. Thus, for example, Paul utilized the shameful death of Jesus as a way to understand the new relationship the "gentiles" enjoy with the God of Israel. Gal 3:1–14 is a prime example of how Paul turned the social stigma of Jesus' death into an opening for those who were shamed in the eyes of the people of Israel, namely the subhuman gentiles. The gentiles' limited and failed ("cursed" in the eyes of the tradition) condition had been preempted by God's choice to join the disgrace of Jesus' death.

The social stigma of crucifixion underlies much of Paul's mentioning of the death of Jesus. Paul was not unaware of the social implications of a crucified cult figure. In fact, he played upon this in Gal 3:1–14, 1 Cor 1:18–25 and Rom 5:6–8. He turned a social and political liability into a conduit of benefit and hope. God's solidarity with this social failure, misfit, and disgraced nobody turns the tables against the entire Roman system. (cf. Rom 7–8). The death of Jesus becomes an identification point for those in the empire who yearn for genuine liberation from the devastating power of the imperial pyramid.[5]

The Emergence of a Narrative Structure

We finally come to what many bible readers consider actual reports on the death of Jesus, namely the canonical gospels. The few who are aware of the existence of the fragmentary Gospel of Peter have been discouraged from seeing it as a significant factor in the development of the gospel tradition.[6] Yet a number of observations must be made before we can move on to the narrative gospels in particular.

First, the canonical death stories of Jesus are not simple reports of what happened. Rather, Source, Form and Redaction Criticism have demonstrated they are increasingly complicated narratives con-

5. Dewey, "EIS TEN SPANIAN."
6. Brown, *The Death of the Messiah*, pp. 1317–49

structed to speak to the concerns of the particular first century communities. At best the canonical gospels are indirect witnesses to the historical Jesus. They are historical in so far as they indicate and witness to their communities concerns and questions. Second, we know that there are material relationships among the canonical gospels. The majority of New Testament scholars would accept the historical priority of Mark as well as the independent use of Mark by Matthew and Luke. Members of the Jesus Seminar have gone on record, reaching a consensus by a slim margin that the writer of John knew Mark. They have also concluded that there is only one basic passion narrative behind all the gospel accounts.[7] This judgment is greatly due to what may be the most intriguing aspect to all the passion accounts: one coherent and consecutive story runs through all five versions of the death of Jesus. Such a dramatically similar pattern cannot be accounted for if each writer worked independently of the rest. A subsequent question concerns the direction of the relationships. Which account of the existing five passion narratives was the earliest? We know that Matthew and Luke used Mark. If John knows Mark then it would seem that Mark is the root narrative. Yet, both John Dominic Crossan and I have argued that there is a further nuance to this complicated discussion. The Gospel of Peter may contain the germ of the earliest passion account, which was then used by Mark.

Before we continue discussing the gospel interrelationships, we must not forget that a major watershed was reached either with the first version of Peter or Mark. The citations tradition has given way to a full-blown narrative. What has happened to bring about such an extended story? Second, there is consensus that this structure is of a particular format. The Tale of the Vindicated Sufferer forms the template for all of the passion stories. In this Tale the actions and claims of an innocent person provoke his opponents to conspire against him. This leads to an accusation, trial, condemnation, and ordeal. In some instances this results in his shameful death. The hero of the story reacts characteristically, expressing his innocence, frustration, or trust in prayer, while there are also various reactions to his fate by characters in the tale. Either at the brink of death or in death itself the innocent one is rescued and vindicated. This vindication entails the exaltation and acclamation of the hero as well as the reaction and punishment of his opponents.

7. Funk, *Acts of Jesus.* pp. 246–247

The Earliest Version of Peter: P

The earliest layer (P) of the Gospel of Peter may well have been the mythic construction utilized by the Hellenistic community.[8] The earliest layer of P was fabricated out of biblical citations and set out according to the literary components of the Tale of the Innocent Sufferer.[9] We see the typical components of that tale: condemnation (2.3c), ordeal (3:1,2a), investiture, acclamation (3:2b, 3), ordeal (3:4, 4:1a), reaction (4:1b), acclamation (4:2), reaction (4:3–5), punishment: (5:1a), ordeal (5:2), punishment (5:3,4) prayer (5:5a), rescue (5:5b) vindication (5:6–6:1) reaction/acclamation (8:1b). In contrast to the prevailing style of this tradition (e.g., 2 Macc 7, where specific characters are given for protagonists and antagonists), this story apparently follows more closely the narrative style of the Wisdom of Solomon, where the only one entitled is the "just one", the "son of God." With the use of the title "the Lord" we are only one step removed from reading the story of the righteous one as a type. The midrashic character of the narrative fits very much the situation of a mixed Hellenistic community. There is no assigning of blame for the killing of Jesus to any of the authorities. Rather the "people" are responsible for the death of Jesus. Moreover, the vindication of the victim occurs at death, where the Lord is "taken up." The rhetorical effect of the early fragment is twofold: to convince the audience that the Lord is *dikaios* and the "people" are sinful, yet able to repent. The example of the Lord who is nobly patient to the end delivers narrative proof of his *pistis*.

The heroic allusions we have noted earlier in the early pre-Pauline traditions are becoming fleshed out. The rescue of his spirit by God and the accompanying tremors substantiate the validity of such a virtuous one. Not only is this man sarcastically dubbed a son of God and ironically entitled "King of Israel," but he is declared in the midst of his humiliating ordeal a "savior of humanity." This narrative as such can appeal to two different audiences: Jews and gentiles. By the fact that they would have been carrying the social stigma or blame of inferiority (vis-à-vis the truly human Jews), the gentiles would be able to identify with the victim so humiliated. The Jewish audience would be startled by the role of the "people" in this narrative. The people,

---

8. GP 2:3c–5:1a, 5:2–6:1, 8:1b. Dewey, "Passion Narrative."
9. GPet 3:4, Isa 50:6–7, Zech 12:10; GPet 4:1a, Isa 53:12; GPet 4:1b, Isa 50:7, 53:7; GPet 4:3, Ps 22:18; GPet 5:1, Amos 8:9; GPet 5:2, Ps 69:21; GPet 5:5a, Ps 22:1.

at first caught up in the persecution and execution of the innocent one, are able after decisive signs of divine approval are given to turn in repentance, thereby offering to the audience a model of reconsidering their stance and status. Both sides could identify with the "just one." The midrashic fabulation would create the mythic grounds for a mixed and reconciled association. The title of "Lord" is woven into the narrative threads of the vindicated just one, whose beneficial function for humanity is to unite listeners of the story in a novel association.

The attempt to join a mixed community into a new association is an effort to remove the social stigma and shame that went hand in hand with social negotiation in the first century. The full-bodied telling of the story of the vindicated innocent concretizes the possibility of imaginatively crossing social boundaries first in the narrative and then in social interaction. Those who saw themselves as inferior, within the pyramidal power structure of the Roman world, who were understood as less than human, could see in such constructions a way to reframe *their* existence and future. It was never a question of reporting the story of the death of Jesus. No one was interested in handing on some factual account for posterity. Rather, the construction of the story of the fate of Jesus attempted to breach the *mythoi* that were dominating the social world of the first century.

The Passion Narrative of Mark

The passion narrative of Mark carries the skeletal structure of the Suffering Innocent Tale:

Provocation (11:15–17, 12:1–11; 14:3–9?)
Conspiracy (11:18; 12:12–13; 14:1–2; 14:10–11)
Decision, (14:3–9; 14:35–36; 14:41–42; 14:62?, 15:29–32?)
Trust, (14:35–36),
Obedience, (14:3–109; 14:35–36; 14:62?)
Accusation (14:57–61; 15:2–3)
Trial, (14:53–64; 15:1–15)
Condemnation, (14:64; 15:15)
Protest (Eliminated when accusation is true)
Prayer, (35–36; 15:34)
Assistance (15:9–14; 15:21)
Ordeal, (14:65; 15:16–20; 15:29–30; 15:31–32; 15:36)

Reactions, (14:63; 15:5)
Rescue, (14:62)
Vindication, (12:10–11; 14:62; 15:38; 15:39; 16:4–7)
Exaltation, (14:62; 15:26?)
Investiture, (15:17)
Acclamation, (15:18; 15:26; 15:39)
Reactions, (15:39)
Punishment, (12:9; 12:36; 12:40; 13:2; 14:21; 15:38)

The Gospel of Mark was written soon after the fall of Jerusalem. The Markan community saw themselves as a mixed association who were living dramatically in the last times. The employment of the Suffering Innocent Tale would have been quite understandable to a community that was attempting to reflect on their fate. Mark has linked the death of Jesus with the subsequent fall of Jerusalem (cf. Mark 12:1–11). Now the Tale is retold tying the fate of Jesus to that of his people. He dies a martyr's death on behalf of "many" (14:24). As the story is more finely drawn, lines of loyalty are indicated. Blame begins to take on human features. The leaders of the people figure greatly in the tragic events. We have gone beyond the general critique of the "people" in Peter. The Markan version of the Tale becomes another way of defining the followers of Jesus. In brief, the death story of Jesus was not told to bring the community back to the actual event. Rather, the story is told to make sense of the persecution and deaths experienced by those in the Markan community. They saw that, just as their leader was given up to the demonic powers and was vindicated, they too were to endure tribulation in order to look with hope to their imminent vindication.

The Death Story of Jesus in Matthew

The Gospel of Matthew was written for a Jewish community sometime after the fall of Jerusalem (85 C.E.). As Jews attempted to rebuild after this seismic disaster, two groups remained who contended for determining the future of Israel. While the Pharisees were gathering at Jamnia, recollecting the oral traditions through the composition of the Mishnah, the community of Matthew held that they had the true interpretation of Torah. Jesus the Anointed, the embodiment of God's Wisdom, was the prism through which they interpreted the traditions (5–7; 22:34–40). The Matthean community saw the Pharisees as the primary competition for Jewish leadership. The polemic of Matt 23 comes from that perceived threat.

The death story of Jesus in Matthew is taken principally from its Markan source. Matthew is quite self-conscious of Mark's use of the tale of the suffering innocent one. Indeed, when one inspects the additions Matthew makes to the Markan material, one can see that he intensifies this thematic.

Matthew adds particular material: 26:3, 57 ("palace of Caiaphas"); 26:15 ("30 pieces of silver"); 26:25 ("Judas . . . so"); 26:28c ("for forgiveness of sins"); 26:50 ("Friend . . . "); 26:52–54 ("Put up sword . . . scriptures fulfilled"); 27:3–10 (Death of Judas); 27:19 (Pilate's wife); 27:24–25 (Blood curse); 27:40b, 43 ("Son of God"); 27:51b–53; 27:62–66 (tomb guard). We can observe that Matthew continues to reinforce the elements of the Tale of the suffering innocent one. More characters are introduced as opponents/aids (Caiaphas, Pilate's wife). Further details are given ("palace of Caiaphas," "30 pieces of silver," Judas' death, Pilate's wife's dream). The innocence of Jesus is further underscored (no violence, why Judas dies, the request of Pilate's wife, the blood curse scene [hand washing, irony], the explicit use of "son of God" [cf. Wis Sol]).

A Note on The Blood Curse

Throughout the sad history of Jewish-Christian relations this particular scene has been the basis for enormous damage. People have read this text as literal history, taking it as a theological justification for the persecution and death of Jews. What people have missed is that this is a Matthean addition to underscore Jesus' innocence, capitalizing on the fiction of the suffering innocent one. This scene is historical, however, in the sense that it reflects the concerns of the Matthean community in the last two decades of the first century. The scene tries to argue that the Roman involvement in the death of Jesus was minimal. Here Pilate the procurator declares Jesus is innocent and that, officially, Rome is not involved. Matthew attempts to paint the Jesus movement as unthreatening to the late first century Empire. It wrestles with the haunting memory that the historical Jesus died a Roman death under the more scandalous circumstances

But there is a further nuance to this scene. The blood curse holds a triple irony. First, the people within the narrative do not see themselves at fault. From their perspective they are innocent of this man's blood. But from the Matthean perspective the people unwittingly bring a curse upon themselves for participating in the death of an innocent man. Yet if one recalls Matt 26:28c, where Jesus' blood of the covenant is to be poured out *for the forgiveness of sins,* the people are unwittingly calling for forgiveness. This ironic twist could have been used by the Matthean community to win over unpersuaded fellow Jews to the Jesus cause. Their refusal to accept Jesus could be turned around; his death can become their occasion of God's forgiveness. A third ironic note would be from the perspective of subsequent history: Matthew's attempt at reconciliation was very much an historical failure.

The Lukan Death Story of Jesus

Written towards the end of the first century the Gospel of Luke absorbs the Markan passion structure and delivers a typology of Jesus for the Lukan community to imitate. The death of Jesus is not redemptive (as in Mark); nor is it revelatory (as in John). The death of Jesus becomes a pattern for imitation. Luke presents Jesus as an innocent sufferer par excellence who undergoes the agony of martyrdom.

Luke's insertions (23:6–16; 23:27–32; 23:40–43) into his Markan source provide a constant repetition of the innocence of Jesus during the trial and death scenes. Each addition illustrates Jesus in extremis and yet "in command" of the situation. The martyrdom of Jesus becomes the paradigm for making sense of the ambiguities the community will meet as they continue to exist in the Empire.

The Johannine Intimations

The death of Jesus is the focal point for the Gospel of John. Even before the passion narrative (chaps.18–19) the writer prepares his audience with three passion predictions carrying a distinct nuance. John 3:14, playing upon the image of Moses lifting up the bronze serpent for all to see and be healed, focuses upon the "elevation of the Son of Adam" so that, by believing, people can have real life. In John 8:28 the Johannine Jesus declares that when he is "elevated" people will know that "I Am" (*ego eimi*). The death of Jesus becomes a means of revealing the divine (name). Lastly, in John 12:32–34 Jesus declares that, when elevated, he will be the focal point for all. In sum, instead of predicting the fate of Jesus, the Johannine passion sayings throw the audience forward in anticipation. By the time one comes to the death scene of Jesus the listeners will have been tutored into seeing this death as a revelatory possibility.

The passion narrative in John has been greatly recast by the Fourth Evangelist. One sees this story from an ironic perspective. The dramatically structured trial before Pilate, the crucifixion and death, and the events immediately following Jesus' last breath, demand a perspective that has already been gained from experience with the first part of the gospel.

The attentive reader begins to hear these scenes within the earlier overtures. The death of Jesus is not redemptive, not a martyr's scene. It is the epiphany that had long been intimated.

If the historicizing of prophecy was the earliest layer of the tradition concerning the death of Jesus and, if this prophetic tradition was formatted into an extended narrative through the genre of the Suffering and Vindication of the Innocent One, then what we find, for example, in John 19:31–37 is a further layer of this creative work. Here we can see how the use of scripture is connected to the developing narrative tradition, thereby augmenting it and causing further interpretive growth. V.35 is a later (and distinctly Johannine) insertion into a scene that had been generated from the scriptural quotation (and thus, in keeping with the historicizing of prophecy). The bone-breaking scene in Peter may have had a scriptural basis (Ps 34:20). The water and blood, on the other hand, may be John's creation, perhaps reflecting the community's prior reflection on the paschal lamb and Zechariah (cf. Zech 12:10). Such an abbreviated analysis does little justice to the involved weaving of the Fourth Evangelist's imagination. Each scene is constructed to bring the hearer of the story in direct confrontation with the Word. With the Fourth Gospel one never really leaves the foot of the cross. Every reading becomes a possible realization of the revelation of the One who so loved the universe.

The Matter of Imagination

From the evidence that we have considered it is clear that the traditions about the death of Jesus are hardly monolithic. The death of Jesus tradition is marked by constant reinterpretation. Frankly stated, the death of Jesus was left to the imaginations of the various Jesus communities. In using our historical imagination we have been concerned to respect the texture of the evidence. The literary clues and structures, as well as the probable historical situations for the particular texts, have given us much to sort out. What becomes painfully clear is that none of the traditions is really interested in our historical investigation. They were not referring to the death of Jesus or telling an extended story in order to return to "that point in time." Rather, in a fashion typical of an oral culture, they spoke of the death of Jesus to bring it forward into their lives. In other words, their experience, their imaginative resources, and their dreams filled in the gaps in their stories. This paper has indicated how diverse and imaginative these retellings were. We shall be continually frustrated to get behind these formats to what actually happened. Instead of consulting accurate reports, we find ourselves nibbling at the margins of the fragmentary evidence. In order to discern what might have happened we have to use our historical imaginations to construct reasonable scenarios. However, we cannot fall prey to the "plausibility syndrome." We cannot go so quickly from "it is likely" to "it was thus." Instead, we must not only recognize the historical gaps but also refuse to make the unknown unwittingly into our own image.

The Jesus Seminar concluded most overwhelmingly that Jesus of Nazareth was executed by the Romans.[10] Despite their consensus that Jewish authorities were somehow involved in the death of Jesus, the Seminar did not see any basis for a Jewish trial. Indeed, the trial before Pilate was considered too intentionally fabricated. Further, the seminar concluded that detailed information about the crucifixion of Jesus is derived from prophecy historicized. What actually happened to Jesus, when Roman authorities took him, can only be imaginatively surmised. We are left with reviewing the information available from the first century. We can hazard educated guesses as to what might have occurred. But we must be clear – these are studies in plausibility.

In the paper I presented last fall on Christology, I argued that Christology is not really about Jesus.[11] I would now add that the death of Jesus tradition is not about the death of Jesus. The historical investigation shows that the telling of the stories of the death of Jesus is very much a way for those first century communities to gain a sense of meaning within the jeopardy of their existence. At each level we

10. Funk, *Acts of Jesus*. p. 133.
11. Dewey, "Some ragged lines."

can see human beings choosing to create meaning in the face of extremity. Such constructions were not attempts at distancing Jesus from the community. Rather, he was given distinctive titles and his death was seen as heroic, redemptive, revelatory, etc., precisely for the sake of the "people."

We cannot, however, simply duplicate this tradition of construction. There are many today who would simply wish to maintain the "traditional ways" without the bother of any historical work. But such a position avoids the realization that all of the images and structures employed to speak of the death of Jesus were culturally embedded. This means that we cannot overlook the historical forces in which these images and structures had their play. The sacrificial model, for example, which we found in the pre-Pauline tradition, was not isolated from its culture. Noble sacrifice was but one facet of a society built upon the system of domination. To continue to speak of the "virtue" of sacrifice without any sensitivity to a society, which demanded the sacrifice of life for its maintenance, may well mean a fundamental misreading of the evidence. Indeed, to carry this image forward uncritically may actually support the domination model, which the image originally was constructed to dethrone. Certainly, the conditions of social stigma and shame have to be understood in order to see the creative move by Paul in Gal 3, as he magically turns a disgraceful memory into a promising situation. Additionally, the emergence of the Tale of the Innocent Sufferer cannot be understood without a realization that this story form emerges from the Jewish psyche at moments of seemingly great injustice. The Tale is not told to reiterate an "old saw" but to engage in the quest for justice. Once we begin to see this then we can follow up the trail of the Suffering Innocent Tale. The saddest commentary on this death story tradition is that the canonical versions were eventually used to kill innocents. Pogroms were engendered from sermons enkindled by these narratives. More immediately in regard to the evidence at hand, we can further ask whether the concern for God's justice becomes muted as the tradition progresses even through the gospels. Has the writer of John, for instance, relinquished that justice concern, or has the confrontation with Reality taken a different tack?

Such a line of investigation inevitably brings up the charge that all such critical work intends the unraveling of Christianity. Will not these critical "deregulations" come at too high a price for the religious consumer? But that objection keeps the pressure off those holding teaching authority within the various Christian churches. Why have they not provided the conditions of growth by educating the "faithful" into maturity, into understanding their lives within the world? Why are the bible readers not ready to embark on an honest historical quest?

Some scholars recently have tried to bring some sanity back to the historical debate.

Ehrman and Wright (Veitch) have recycled the Apocalyptic Jesus of Schweitzer. Now from the findings of the Jesus Seminar it is quite dubious that Jesus was an apocalyptic thinker. Yet, this apocalyptic scenario, wherein a wild-eyed Jesus attempted to precipitate the final breakthrough of God by his death, brings with it an oddly comforting note. For Wright the traditional constructions of the churches are maintained. But for Ehrman Jesus the visionary was a failure. One need not, then, be worried over this lost apocalyptic game plan. It is enough to carry on ethically in a radically different world.

Such apocalyptic scenarios are founded on the notion that Jesus was curiously unique. His death can be explained away as a failed religious coup d'état. The response by both the Roman and Jewish authorities fits nicely in the plausibly constructed scenario of Jesus' "last days." The apocalyptic Jesus is a rarity, almost of necessity distant from the rest of humanity. But what happens when we cannot justify the Roman and Jewish reaction to this peasant wordsmythe? How certain can we be in drawing straight lines between apparently connecting points? What do we say when we simply do not know what happened? Can we allow this?

We come at last to where we began. We become aware that our historical task is a matter of imagination. But the way in which we imagine the death of Jesus can be used as a cover up, a way to avoid our mortality, our temporality. We fear the erosion of the triumphal arch of our own imaginations. Yet, I would contend that the early Jesus believers did not avoid the issue. As soon as we place their discourse within its historical context we see that, for all its limitations, it became a diversified language of engagement. On the other hand, a decontextualized usage of the same language today would be an exercise in escapism. We need to recall that these ways of speaking were constructed to provide a living space for those in the Empire who were "nobodies." Just as the Viet Nam War Memorial in Washington, D.C. provides a graphic space for people to come to grips with the tragedy of that desperate War, so too the various ways of talking of the death of Jesus became public spaces in which the early Jesus believers had a chance to come alive.

But the act of coming alive occurs amid the images of death. Each way of speaking of the death of Jesus, as we mentioned, has its historical limitations. But there is more. In speaking of the death of Jesus in particular ways, the early believers are exposing the very forces of their society, which contributed to Jesus' death. The very fact that we really do not know the specifics of the death of Jesus reveals volumes regarding the fate of "nobodies" in a domination system. The whole point of their liquidation is that nothing can be said of them. The system has spoken and silenced them forever. It is against this harsh political reality that we should gauge what fragments we possess from the first century. To assume that we know the "whole story" from an uncritical reading of the canonical gospels may well be a refusal to see the larger social picture.

It is crucial to see that this investigation does not conclude that there is only one model for understanding the death of Jesus. Recently theological writers from non-Western countries have begun seeing the connection of the "suffering servant" and the "crucified people" around the world. They have begun to see how the death of Jesus relates more directly to the exploited conditions of the oppressed. They have become critical of the classic Christology, which keeps Jesus aloof from the daily death of men and women.

The variety of ways in which the Jesus believers of the first century remembered is quite telling. There should have been silence (at least from the Roman perspective). The disturbance — even a minor fleabite — should have been settled. Instead, we see a vocabulary of resistance developing over time and space. The violence perpetrated came back to haunt the tenement houses of the Empire. But with a twist. The lost one, the zero, became a point of identification. Something human was detected in the very midst of the forces of domination and dissolution. The citations whispered as scrolls were unrolled turned into magnified tales. The voice considered silenced gained new strength and new legs. Jesus' death was left to the imaginations of the early Jesus believers. They filled in the gaps with their hopes and their fears. This was not living vicariously. The death of Jesus was not a substitute for their genuine commitment to their life together. Rather, it was an occasion for coming to life.

Today the death of Jesus has been left to our historical imagination, to our hopes and our fears. The historical Jesus is still at the mercy of those who would remember him. Are we able to get near to those human remains beyond the outmoded imaginations of the past? Or will we avoid the fragmented evidence? Can we quiet the ravings of our dogmatic power plays and religious goose-stepping? Can we go about the human task of picking up the fragments? Can we make out some human lines despite our primordial match with death, where deals are made to gain some shred of illusory control? Can we get beyond that constant temptation to barter away our humanity out of fear? Can we see through that alienating tension, where we have surrendered to the forces that impinge upon us in order to achieve a modicum of control? Can we learn to resist the need to play the heavenly ventriloquist? Can we give up the fixation with a dictating voice and recognize that we are the only ones making choices in the face of extremity? Can we finally grow up and act like hospice workers, those midwives of the end of life, patiently attending to the barely audible human struggle? Can we give up wanting to turn the death of Jesus into more than a human affair? Can we, at last, let Jesus die?

Works Consulted

Brown, Raymond E. *The Death of the Messiah*. Vols.1–2. New York: Doubleday. 1993.

Crossan, John Dominic. *Who Killed Jesus? Exposing the Roots of Anti-Semitism in the Gospel Story of the Death of Jesus*. San Francisco: Harper. 1995

Dewey, Arthur J. "EIS TEN SPANIAN: The Future and Paul," in *Religious Propaganda and Missionary Competition in the New Testament World*, eds., Lukas Bormann, Kelly Del Tredici, Angela Standhartinger. Leiden: Brill, 1994. 321–349

_____. "Jesus as . . . What, Exactly?" *The Harvard Divinity Bulletin*. 29(2000) 1. 25–27. Review of Bart Ehrman's *Jesus, Apocalyptic Prophet of the New Millennium* and Paula Fredriksen's *Jesus of Nazareth, King of the Jews*.

_____. "The Passion Narrative of the Gospel of Peter" **Forum** (new series) 1,1 (1998) 53–69.

_____. *Proclamation 6, Series B, Advent Christmas*. Minneapolis: Fortress.1996. 62–63.

_____. "Some ragged lines: From Christology to Christopoetics," **Seminar Papers**. Westar Institute Fall 2000 Meeting. Santa Rosa, CA. 1–9.

Dillenberger, Jane Daggett. *The Religious Art of Andy Warhol*. New York: Continuum. 1998.

Ellacuria, Ignacio. "The Crucified People," *Mysterium Liberationis* (Maryknoll, N.Y.:Orbis Books. 1993. 580–604.

Funk, Robert W., Roy W. Hoover and the Jesus Seminar. *The Five Gospels*. New York: MacMillan. 1993.

Funk, Robert W. and the Jesus Seminar. *The Acts of Jesus: What Did Jesus Really Do?* San Francisco: HarperCollins. 1998.

Georgi, Dieter. *Theocracy: in Paul's Praxis and Theology*. Minneapolis: Fortress. 1991.

Hammarskjold, Dag. *Markings*. New York: Ballantine. 1991.

Koyama, Kosoke. "The Crucified Christ Challenges Human Power," & Chung Hyun Kyung, "Who is Jesus for Asian Women?" in *Asian Faces of Jesus*. ed., R. S. Sugirtharajah. Maryknoll, N.Y.: Orbis Books. 156, 224

Mack, Burton L. *A Myth of Innocence*. Philadelphia: Fortress Press. 1988.

Nickelsburg, George W. E., *Resurrection, Immortality, and Eternal Life in Intertestamental Judaism*. Cambridge: Harvard Theological Studies. 1972;

_____. "The Genre and Function of the Markan Passion Narrative," *Harvard Theological Review* 73 (1980) 153–80

Seeley, David. "The Concept of the Noble Death in Paul." Ph.D. diss., Claremont Graduate School. 1987.

Veitch, James. "Patrolling the Right Path," *Forum*. New Series. 1.2 (1998) 349–385.

Waliggo, John M. "African Christology in a Situation of Suffering," *Faces of Jesus in Africa.*, ed. Robert Schreiter. Maryknoll, N.Y.:Orbis Books. 1995. 164–180.

Williams, Sam K. *Jesus' Death as Saving Event: The Background and Origin of a Concept*. Missoula. Scholars Press. 1975.

White, John. *The Apostle of God*. Peabody: Hendrickson Publishers. 1999.

Consider Yourself Dead

On the Martyrological Understanding of Jesus' Death

Stephen J. Patterson

If any want to become my followers, let them deny themselves and take up their cross and follow me.

— Mark 8:34

In our current work in the Jesus Seminar we are presently occupied with the question of how one might legitimately begin to make meaning from the history and tradition we have exposed and clarified in the first phase of our work. Part of this current work should give attention to the ways in which early Christians themselves began to construct meaning around what they had experienced in connection with Jesus: his words, his deeds, and his fate. The present essay is so focused. It is concerned in particular with Jesus' fate: his death as a victim of Roman imperial justice, and how his followers began to think of this very ignoble death as meaningful after all — even noble. They did so, of course, by drawing on the cultural resources available to them from the complex Hellenistic and Jewish culture in which they lived. This was not the first time Jewish comrades had seen one of their own die at the hands of the enemy; it was not the first time they had seen someone killed in the struggle for some counter-cultural cause. They knew what a dissident was. They knew what a martyr was. The Hellenistic Jewish tradition was rich with images and models for how to live, and die, in faithfulness to God, even in the face of brutal foreign oppression and humiliation. It is with this tradition that I shall begin.

The Death of God's Righteous One

In the period of Christian origins a number of popular stories — some of them very ancient — circulated among the Jews, which focused on

Jewish heroes living in the court of a foreign ruler.[1] In these "court tales" the hero, caught in the web of foreign rule, must decide between bowing to the wishes of the heathen king or remaining faithful to the God of the Jews. The legends surrounding Daniel, Susanna, Esther, the Maccabees all unfold in just this way. These great heroes of the Jewish people all faced great danger, torture, even death, but in the end, remained faithful to God against the tyrant king.

Understandably, such stories were very popular among Jews living under Roman rule. The example of their heroes was meant to inspire faithfulness and to strengthen Jews against the betrayal of their tradition. In his study of these court tales, George Nickelsburg was able to identify a set of themes, or plot, common to many of them.[2] Together they create the basis of a genre of story Nickelsburg called "The Story of the Persecution and Exaltation of the Righteous Man." In this generic story line, the hero becomes the victim of provocation and conspiracy. Eventually he or she must decide between obedience to God and giving in to the demands of a foreign ruler. The hero trusts God, is obedient, but must as a consequence suffer persecution, slander, false accusation, trial, and ultimately condemnation. But this is not the end. It is God who owns the final word. The hero is rescued and redeemed, and in the end, vindicated against his or her enemies. Finally the hero is exalted and made an example for all to see and — presumably — to imitate.

This pattern was not limited to works of narrative fiction and martyrology. One finds it in the more poetic wisdom literature of the period as well. The martyrs had a lesson to teach, and it was taught in hymns, poetry, and classroom literature. One of the most compelling presentations of this idea of the suffering righteous one is found in a Jewish work from the First Century, B.C.E., the Wisdom of Solomon. In the following excerpt the author gives voice to the thoughts of the wicked who would oppress God's righteous one:

Let us lie in wait for the righteous man,
    because he is inconvenient to us and opposes our actions;

---

1. For discussion, see Lawrence M. Wills, *The Jew in the Court of the Foreign King*.
2. G. W. E. Nickelsburg, *Resurrection, Immortality, and Eternal Life*, esp. pp. 48–62.

He reproaches us for sins against the law,
and accuses us of sins against our training.
He professes to have knowledge of God,
and calls himself a child of the Lord.
He became to us a reproof of our thoughts;
the very sight of him is a burden to us,
because his manner of life is not like that of others,
and his ways are strange.
We are considered by him as something base,
and he avoids our ways as unclean;
he calls the last end of the righteous happy,
and boasts that God is his father.
Let us see if his words are true,
and let us test what will happen at the end of his life;
for if the righteous man is God's child, he will help him,
and will deliver him from the hand of his adversaries.
Let us test him with insult and torture,
so that we may find out how gentle he is,
and make trial of his forbearance.
Let us condemn him to a shameful death,
for, according to what he says, he will be protected.

(Wisdom of Solomon 2:12–20)

So plots the wicked against God's righteous one. But it is to no avail.
In the next chapter, there is redemption:

But the souls of the righteous are in the hand of God,
and no torment will ever touch them.
In the eyes of the foolish they seem to have died,
and their departure was thought to be a disaster,and their
going from us thought to be their destruction;
but they are at peace.
For though in the sight of others they were punished,
their hope is full of immortality.
Having been disciplined a little, they will receive great good,
because God tested them and found them worthy of himself;
like gold in the furnace he tried them,
like a sacrificial burnt offering he accepted them.
In the time of their visitation they will shine forth,
and will run like sparks through the stubble.

They will govern nations and rule over peoples,
    and the Lord will reign over them forever.
Those who trust in him will understand truth,
    and the faithful will abide with him in love,
        because grace and mercy are upon the holy ones,
        and he watches over the elect.

(Wisdom of Solomon 3:1–9)

When Christians first began to formulate their convictions about Jesus in light of his death, texts and traditions such as this one became very important. They gave the followers of Jesus a framework for understanding his fate. Like God's righteous servant, Jesus came to be seen as the target of enemies who conspired against him. He irritated his opponents, accusing them of transgressing against the law, and of hypocrisy. He claimed to know God, to be a servant of God. His words and deeds were an offense, his manner of life strange. He boasted that God was his father. In the end, his enemies captured him, and subjected him to the most shameful death. But he was not lost, ultimately. God redeemed him, accepted him like a sacrificial burnt offering. One day, they hoped, he would return to rule the nations of the earth. In the mean time, those who trust in God know the truth, and they abide in his love.

Christians did not arrive at these ideas from out of the blue. Nor did they derive naturally from the events of Jesus' life. They were the product of thinking about his life in light of the Jewish tradition of God's suffering righteous ones. Certain aspects of his life — his counter-cultural lifestyle, for example — could take on special significance and become meaningful in new ways when viewed through the lens of this tradition. His shameful death was no longer a disaster, but could be seen as the expected fate of one who remained true to God in the face of wicked adversaries. And his followers could see the cross as a powerful moment of witness, but not the end of Jesus' mission. Christians could hope for a new day, when Jesus would finally be vindicated before his enemies.

The Passion Narrative and the Wisdom Tale

Among the first written attempts to account for what had happened to Jesus was the story of his final days, his trial, and death, known as the Passion Narrative. This is the source that many believe was used by the writers of Mark and John, and perhaps also another fragmentary gospel, the Gospel of Peter, to give account of Jesus' death.[3] Not surprisingly, when Nickelsburg looked at the Passion Narrative against the backdrop of the Wisdom Tale, he found that the parallels were extensive.[4] In fact, he could argue that it was this old Jewish tale of suffering and vindication that gave the Passion Narrative its basic plot and structure. The chart in Figure 1, p. 166, adapted from Nickelsburg's study, and incorporating additions from Burton Mack's similar treatment,[5] makes it possible to see how extensive the parallels are.

Nickelsburg's quite plausible theory of how his "Wisdom Tale" gave rise to the story contained in the Passion Narrative serves, of course, to underscore what we have said throughout our work: the gospels and their sources are not historical archives. Committing to memory the things that took place, exactly as they took place, was not the task early Christians found laid at their feet in the years following Jesus' death. What was absolutely imperative for their own survival as a community was the task of discerning meaning in the life and death of the one who had brought them together in the first place. The writer responsible for the Passion Narrative did not begin with the question, "What really happened?" Whether he knew the details of Jesus' final days or not, he surely knew enough: that the one in whom they had come to believe was now dead, shamefully executed on a Roman cross. Beyond this, any further historical detail

---

3. The existence of a pre-Markan passion narrative is to be sure a fractious debate not to be settled here. For an informative, if tendentious discussion, see Burton L. Mack, *A Myth of Innocence*, pp. 249–68. Mack notes well the troubling apologetic interests involved in the quest for a pre-Markan Passion Narrative as an historically reliable account of Jesus' final days. Yet, Mack's conclusion, drawn from the work of Werner Kelber, et al. in *The Passion in Mark*, that Mark created the passion sequence on his own is unsatisfactory since it necessitates the dependence of the Gospel of John and the Gospel of Peter on Mark for the episodes they all share in common, something I find unlikely. Consequently, I would continue to foster the theory of a pre-Markan Passion Narrative, but without the usual accompanying assumption of its basic historicity. The *fictional* work Mack and others ascribe to Mark must simply be moved back to a pre-Markan stage.

4. "The Genre and Function of the Markan Passion Narrative," pp. 153–84. Nickelsburg's treatment is the most elegant, but his insights about the use of the tradition of the suffering righteous one were anticipated by several, including C. H. Dodd, *According to the Scriptures,* Barnabas Lindars, *New Testament Apologetic,* Eta Linnemann, *Studien zur Passionsgeschichte.* Detlev Dormeyer's study, *Die Passion Jesu als Verhaltensmodell,* adds independent weight to the discussion.

5. Mack, *A Myth of Innocence*, p. 267.

would be utterly superfluous. The important question was not what really happened. The question — the truly important question — was now, "Were we right about him or not?" "Were we right to follow him?" "Was his cause just?"

The writer of the Passion Narrative had somehow answered these soul-searching questions with "yes." He had come to believe that Jesus was not a criminal; nor was he simply a victim. He was one of God's righteous ones, who died true to his convictions. And so he wrote the story of Jesus' final days as the story of God's persecuted

---

Figure 1
Stories of Persecution and Vindication
And the Passion Narrative (as used by Mark)
( ) = items out of sequence

Elements of Nickelsburg's *Wisdom Tale*	In the Passion Narrative *(as used by Mark)*
Provocation	Mark 11:15–17
Conspiracy	Mark 11:18; 14:1
Decision	Mark 14:3–9; 35–36; 41–42
Trust	Mark 14:35–36
Obedience	Mark 14:3–9; 35–36
Accusation	Mark 14:57–61
Trial	Mark 14:53–64
Condemnation	Mark 14:64
Protest	
Prayer	Mark 14:35–36
Assistance	
Ordeal	Mark 15:29–30
Reaction	(Mark 14:63)
Rescue	(Mark 14:62)
Vindication	Mark 15:38
Exaltation	(Mark 14:62)
Investiture	
Acclamation	Mark 15:39
Reactions	Mark 15:39
Punishment	(Mark 15:38)

righteous one. For Christians, Jesus would become the preeminent suffering righteous one. His faithfulness and obedience would become a witness to the value of his cause, and an example for anyone willing to take up the cross as their own fate.

A Noble Death

These ideas about death and persecution were not unique to Jewish culture in the period of Christian origins. They were part of a broader cultural view of what constitutes a meaningful death in the Hellenistic world. To die nobly for a cause, to remain true to one's principles to the very end — this was a time honored ideal in Hellenistic culture generally speaking. In this period popular philosophers were forever discussing death, and how to face it with equanimity and courage without compromising one's convictions.[6]

The most illustrious example of one who had died thus was, of course, Socrates. Who can forget one of the most memorable scenes in all of literature, the death of Socrates, recounted in Plato's Phaedo. Socrates, already condemned for impiety and corrupting the young men of Athens, is met by his disciples one last time before he must die. As they arrive at the prison, he is just being released from his chains, for this is to be the day of his execution. As they enter the prison, his wife, Xanthippe, bursts into tears at the sight of them. Socrates, nobly, asks his disciple Crito to see to her needs as she is lead away, baby in her arms. At length he discourses with his disciples: on how to endure pain and suffering; on how to face death; and on the nature of the world. Finally, when he has finished, Crito asks: "And have you any commands for us, Socrates . . . ?" He replies:

> If you take care of yourselves you will serve me and mine and yourselves, whatever you do, even if you make no promises now; but if you neglect yourselves and are not willing to live following step by step, as it were, in the path marked out by our present and past discussions, you will accomplish nothing, no matter how much or how eagerly you promise at present."[7]

6. Among recent treatments of the Noble Death tradition and its significance for understanding the New Testament are those by David Seeley, *The Noble Death*, and by Arthur J. Droge and James D. Tabor, *A Noble Death*. Earlier, see Martin Hengel, *The Atonement,* pp. 1–32. All have proven invaluable in formulating the ideas in this essay.

7. Phaedo 115b–c (LCL).

At last Socrates drinks the hemlock, and dies, in peace, true to his principles to the very end.

This was the paradigmatic noble death, the death of Socrates, who was "of all those of his time . . . the best and wisest and most righteous man," says Phaedo.[8]

> Both in his bearing and his words, he was meeting death so fearlessly and nobly. And so I thought that even in going to the abode of the dead he was not going without the protection of the gods, and that when he arrived there it would be well with him, if it ever was well with anyone. And for this reason I was not at all filled with pity, as might seem natural when I was present at a scene of mourning.[9]

Plato's masterful depiction of Socrates' death was not meant to evoke pity or regret. His death was a witness — a martyr's death. In it we are to see how one might die nobly. Indeed, says Socrates, "is not [philosophy] the practice of death?"[10] Perhaps not always. But when your convictions place you in harm's way, the philosopher's highest calling is to die nobly, true to one's principles.

At least this is how the death of Socrates was appropriated in the Hellenistic philosophical tradition. In the first century C.E. the problem of death, and how to face it with dignity, was ubiquitous in philosophical discourse. This is perhaps understandable. Rome's Empire was totalitarian. It could not tolerate dissent. And the philosophers often dissented. Then, indeed, philosophy was the practice of death. Many faced the choice that Socrates had faced: to live in compromise or to die with honor. For such folk, Socrates became a martyr, a model. The first-century Cynic philosopher, Epictetus, writes:

> Socrates does not save his life with [the] dishonor [of escaping death by compromising his principles], the man who refused to put the vote when the Athenians demanded it of him, the man who despised the tyrants, the man who held such noble discourse about virtue and moral excellence; this man it is

8. Phaedo 118a (LCL).
9. Phaedo 58e–59a (LCL).
10. Phaedo 80e–81a (LCL).

impossible to save by dishonor, but he is saved by death, and not by flight.[11]

Here death is not a disaster, an ending. It is salvation. Death in this tradition is transformed from defeat into victory. In fact, a noble death may become the capstone to a well-led life, one that transforms that life and makes it ultimately more useful to others. Epictetus continues:

> . . . if we had been useful in our way of living, would we not have been much more useful to people by dying when it was necessary and in the manner called for? And now that Socrates is dead, the memory of him is no less useful to people. In fact, it is perhaps even more useful than what he did or said while he stilled lived.[12]

For Epictetus, death was not the end of Socrates and his benefits for humankind. To the contrary, his manner of death transformed him into something more than what he had been in life.

The idea of dying nobly, with unflinching bravery and loyalty was not limited to the philosophers. It was a standard theme in stories of military heroes, or anyone who was called upon the face death with dignity. It appears again and again, for example, in the tragedies of Euripides, as the ideal way for one to face whatever the gods might ordain, including and especially death. In his study of the Noble Death tradition in Hellenistic literature, David Seeley identifies five key ideas that usually appear in various discussions and depictions of the noble death of individuals whose lives are seen as exemplary:[13] 1) The one who dies nobly dies in *obedience* to his or her principles, or often, to some higher (divine) calling or mandate. 2) In doing so, the hero demonstrates how to *overcome physical vulnerability*, to face torture and death without fear. 3) The standoff with the hero often involves a *military setting* — loyalty is often at stake. 4) Such a death is often seen as *vicarious* for others insofar as it may be imitated. Vicariousness comes through mimesis in this tradition. 5) Finally, there are often *sacrificial overtones* as the death of the hero is described and interpreted.

---

11. Discourses IV.1,164–65 (LCL).
12. Epictetus, *Discourses* IV. 1. 168–69; LCL alt.
13. Seeley, *The Noble Death*, pp. 13, 83, 87–99, et passim.

The idea of the Noble Death influenced Jewish writers of this period as well. Jews had their own heroes who had died true to their principles. Perhaps the best example of the idea of the noble death in Jewish literature is to be found in the book known as Fourth Maccabees, a Hellenistic Jewish work written in the period of Christian origins, probably in Antioch — a city of much Christian activity, where Paul spent of good deal of time early in his ministry. Ostensibly, the book is a defense of the idea that reason — i.e., "the mind making the deliberate choice of the life of wisdom" (1:15) — can rule over the bodily passions. To prove the point, the author takes the example of an aged priest, Eleazar, seven pious brothers, and their mother, all of whom were tortured to death during the Jewish struggle for freedom against Antiochus IV Epiphanes in the Second Century, B.C.E. In spite of their gruesome ordeal, these martyrs all remained faithful to God. Their noble deaths two centuries earlier, became an inspiration for Jews living under Roman rule, who faced many of the same challenges their ancestors had faced under Antiochus.

In Fourth Maccabees one may clearly see the marks of the Noble Death tradition, as described by Seeley.[14] The story unfolds in the context of a war — thus the *military setting*. The overarching theme of Fourth Maccabees is, of course, *obedience*. As the torturer stokes the fires that will soon sear his flesh, the elderly Eleazar takes his stand:

> We, Antiochus, who firmly believe that we must lead our lives
> in accordance with the divine Law, consider that no compul-
> sion laid on us is mighty enough to overcome our own willing
> obedience to the Law. (5:16)

Eleazar may speak with such confidence because in his resolve, he has *overcome* the sense of *physical vulnerability* that might cause him, out of fear, to capitulate to the Tyrant's demands. He mocks Antiochus and his threats of torture:

> I will not violate the solemn oaths of my ancestors to keep the
> Law, not even if you gouge out my eyes and burn my entrails.
> I am neither so old nor short of manliness that in the matter

---

14. Seeley's analysis of Fourth Maccabees is most helpful: *The Noble Death*, pp. 92–99.

of religion my reason should lose its youthful vigor. So set the torturer's wheel turning and fan the fire to a great blaze. I am not so sorry for my old age as to become responsible for breaking the Law of my fathers. I will not play you false, O Law, my teacher; I will not forswear you, beloved self-control; I will not shame you, philosophic reason, nor will I deny you, venerable priesthood and knowledge of the Law. (5:28–36)

And so the ordeal begins, described in graphic detail by the author for his enrapt audience. Eleazar is stripped and scourged, and abused by his torturers. His friends try to offer him a way out. "Just pretend to taste the swine's flesh," they counsel. But he refuses. The death he dies is not a private, solitary act. It is public, a witness to others. He will not "become a model of impiety to the young by setting them an example of eating unclean food." In this sense his death is *vicarious*, 'for others': it gives others an example to emulate. "Therefore, O children of Abraham, you must die nobly for piety's sake." (6:22)

And so the torture continues: Eleazar is branded; an "evil-smelling concoction" is poured in his nose; he is thrown into the fire itself. At last, as he about to expire, he lifts his eyes to God and prays:

> You know, O God, that though I could have saved myself I am dying in these fiery torments for the sake of the Law. Be merciful to your people and let our punishment be a satisfaction on their behalf. Make my blood their purification and take my life as a ransom for theirs. (6:28–29)

Thus, Eleazar's death becomes vicarious in another way: it is a *sacrifice* for the purification of the land.

Obedient Unto Death

The idea of the Noble Death was a common one in the culture of Hellenism, and in the Hellenistic Judaism that emerged in the period of Christian origins. It may have been particularly strong in the city of Antioch, the home of a shrine to the Maccabean martyrs. Antioch was also the first mission field of Paul the Apostle. And it may have been the home of the gospel writers responsible for the Gospel of Mark and the Gospel of John. It is therefore not at all surprising to find many of the ideas associated with martyrdom and the Noble Death tradition in the literature of early Christianity. Jesus was tortured to death by an Empire that Christians regarded as tyrannical. This made the tradition of the Noble Death relevant. When one examines how the death of Jesus is treated in the texts and traditions that emerge, especially from Antiochene Christian circles, one sees immediately the profound influence of the Noble Death.

Let us begin with Paul. He, more than any other early Christian missionary, is usually credited with the most active and imaginative interpretive effort in presenting Jesus, the crucified Messiah, to the wider Hellenistic world. But when Paul began to develop his characteristic preaching, he did not begin from scratch. He came into the Christian movement relatively late, when many traditions had already been formulated. Some of these traditions he would have encountered first in Antioch.

One of the earliest pieces of Christian tradition we can lay our hands on is a hymn to Christ that Paul quotes in one of his letters, to the Philippians. It is a complex hymn, blending ideas of the Hebrew prophets, language from the Roman imperial cult, and the mythic pattern of the descending/ascending redeemer known from many Ancient Near Eastern religions.[15] But at the very center of this hymn is a single line — perhaps the only clearly Christian contribution to the hymn at all — in which we find that central theme of the martyrological tradition: obedience:

> Who, though he was in the form of God,
> did not count equality with God a thing to be grasped,
> but emptied himself, taking the form of a slave,
> being born in human likeness,
> *And being found in human form he humbled himself*
> *and became obedient unto death, even death on a cross.*
> Therefore God has highly exalted him
> and bestowed on him the name which is above every name,
> that at the name of Jesus every knee should bow,
> in heaven and on earth and under earth,
> and every tongue confess that Jesus Christ is Lord,
> to the glory of God the Father.
>
> (Phil 2:6–11, emphasis mine)

---

15. See David Seeley's insightful analysis in "The Background of the Philippians Hymn (2:6–11)," pp. 49–72.

Paul dictated this traditional hymn into a letter he was writing from a Roman prison cell, probably in Ephesus. He is in trouble, again. This time, he does not know whether he will live or die. And now he has received word from Philippi, that the church he founded there is in trouble too. They have sent word to him, inquiring: what does this mean that you are in prison and we suffer here in Philippi? Perhaps some have raised questions about his credibility: how can a true apostle get into so much trouble (see 1:15–18)? But Paul does not see his current troubles as a mark against him. Rather, they are his opportunity to bear witness to the cause of Christ. Thus Paul addresses the Philippians in terms that should by now be familiar:

> I know that through your prayers and the help of the Spirit of Jesus Christ this will turn out for my deliverance, as it is my eager expectation and hope that I shall not be at all ashamed, but that with full courage now as always Christ will be honored in my body, whether by life or by death. For to me to live is Christ, and to die is gain. (Phil 1:19–21)

Paul is prepared to die nobly. "I shall not be ashamed, . . . Christ will be honored in my body," he vows. And he urges the Philippians also to "stand firm," and not be frightened. It is their privilege to "suffer for his (Christ's) sake" (1:27–30). It is in the midst of this exhortation to bear up nobly for the cause of Christ that Paul includes the hymn, perhaps a hymn already familiar to the Philippians. Christ died nobly, obedient to the end. This is Paul's aim as well. As Jesus sacrificed his life for the cause of his new Empire of God, so also now Paul will offer his own life for the sake of those who would be faithful to that new reality and hope. He is ready, he says, "to be poured out as a libation upon the sacrificial offering of your faith" (2:17).

This is how the martyrological tradition works. The martyr's death is vicarious insofar as it sets an example to be emulated by others.[16] Its benefits are experienced through imitation. Jesus' death became, in this tradition, the expression of obedience. He was no longer simply a victim. He died willingly, nobly, for a cause. His obedience unto death, even death on a cross, became a model for his followers who might also find themselves imprisoned, tortured, even executed for the cause of God's new Empire. Paul has taken this

---

16. This is Seeley's insight; see *The Noble Death*, pp. 92–94, et passim.

witness to heart. Now he offers himself as a sacrifice, obedient to
the cause, even under the threat of death. And he also expects that
the Philippians will come to see their own suffering and threat of
death in the same way. The death of Jesus has become part of the
Christian way of living. This way of life always carries with it the
threat of death. As Paul writes to another church — in Corinth —
again, defending his record of constant trouble and conflict with the
authorities:

> We are afflicted in every way, but not crushed; perplexed, but
> not driven to despair; persecuted, but not forsaken; struck
> down, but not destroyed; always carrying in the body the
> death of Jesus, so that the life of Jesus may also be manifested
> in our bodies. For while we live we are always being given up
> to death for Jesus' sake, so that the life of Jesus may be mani-
> fested in our mortal flesh.[17] (2 Cor 4:8–11)

Consider Yourself Dead

While Paul used the traditions of the early church in his preaching
and writing, he was also an innovator, a creative practical theologian. The idea that Jesus' death was a vicarious death, at once his
and ours, was intriguing to him. As he pondered this martyrological
notion, he also had before him his own experience of Jesus as a spiritual force in his life. The spirit of Jesus, the risen Lord, had taken
over Paul, such that he could say quite seriously, "It is no longer I
who live, but Christ who lives in me" (Gal 2:20b). Finally, he had
before him the liturgical life of the early Christian movement, especially its practice of baptizing persons who wished to dedicate themselves to Jesus. In Paul's last known letter, to the Romans, all of these
things come together in one of Paul's most elegant formulations
expressing the significance of Jesus' death.

The issue that consumes Paul in this part of Romans is the question of sin. Recall that in Paul's version of Christianity, the Jewish

---

17. Note that the Stoic parallels commonly listed in connection with Paul's antitheses in vv. 8–9 (see, e.g., Victor Paul Furnish, *II Corinthians*, p. 281) express precisely
the same sentiments as one finds in the Jewish martyrological literature, 2 and 4
Maccabees: freedom from concern over what might happen to one's body and the con-
sequent freedom to act in accord with one's conscience, in spite of dire threat. Paul's
perspective is distinctive, to be sure — his perseverance testifies not to the power of his
reason, but to the transcendent power of God working through his earthen vessel of a
body — but the martyrological context of such discourse is to be noted.

ness could be distinguished from sin. In trying to live without it, was Paul not embracing a life of sin? "Are we to continue in sin that grace may abound?" he asks, hypothetically (Rom 6:1). "Not at all!" he replies.

> How can we who died to sin still live in it? Do you not know that all of us who have been baptized into Christ Jesus were baptized into his death? We were buried therefore with him by baptism into death, so that as Christ was raised from the dead by the glory of the Father, we too might walk in newness of life. (Rom 6:2–4)

For Paul, baptism is baptism into Christ's death. What could he mean by this, and how did such an idea address the problem of sin? To understand Paul's meaning one must realize that for Paul sin is not just bad behavior. It is a cosmic power, a force loose in the universe to which we poor human beings are subject. Sin, for Paul, is the cumulative force of evil exercising power over humanity. Such an idea, foreign perhaps to moderns, was a common way of thinking in antiquity. The universe, for ancients, was full of such hostile forces against which mere mortals were powerless. Sin, as an evil power, exercised its control over a person through the flesh — the "sinful body" says Paul (6:6) — the seat of all the passions in Paul's ancient anthropology. If this was so, then ultimately a person's only escape from sin's power is death, when the body of flesh passes away. From out of this thought world Paul arrived at a new way of considering Jesus' death as a vicarious event. If Jesus' death is at once the death of anyone who would follow him, then in his death lies the key to ultimate freedom: freedom from the power of sin:

> We know that our old self was crucified with him so that the sinful body might be destroyed, and we might no longer be enslaved to sin. For he who has died is freed from sin. But if we have died with Christ, we believe that we shall also live with him. For we know that Christ, being raised from the dead will never die again; death no longer has dominion over him. The death he died he died to sin, once for all, but life he lives he lives to God. So you also must consider yourselves dead to sin and alive to God. (Rom 6:6–11)

But how could this be? How could a person really become united with Jesus in his death? Paul decided that this was the meaning of baptism. He took a concept that had been expressed primarily in a literary mode — the vicarious death of a martyr — and gave it ritual power. He could do this because Jesus had become for him more than a martyr. He was a divine being, an epiphany, a spiritual force in his own right. Worship and ritual worked with him: you could be united with Jesus spiritually, ritually. That he chose the ritual of baptism to bear this burden of meaning is quite understandable. On the one hand, death and water were connected in various ways symbolically and mythically in antiquity. And Jews had long associated ritual washing with purification against sin and ritual uncleanness. All of this must have been wrapped up together in the poetics of Paul's new formulation of the meaning of baptism.

But what is most impressive about Paul's interpretive work here is the extent to which he seems to understand how ritual really works in the life of a believer. However powerful and poetically effective a ritual might be, it is not magic. Ritual can create a very real experience of altered reality, an intense moment — in this case — of freedom. But when the event is over, life stands waiting outside the door, ready to reassert itself when the priests have disrobed and the ritual fires have been extinguished. Paul understands all of this very well. Consequently, he does not say that those who have died with Jesus in the act of baptism have also been raised with him. That final and permanent freedom lies still in the future.[18] Rather, Paul very carefully asserts that "as Christ was raised . . . , we too might walk in newness of life" (6:4). Life is still there, waiting to be walked. Baptism has not changed that reality. You're not dead yet. So, he insists, you "must *consider yourselves dead* to sin and alive to God" (6:11). The future of freedom remains still to be constructed. "Let not sin therefore reign in your mortal bodies, to make you obey their passions, . . . but yield yourselves to God as people who have been brought from death to life" (6:12–13).[19] So long as you still have a body, you still have before you the martyr's challenge: obedience. The death of Jesus is vicarious, for others, only insofar as they choose to embrace his death and his life as their own.

---

18. Note the "caution required by the apostle's eschatology" (Ernst Käsemann, *Commentary on Romans*, p. 166).

19. That Paul must balance his indicatives here with imperatives underscores his realism about the continuing human situation — so Guenther Bornkamm, "Baptism and New Life in Paul (Romans 6)," in *Early Christian Experience*, pp. 71–86.

The One Who Endures to the End

This idea, drawn from the tradition of the Noble Death, that the death of the martyr could have vicarious effects for others, was a powerful one. As Paul worked out its implications in ritual, others continued the literary tradition of martyrology, telling the story of Jesus in a way that invited its imitation, in life and in death. The Gospel of Mark is one result of this literary effort.[20]

The idea of Jesus the martyr had obvious relevance to the writer of this first gospel. Mark was written during, or just following the years of the Jewish War for independence from Rome (66–70 C.E.). As a messianic Jew who believed in Jesus, Mark's author would have found no comfort with Rome. But his beliefs about Jesus would have put him at odds with most Jews as well — at a time when solidarity and loyalty to the Jewish tradition were in high demand. He was a person caught between the two sides of a war-torn world. And he was part of a community that found itself in this precarious situation as well. He and his community had come to a moment of truth. Are we right or are we wrong? Is the followership of Jesus worth the risk we must now take? The issue of faithfulness and loyalty runs ubiquitous through Mark.

We have already seen how the Passion Narrative took up the question of Jesus' death, as the death of God's persecuted righteous one. Mark knew this early text. But he wanted more from his narrative than just an account of Jesus' unjust death. He wanted to create a narrative that would involve his audience, that would tie their fate together with that of Jesus. And so, Mark took up the Passion Narrative, but used it to write his own story of Jesus. In it he weaves the Passion Narrative into a skillful plot that focuses the martyr's question on the lives of those for whom he writes: can you remain faithful in the midst of adversity?

One way he does this is by creating a narrative pattern to which Norman Perrin called attention some years ago.[21] Perrin noticed that the fate of John the Baptist and Jesus is essentially the same in the Gospel of Mark. Mark speaks of John as "preaching," (1:7), but then he is "delivered up" (*paradidonai*) to his enemies (1:14). Thereupon Jesus makes his own debut, like John, "preaching" (1:14). And what is his fate? He, too, must be "delivered up" (*paradidonai*: 9:31;

---

20. The martyrological aspects of Mark are emphasized especially by Mack (*Myth of Innocence, passim*)

21. Norman Perrin, *The New Testament,* pp. 144–45.

10:33). As Mark approaches the passion narrative, he creates successive scenes in which Jesus predicts his own betrayal and death in Jerusalem. But the disciples cannot understand or accept what he is saying. Peter rebukes him (8:32); the disciples cannot understand his meaning (9:32); James and John can only speak of the glory that is to come (10:37). Finally Jesus asks them: "Are you able to drink the cup that I drink, or to be baptized with the baptism with which I am baptized? (10:38). They reply, "We are able" (10:39). Are they?

Now, with the stage set, Mark heads into the Passion Narrative. Jesus provokes the authorities (11:15–17), who begin to conspire against him (11:18). What Jesus has predicted is beginning to take place. Mark enhances the developing tension. Jesus defends his authority against those who would question him (11:27–33). He prophecies against Jerusalem in parable (12:1–12). He gives a smart-alecky answer to the question of whether or not to pay the tribute (12:13–17). He denounces the scribes (12:38–40). Something bad is going to happen to this man — one can sense it. But he wades deeper into the trouble, true to his cause, unflinching in the face of the growing danger.

Now Mark comes to what is arguably the high point of his entire narrative — at least for his audience: the apocalypse. Here Jesus foretells what is to happen in the future — about a generation away (13:30). When? "When you see the desolating sacrilege set up where it ought not to be (let the reader understand), then let those who are in Judea flee to the mountains. . . . " (13:14). Here Mark, with an inside nod to his audience, makes reference to the imminent destruction of the Jerusalem Temple. He is speaking of the very war that is just now raging around them. When will all of this take place? Now! Says Mark. It is happening now! And what will it mean for those who are reading these words? Jesus speaks to them out of the past, foretelling the future — their future:

> But take heed to yourselves; for they will deliver you up (*para-didonai*) to councils; and you will be beaten in synagogues; and you will stand before governors and kings for my sake, to bear testimony before them. And the gospel must first be preached to all nations. And when they bring you to trial and deliver you up (*paradidonai*), do not be anxious beforehand what you are to say; but say whatever is given you in that hour, for it is not you who speak but the Holy Spirit. And

brother will deliver up brother to death, and father his child, and children will rise against their parents and have them put to death; and you will be hated by all for my name's sake. But he who endures to the end will be saved. (Mark 13:9–13)

Now it is clear. John preached, and was delivered up. Jesus preached, and he was delivered up. And now Mark's readers see their own fate. They will be called upon to preach, and they too will be delivered up. And how will they face this fearful prospect? Mark hopes that the martyr's story will now do what it is designed to do. Jesus, the persecuted righteous one, is to be their model. The disciples will flee (14:50). But Jesus will remain faithful to the end. Mark insists that his readers must emulate the steadfast faithfulness of Jesus, true to their cause to the very end. For those who can do this, there is reward, as Jesus says: "But anyone who endures to the end will be saved" (13:13b).

This final admonition recalls to mind the words of Epictetus on the death of Socrates: "he is saved by death, not by flight." Mark hopes to convince his readers not to flee. Death may lie before them, but it is not to be feared. This idea, that death must not be feared, is central to the Noble Death tradition. Seneca argued that this was precisely why Socrates chose to face death, even when the opportunity of escape presented itself. In his letter to Lucilius (On Despising Death) he writes:

Socrates in prison discoursed, and declined to flee when certain persons gave him the opportunity; he remained there, in order to free humankind from the fear of two most grievous things, death and imprisonment. (Epistle XXIV, 4; LCL)

This theme is indeed relevant to Mark and his audience. They live in fearful times. Throughout Mark's gospel fear confronts those who would believe in Jesus. Fear is the enemy, the polar opposite of faith, for Mark. "Do not fear, only have faith," says Jesus to those who fear that the ruler's daughter, whom he might have healed, is already dead (5:36). "Why are you afraid? Have you no faith?" asks Jesus when the disciples respond in fear to Jesus' powerful act of calming the sea (4:40). As Mark's story unfolds, the disciples' fear only intensifies. In the end, they all flee in fear. Peter is paralyzed by fear (14:66–72). Fear even stalks the women, who, in Mark's final scene, discover the tomb of Jesus empty. The angel standing guard instructs them to go and tell the disciples what they have seen. But they do not, for they cannot. "They said nothing to anyone, for they were afraid" — *ephobounto gar* (16:8). With this awkward phrase, Mark brings his story to a close with a colossal loose end. It begs the question: who will have the courage to tell the story? Who will bear witness? Who would be a martyr?

The Glory of Death

In many ways these concerns about survival, fear, and faithfulness were John's concerns as well. The fourth evangelist wrote some years after Mark, but he too faced times that posed a threat to him and his church. It was a time when Jews and Christians were going their separate ways. Jews who were followers of Jesus found themselves having to choose between the security of the larger community in which they lived and the risky human experiment that was the church. John even avers that those who would dare to expose themselves as Christians in his community might face death (16:2). The pressure felt by those within John's church was intense. In fact, some might have begun to renounce their faith (16:1; 9:22).[22]

Like Mark, John turns to the martyrological tradition to try to shore up the flagging zeal of his folk.[23] In presenting the death of Jesus as that of a martyr, John had many of the same basic elements used by Mark. He probably had a Passion Narrative similar to that of Mark, likewise built on the idea of God's suffering righteous one. He was a Jew, quite likely from Antioch, and so must have known the Maccabaean martyrological tradition well. And he was part of the larger Hellenistic world, with its philosophical discussions of how to die nobly, true to one's cause.

But John's creative act of building his own story of Jesus did not imitate that of Mark. There may be many reasons for this. John, after all, is a very complex book. One reason, however, is clear. John had a different way of thinking about Jesus; he had a different Christology. In Mark, Jesus is a human being, the son of Man, who is designated as God's Son at the event of his baptism by John the Baptizer. In John,

22. On the Johannine situation and the question of martyrdom see the benchmark study by J. Louis Martyn, *History and Theology in the Fourth Gospel*; also, *The Gospel of John in Christian History*, pp. 90–121.

23. The complexity of themes and issues in John serves often to obscure what otherwise might be quite obvious. The martyrological aspects of John are seldom commented upon, though a notable exception is Paul Minear's subtle treatment in *John*.

Jesus is not a human being. He is "a god striding across the earth."
He is the Logos of God, God's own Word, at one with God from the
beginning of time. Apart from him, nothing in all creation came into
being (John 1:1–5). This very "high" Christology may, in part,
explain how Jesus faces the final days of his life in John. Through the
final chapters of the gospel, from Gethsemane, to the arrest and trial
scenes, and finally the cross, Jesus is in control. In Gethsemane, for
example, Judas brings an entire cohort (a *speiran*) of Roman soldiers
(about 600 men) to execute the arrest of Jesus. But with a word from
God's Son — *ego eimi* ("it is I") — they all fall to the ground, powerless before him (18:6). These words, *ego eimi*, are not innocent in
John. They are the epiphanic words of self-revelation spoken by the
one who is God incarnate. In John, Jesus is no ordinary victim of
Roman justice. He is a powerful, willing captive, orchestrating his
own death according to a grand plan.

Initially this may seem to diminish the power of Jesus' death as a
witness to others. What he, the Logos of God, could do was super-
human, not to be attempted by mere mortals. John does risk this conclusion. But the willingness of a martyr to embrace death, even to
orchestrate its arrival, is not without precedent. Socrates rejected his
friends' plot to spirit him away from Athens. He chose instead to die
nobly, willingly, in control to the end. And in the Christian tradition
itself, to choose to die, to dream about it, to plan it out, became the
highest expression of martyrological zeal. In one famous scene from
a third century Christian martyrological text,[24] the young and beautiful Perpetua, a girl barely past her teens, faces her executioners with
a resolve that is almost super-human. Her executioner is a young
gladiator whose hand is trembling so much he cannot make his sword
perform the final deed. So Perpetua, to the astonishment of the
crowd, reaches out, takes his hand, and guides the blade to her own
throat (*Perpetua and Felicitas*, 21). Such is the martyr's zeal.

Even though John's Jesus is in control, almost orchestrating the
unfolding drama of his death, John still tried to connect the fate of
Jesus with that of his audience using martyrological motifs and ideas.
Let us take, for example, the way John handles the final days of Jesus
in Jerusalem, the ground covered by the Passion Narrative. Jesus and
the disciples arrive in Jerusalem in triumphal procession. This much

---

24. *The Martyrdom of Saints Perpetua and Felicitas*; for the text in translation see
Herbert Musurillo, *The Acts of the Christian Martyrs*.

comes from the Passion Narrative. But as he arrives, he is already under a cloud. There is no need of an incident in the Temple to provoke the authorities; Jesus has been provoking them all along with his outrageous words. The threat of death already stalks him (see, e.g., John 5:18; 7:19, 25, 32, 44; 8:59; 10:31; 11:45–53). Thus, John has moved what would have been the next scene in the Passion Narrative, the Temple incident, up to the opening scenes of the gospel, using it already in chapter two as a kind of first provocative act (2:13–22). With the tension building, Jesus turns to face what awaits him in this last visit to Jerusalem, evoking familiar ideas from the martyrological tradition:

> The hour has come for the Son of man to be glorified. Truly, truly, I say to you, unless a grain of wheat falls to the earth and dies, it remains alone; but if it dies, it bears much fruit. He who loves his life loses it, and he who hates his life in this world will keep it for eternal life. If anyone serves me, he must follow me; and where I am, there shall my servant be also; if any one serves me, the Father will honor him. (John 12:23–27)

John has packed so much into these verses: the idea that in death a life is transformed; the idea that to gain authentic life, one must be willing to part with life, "to hate life in this world;" the idea that anyone who would serve Jesus must follow him, even into death. All of these ideas are developed from the martyrological tradition, as we have seen. And embracing this entire thought is the idea that Jesus' death is not a crisis or a catastrophe to be dreaded. It is to be his moment of glory. And those who follow him into death, God will honor.

This is different from what we have seen in Paul or in Mark, where Jesus' death, though significant in martyrological terms, is still the nadir of the story. It is a crisis to be faced with dignity. In John, Jesus' death is the climax of the story, the moment in which he is to be glorified. And not he alone. In this act God is glorified as well:

> Now my soul is troubled. And what should I say — "Father, save me from this hour'? No, it is for this reason that I have come to this hour. Father, glorify your name." Then a voice came from heaven, "I have glorified it, and I will glorify it again." (John 12:27–28)

Here John invokes the memory of Jews throughout time who have been martyred in faithfulness to God. To die as a martyr is to glorify God. One sees this in the Maccabaean literature (e.g. 4 Maccabees 1:12; 18:23) And to die thus is bring to oneself honor and glory — this, too, is a martyrological theme (e.g. 4 Maccabees 7:9). Glorious is the martyr's death in every respect. This why John repeatedly refers to Jesus' death as his glorification (e.g. 7:39; 13:31–32; 17:1, etc.).

At this point in John's story, we would expect him to follow the Passion Narrative into the scene in Gethsemane, with the betrayal and arrest of Jesus. But before moving on to these crucial events, John pauses. In John's story, Jesus now retreats with his disciples for one final private discourse. The pause is long — chapters 13–17 — and includes instruction on how to care for one another, how properly to understand him, and on the nature of the world. And he gives the disciples one last commandment:

> I give you one final commandment, that you love one another. Just as I have loved you, you also should love one another. By this everyone shall know that you are my disciples, if you have love for one another. (John 13:34–35)

And then, again:

> This is my commandment, that you love one another as I have loved you. No one has greater love than this, to lay down one's life for one's friends. You are my friends if you do what I command you. (John 15:12–14)

Here are the basic ideas of the martyrological tradition. The fate of the martyr is united with those who would follow him in life and in death. As Jesus loved, so they are to love. As Jesus died, so must they also be willing to die for one another. His death is a witness to them, an act to be imitated. The relevance of this idea soon becomes clear as Jesus' discourse continues:

> If the world hates you, be aware that it hated me before it hated you. If you belonged to the world, the world would love you as its own. Because you do not belong to the world, but I have chosen you out of the world — therefore the world hates you. Remember the word that I said to you, "Servants are not greater than their master." If they persecuted me, they

will persecute you; if they kept my word, they will keep yours also. . . . I have said these things to you to keep you from stumbling. They will put you out of synagogues. Indeed, the hour is coming when those who kill you will think that by doing so they are offering worship to God. (John 15:18–20; 16:1–2)

The farewell discourse of Jesus in John is a long exposition of John's typical theology: the Logos of God is returning to the place from whence he has come. But by lacing these chapters with ideas clearly drawn from the martyrological tradition, John manages to keep Jesus from drifting off into transcendental irrelevance. The Logos is also Jesus, the teacher and martyr. His life and death stand as a witness for how to live and die. As Jesus retires with his disciples and instructs them thus, one cannot help but think of that last meeting of Socrates with his companions. As he goes forth from the upper room to face arrest with dignity, to defy his tormentors with words that witness to his resolve, to defy Pilate himself, one cannot help but think of the heroic witness of Eleazar, denouncing the tyrant who's instruments of torture have become powerless over him. In the end, Jesus dies with dignity. In the final death scene (19:25b–30) there is no cry of anguish, as in Mark. From the cross he calmly sees to his mother's future; he drinks from a bowl of sour wine (again, vague allusions to Socrates' final acts); and then utters the final word: *tetelestai* ("it is finished"). This noble end is not a disgrace. It is his moment of glory.

To Live and Die With Jesus

For the early followers of Jesus, his death was not simply the death of a victim. Jesus died as a martyr. *Martys*, of course, is the Greek word for "witness." For early Christians, Jesus' death was a "witness" in a double sense. On the one hand, Jesus' faithfulness to his cause testified to the proposition that there are things worth dying for. Jesus died for God's new Empire, that new way of being in the world he tried to exemplify in his words and deeds. His death was an invitation — a dare, really — to others to try to live as he had lived. On the other hand, it testified to the fact that it is possible to face such a death nobly, without fear. The martyr's death is ultimately an act of freedom: freedom from fear. Once one has learned to face death without fear, then there really is nothing to be feared. As Seneca tells his friend Lucilius, "death is so little to be feared, that through its good offices nothing is to be feared" (Ep. XXIV, 11). Jesus' death, as a martyr's death, is one that frees one from fear — not only the fear of death, but all such fears that would dissuade one from embracing Jesus' radical new way of thinking about human life and relationships. In this sense, the power of death, and of those who wield its instruments, is vanquished.

For Christians who embraced Jesus' dissident stance over against the Empire and its ways, grasping this sense of freedom was a very important thing. If Jesus could face false charges, arrest, torture, and death, even death on a cross, without fear, then what power should these things have over his followers as they pursued that same vision of God's Empire for which Jesus had willingly died? As Paul wrote to those Christians living in the heart of Rome itself:

> If God is for us, then who is against us? He who did not spare his own Son, but gave him up for us all, will he not also give us all things with him? Who shall bring any charge against God's elect? It is God who justifies. Who is to condemn? It is Jesus Christ who died, yes, who was raised from the dead, who is at the right hand of God, who intercedes for us? Who shall separate us from the love of Christ? Shall tribulation, or distress, or persecution, or famine, or nakedness, or peril, or sword? As it is written, "For thy sake we are being killed all day long; we are regarded as sheep to be slaughtered." No, in all these things we are more than conquerors through him who loved us. For I am sure that neither death, nor life, nor angels, nor principalities, nor things present, nor things to come, nor powers, nor height, nor depth, nor anything else in creation, will be able to separate us from the love of God in Christ Jesus our Lord.[25] (Rom 8:31–39)

This is the power of the martyr's death: it enables one to live faithfully to God, free from fear of the consequences that might come from such an act of defiance. The martyr's death is an act that conquers the power of death itself, but only insofar as one chooses to embrace the martyr's death as one's own. When one embraces the

---

25. For the martyrological sense of the passage, esp. of the quote from Ps 43:23, see Käsemann, *Romans*, pp. 245–52, esp. 249–50.

martyr's death, then the martyr's life becomes possible too. And this, finally, is the point of seeing Jesus as a martyr. The martyr frees one to live the martyr's life by showing one how to die the martyr's death, free from the all-consuming fear of death. The martyrological tradition gave early Christians a way of using the death of Jesus, terrifying though it was, as a source of power for those who would take up his dissident way of life, and his cause of a new Empire of God.

And what of those of us who would look to the ancient roots of Christianity for ways to understand Jesus and his fate as somehow significant for our own quest for meaningful existence: could the martyrological tradition prove meaningful even today? Are there things worth dying for? Are there causes worth living for? Certainly these are the questions raised by the ancient tradition of martyrdom. But early Christians did not pose these questions in the abstract like this. They had in mind a particular cause, a particular vision of human existence lived before God that they had come to see in Jesus' words and deeds. They — some — would willingly die for that vision, the Empire of God. But the martyrological tradition has also been used to coax people to die for things far less noble, far less worthy than this very unusual vision of life. From antiquity to modernity one sees this again and again in Christian history. There is a fine line between the martyr and canon fodder.

In spite of its frequent misuses through the ages, the martyrological tradition is nonetheless important. It reminds us that Jesus' death was connected to his life, and that his life and fate became exemplary for his followers as they considered, in the wake of his death, just how committed they would be to the things Jesus had said and done. Here is a way of understanding Jesus' death (and life) as vicarious for the believer in a way quite different from classical theories of atonement. The life and death of a martyr are meaningless if those who witness them remain unmoved by their witness. They become vicarious "for us" only insofar as they are embraced as the life one would dare to lead, and the death one would be willing to risk.

Works Consulted

Bornkamm, Günther. "Baptism and New Life in Paul. Romans 6." Pp. 71-86 in *Early Christian Experience*. New York: Harper & Row, 1969.

Dodd, C. H. *According to the Scriptures: The Sub-Structure of New Testament Theology*. New York: Charles Scribner's Sons, 1953.

Dormeyer, Detlev. *Die Passion Jesu als Verhaltensmodell: Literarishe und theologische Analyse der Traditions- und Redaktionsgeschichte der Markuspassion*. Neutestamentliche Abhandlungen 11. Münster: Aschendorff, 1974.

Droge, Arthur J., and James D. Tabor. *A Noble Death: Suicide and Martyrdom Among Christians and Jews in Antiquity*. San Francisco: HarperSanFrancisco, 1992.

Furnish, Victor Paul. *II Corinthians*. Anchor Bible 32A. New York: Doubleday, 1984.

Hengel, Martin. *The Atonement: The Origins of the Doctrine in the New Testament*. Philadelphia: Fortress, 1981.

Käsemann, Ernst. *Commentary on Romans*. Trans. and ed. Geoffrey W. Bromiley. Grand Rapids: Eerdmans, 1980.

Kelber, Werner et al. *The Passion in Mark: Studies on Mark 14–16*. Philadelphia: Fortress, 1976.

Lindars, Barnabas. *New Testament Apologetic: The Doctrinal Significance of the Old Testament Quotations*. Philadelphia: Westminster, 1961.

Linnemann, Eta. *Studien zur Passionsgeschichte*. Forschungen zur Religion und Literatur des Alten und Neuen Testaments 102. Göttingen: Vandenhoeck & Ruprecht, 1970.

Mack, Burton L. *A Myth of Innocence*. Philadelphia: Fortress, 1988.

Martyn, J. Louis. *The Gospel of John in Christian History: Essays for Interpreters*. New York: Paulist Press, 1978.

_____. *History and Theology in the Fourth Gospel*. Revised, enlarged edition. Nashville: Abingdon, 1979.

Minear, Paul. *John: The Martyr's Gospel*. New York: Pilgrim Press, 1984.

Musurillo, Herbert. *The Acts of the Christian Martyrs*. Oxford: Oxford University Press, 1972.

Nickelsburg, G. W. E. "The Genre and Function of the Markan Passion Narrative," *Harvard Theological Review* 73 (1980), pp. 153-84.

_____. *Resurrection, Immortality, and Eternal Life in Intertestamental Judaism*. Harvard Theological Studies 26. Cambridge: Harvard University Press; London: Oxford University Press, 1972.

Perrin, Norman. *The New Testament: An Introduction*. New York: Harcourt, Brace, Jovanovich, 1974.

Seeley, David. "The Background of the Philippians Hymn. 2:6-11." *Journal of Higher Criticism* 1 (1994), pp. 49-72.

_____. *The Noble Death: Greco-Roman Martyrology and Paul's Concept of Salvation*. Journal for the Study of the New Testament, Supplement Series 28. Sheffield: JSOT Press, 1990

Wills, Lawrence M. *The Jew in the Court of the Foreign King: Ancient Jewish Court Legends*. Harvard Dissertations in Religion 26. Minneapolis: Fortress, 1990.